O U G H T E N
H O U S E
PUBLICATIONS

"Books and Tools for the Rising Planetary Consciousness"

⟨⟩ Dedication ⟨⟩

To the Lightworkers who are dedicated to following Spirit with each breath and each step; who are dedicated to embodying Divinity and living Heaven on Earth; who are dedicated to joyous service, fierce wholeness, impeccability, and the cosmic joke; and who are dedicated to a vision of planetary ascension that is easy, graceful, ecstatic, and high-velocity fun. Ya-hoo!

What is Lightbody?

Archangel Ariel
Channeled by Tashira Tachi-ren

Editing and Typography by Sara Benjamin-Rhodes

Published by
OUGHTEN HOUSE PUBLICATIONS
Livermore, California USA

WHAT IS LIGHTBODY?
ARCHANGEL ARIEL, CHANNELED BY TACHI-REN

EDITING & TYPOGRAPHY BY SARA BENJAMIN-RHODES

Published by:
Oughten House Publications
P.O. Box 2008
Livermore, California, 94551-2008 USA

Library of Congress Cataloging-in-Publication Data
Ariel (Archangel : Spirit)
What is Lightbody / material channeled from Archangel Ariel by Tachi-ren.

p.   cm.
ISBN 1-880666-25-1 : $12.95
1. Spirit writings.   2. Meditations--Miscellanea.   I. Tachi-ren, 1956-
II. Title.
BF1301.A615   1994
133.9'3--dc20   94-31333
                                            CIP

ISBN 1-880666-25-1, Trade Paperback
Printed in United States of America
Printed with vegetable ink on acid-free paper

⋖⋙ Table of Contents ⋘⋗

(continued)

⋘ The Importance of ⋙ Discernment

In editing a book for Oughten House, I strive to take it to the highest level of which I am capable. I draw upon my intuition and experience and try to catch anything that is not accurate or clear. However, there are as many pictures of reality as there are points of awareness to formulate them. There are many destiny patterns unfolding simultaneously. We each need to use our own discernment to distinguish what is "ours" and what is someone else's. No source of information is without its distortion. Even the clearest channels are not, nor have they ever been, 100% accurate. Even within information that is "mostly true," there is some information that is not true. Even within information that is "mostly false," there is some truth present.

Your greatest ally in finding your way to your own "destination" is your own discernment. No one can know your own answers except you. You cannot rely on anyone or anything outside of you: your answers all lie within you. We are all unique aspects of the One. There is no duplication whatsoever, which is pretty amazing in itself. As you read what is in these pages, take what is "yours" and embrace it. The rest may be there for someone else. If it helps you on your path, then it has served.

— Sara Benjamin-Rhodes, Managing Editor

Publisher's Note

The channeled material presented in this book consists of transmitted information. The reader's interpretation of this or any other channeled information is strictly subjective and reflects his or her personal beliefs.

The language used in this book has been transcribed with the intention of presenting the actual transmission, with the least possible alteration in meaning. Because of this, there are a few words used in unconventional ways. The essence of the material remains unchanged.

We at Oughten House extend our wholehearted appreciation and gratitude to each of our Literary Producers for making this publication possible: Marge and John Melanson, Barbara Rawles, Robin Drew, Irit Levy, Debbie Detwiler, Kiyo Monro, Alice Tang, Eugene P. Tang, Brad Clarke, Victor Beasley, Ruth Dutra, Nicole Christine, Dennis Donahue, Fred J. Tremblay, Kathy Cook, Debbie Soucek, and Kimberley Mullen.

⋘ Acknowledgments ⋙

Special thanks to:

Suzane Coronis, my beloved, for her constant wisdom, outrageous laughter, and steady reminders to make it fun.

Tony Stubbs, flow director extraordinaire, for working his hoofies to the bone to make this book happen. You were there for me from the beginning. See, I really couldn't have done this one without you. Awesome!

J.J. Wilson, for your incredible insight, humor, fierceness, and love. You keep Angelic Outreach together, body and soul — we couldn't do it without you.

Gary Johnson, creator of the beautiful Alpha Chamber, for his financial and spiritual support of this project. Because of you, we didn't have to just "beat it flat."

Delightful Dolores Montoya, for transcribing the tapes and covering the planet with rainbows and fairy dust.

Paul Bader, for transcribing the additions to the text in the midst of chaos.

Susannah Redelfs, for proofing the text and making each of us laugh, even when it hurt.

Extraterrestrial Earth Mission, for their excellent stimulation and relentless humor. We just love you guys!

Ralph Edmonds, Lucie Geear, Mark Kramer, Arisha and Zeke Wenneson, Lea Hubbard, Faraday Tabler, Michelle La Prise, Barbara Brooks, Arasia, Antarah, and Sue Gage for their financial and Spiritual support of these projects.

Rob Gerard and Cathy Cook of Oughten House, for their vision of getting ascension-oriented materials out on the planet and wanting to include Angelic Outreach in that vision.

Ariel and the Council of Ein Soph (The Crew), for being the best multidimensional support team this embodied angelic Lightworker could ever want.

Sara Benjamin-Rhodes of Celestial Co✧operatives, for her excellent editing of *What is Lightbody?* It was wonderful to have an editor who was in alignment with this work. I truly appreciate her precision and forthrightness. I look forward to co-creating with you on a future book.

All the Lightworkers who have loved and supported AO, and have, are, and will use the information in this book to co-create Heaven on Earth. Let's get busy!

◁⧓ Channel's Preface ⧓▷

Please take everything you read within these pages as a model and just another opinion. It is impossible to express Truth (with a capital T) in any earthly language. You can only describe realities. I view reality as a verb, not a noun. There is no one great "Reality" with a capital R. It is a constantly shifting co-creation of intersecting individual realities, each absolutely unique. I choose to operate within a reality that planet Earth is ascending into the Light dimensions through Joy and Laughter.

Also, you should know that no channel is one hundred percent accurate. After all, this and all channeled information comes through a filter of human perceptions. So, if something in these pages rings true for you, then it was your Truth all along. If it doesn't, lovingly release it back to the universe. It's just another opinion.

I and my work group ask that you not create me, Ariel, or any channeled entity as an outside authority. You are the only authority over what is "real and true" in your life.

Angelic Outreach (AO) was designed to support incarnate Lightworkers to awaken to their multidimensional vastness, embody Divinity, and to lighten up Planet Earth. In its earthly form, AO created new technologies, techniques, and articulations for the co-creation of Heaven on Earth. With the publication of this book, AO's work is complete. Lightworkers may access AO through tapes, potions, and books like this one.

There are 383 ascending planets, in five local universes, one of which is planet Earth. As a Lightworker, you are probably incarnate on all of them.

Angelic Outreach, at its vastest, is a multidimensional, multi-universal program of full merger with Source. Through all of our incarnations we act like connective tissue between universes, stars, and planets. We help coordinate the various planetary ascension programs within each universe, as well as assist the merger of several universes into one. It acts as the bridge between all of the Creations, joining the Many with the One.

I am a conscious merged channel for Higher Light beings. I expand my consciousness multidimensionally and merge with the vastness of my own Spirit. From there, I merge with my work group of twenty-four Light beings and all of us channel back through my physical body. This is quite an experience, as you can imagine.

My relationship with "The Crew," as I call my work group, is as an equal. We are co-creative Masters, beings of Light, and we see you as Light Masters also.

In this crew, Archangel Ariel usually functions as a Lightbody theoretician. She articulates the Lightbody process, creating models, technologies, and meditations to support the ascension at every level. As one of these embodied aspects of the crew, I function as a channel for the group's energies and as a "hands on" Lightbody technician.

So, the *What is LightBody?* model presented here is Ariel's "gig," and I think she does it quite well. The material for *What is Lightbody?* was developed and presented in small workshops, from 1987 through 1990. It was transcribed, edited, and printed in book form in 1990. In 1993, the material was updated, revised, and put out on audio cassette. In this Oughten House edition, both Ariel and I have added information throughout the text. We hope you find it a useful and delightful map for the road to Lightbody.

This edition also includes the book *Invocations*. Since its publication in 1989, many Lightworkers have loved these 33 poems, often reading them every day. They were created by various members of "The Crew," and you will feel their different frequencies in the Invocations.

Originally, these two books were self-published by Angelic Outreach and we were never able to keep up with the demand for them. So we are ecstatic that Oughten House will make them available to those of you who have waited so patiently, and to all of you who will

read this material for the first time. May your journey into the Light
be the path of Joy.

Of the Source, in Service to the Source,
— Tashira Tachi-ren

⟨⟨⟩ Preface to the New Edition ⟨⟨⟩

On May 30, 1994, a dramatic shift occurred in the Divine Plan for planet Earth. The entire timeframe for planetary ascension was accelerated. In the beginning of June, many of you experienced the surfacing of intense survival fear, enemy patterning, and old pictures of reality from your physical bodies. These energies were emerging out of your genetic encodements. It was as if God had reached into your body and was pulling out the fear and separation by the roots. Old physical traumas or illnesses may have briefly reappeared. Time accelerated and many of you feel frustrated about completing projects.

The levels described in the Lightbody model are still valid. Moving through these mutational stages can take many years or a few minutes, depending on the Will of Spirit. *These levels are not a measurement of personal spiritual achievement*. Your Spirit determines your appropriate Lightbody level, depending on your Divine design, your incarnational grid within the hologram, and what is needed to serve the planetary ascension. Truly, Lightbody is about the evolution of this species and the collective service to all life.

If you look at this planet from the viewpoint of your Oversouls, you see its entire Alpha-Omega cycle (from its beginning to its end in time), and zillions of parallel realities across space. You are incarnate parts of the Oversouls and have many lifetimes throughout the space-time fabric, simultaneously. We call this your holographic grid of incarnations. From the viewpoint of the Oversouls, these lives are all happening NOW and are points of coordination for restructuring the hologram of this planetary game of separation. The entire space/time construct is contained in a membrane that we call a holographic bubble. This bubble of third-dimensional realities is currently three-quarters of the way through the fourth dimension and is "rising" rapidly. The bubble is collapsing and dissolving. People are having many different responses to these changes.

A Parable

*I*magine that once upon this time, there is a sealed fishbowl (made of one-way glass) inside of a large aquarium. The fish in the aquarium can see into the bowl, but the fish in the bowl cannot see out. Their fishbowl is their only reality. Imagine that the large aquarium is filled with salt water and anemones, crabs, and all kinds of wonderous fishes. The fishbowl is filled with fresh water and goldfish.

The glass of the fishbowl is getting thinner and thinner. Small amounts of salt water are seeping through and the goldfish must evolve very fast to handle this change in their environment. As the wall grows thinner, the goldfish begin to get glimpses of the creatures in the aquarium. Some of the goldfish see these other fishes as The Enemy, and fiercely try to defend their bowl from imminent invasion. They see the anemones as Evil, and accuse other goldfish of being "anemone-influenced." These goldfish hide their personal fear by projecting a climate of fear around them.

Some of the goldfish assume that the fishes in the aquarium have been controlling their fishbowl all along. They see themselves and the other goldfish as hapless victims. They assume that the creatures on the other side of the glass have kept them in the fishbowl just so they could be eaten someday. As their bowl dissolves, they meet each passing day with dread.

Some of the goldfish see the fishes on the other side of the glass as holy, all-powerful superiors. These goldfish relinquish all inner authority and wildly swing from feeling especially chosen to feeling worthless. They try to interpret hidden messages from their "masters" and base their actions and beliefs on the messages. They swim here and there in the bowl, creating lots of ripples, but no lasting effects.

Some of the goldfish see the other creatures as brethren and marvel at the miraculous variations "The Great Fish" has used to express Itself. These goldfish know that the evolution of their species, the dissolving of their bowl, and even the reactions of fear, martyrdom, and unworthiness in the other goldfish are in the fins of "The Great Fish." They follow the Spirit of The Great Fish with each gill and each fin. They experience ecstasy as they prepare to swim in vaster waters.

So, the holographic bubble is collapsing, at times causing massive parallel mergers numbering in the tens of thousands per minute. Linear time is collapsing as it evolves towards a simultaneous time structure (Infinite NOW). Linear space is expanding, as it evolves towards simultaneous space (Infinite Presence).

Parallel mergers are often disorienting — lots of dizziness, shaking, shimmering vision, and breaches of continuity. Knowing that the parallel mergers in mid-October 1994 would shift people's Lightbody levels and could be so intense that it could collapse the bubble, an experiment was conducted. We stimulated the complex standing waves of the sub-atomic structures to accept standing waves from a higher dimension. This allowed the sub-atomic wave motions in separate parallels to be synchronized into controlled interference patterns. The result was smooth intensification of manifested Light and gentle cancellation of abrasive discontinuities. The holographic bubble was not destabilized; it was actually strengthened.

This means that the final collapse will be much smoother. We will synchronize the complex standing waves of this reality with the standing waves of the high astral plane, and then with those of the higher dimensions. The dimensional transitions will be less of a shock; instead, it will be a more dreamlike experience. We think that everyone will notice the shift, nonetheless.

In mid-October, without much of the usual drama, the majority of Lightworkers moved into tenth-level Lightbody and the overall population moved into eighth-level. Many of you (including Tachi-ren) have complained about the lack of fireworks from this shift. We, too, want people to notice what is happening. Although our primary interest is to not destabilize the bubble prematurely, we will try to increase the intensity of experience from future mergers.

As Spirit is placing you into a new positioning with regard to the ascension, many of you are feeling complete with your work on this plane. Allow old forms and models to gracefully drop away. A new form is evolving. You may find that you are more expressive or that you must be wildly creative. There are two songs out on the airwaves that sum up what most of you are feeling: "All I want to do is have some fun and I think that I'm not the only one," and "Bring it on — don't wait until tomorrow!"

Which fish are you? Are you busy fighting "The Enemy?" Have you pulled out your Light sword and are righteously battling the secret government, the greys, the dark forces, etc.? Does this truly match your vision of Heaven on Earth? Are you focused on extraterrestrials trying to control the Earth? Are you participating with pictures of reality that hold that humankind are victims, dupes, or a colonized food source? How does this mesh with the view that each person is a vast, multidimensional master? Have you exchanged your connection with your own Spirit for one with a guru, an Ascended Master, or a channeled entity? The entire universe will rearrange itself to accommodate your pictures of reality. What do you want — really? Your Spirit is shifting your positioning in relation to ascension. Allow the sweetness of transfiguration to fill your soul. Follow your own beloved Spirit, with each breath and each step. <u>Live</u> Heaven!

Of the Source, in Service to the Source
— The Council of Ein Soph

⤳ Introduction by Archangel Ariel ⤶

When we look at you, we see you as vast, multidimensional beings. There's just a little bit of you in this body, thinking that you are all of it. Some of you are getting an inkling that's not so. We see you at all dimensions, in the vastness of who you are.

From our viewpoint, because you are reading this, you are a Lightworker and you are here with a job to do. You are here to assist in the transition of planet Earth into Light. You've done it countless times before and you are an expert in your field.

This book presents you with a model which describes what's going on in this process for this planet. It is not truth. It is not real, because when you are attempting to describe a multidimensional, non-linear model, it's impossible to describe it in the English language. But we're going to do our very best. If at times it bounces around, bear with it, because the process itself is not exactly linear. It's a lot more like music.

Now the only way we can present this model is linearly. We have attempted to do it non-linearly and everyone goes brain-dead. We hope that you can feel the shifts you're going through. We know that if your mental body can say, "Ah, this is part of eighth level of Lightbody," it eases the secret fears. There is a need for this information to go out because the fear level is so very high, especially coming from the physical and mental bodies. If you know what's happening to you and know that it's part of a coherent process, then you feel less crazy.

Every time a planet goes to Light, it is a unique expression of returning home from the experience of separation. The process differs, depending on the particular planet and species that's going to Light. This model is for the human species on planet Earth.

There are 383 other planets also going to Light simultaneously, and most of you are incarnate on most of them. This planet is special, however, because it has experienced the maximum separation from the Source and now it is returning. It will be successful. There is absolutely no doubt that this planet's return to the Source will be successful, and there will be no apocalypse in this parallel reality. There was a time when we were not so sure that this planet would be able to go home, but now we are celebrating the certainty of a safe return.

Now, a species can ascend or go to Light without the planet ascending. You are not the first species to ascend from this planet — there have been four other races before you. What makes this particular process so exquisitely wonderful is that planet Earth is ascending also. She is a conscious, living entity who agreed to support this game of separation on the condition that she would ascend at its conclusion.

We'd like to mention the exquisiteness of this game as it returns to the Source. The beauty of your Divine Expression as you return is so wondrous for us to watch. Even though you stepped away from the Source for what is to us only a brief time, your reunification is one of the most exquisite energies in the universe. We look forward to you consciously experiencing this for yourselves. Because we exist in simultaneity, we have already seen you enjoy your reunification, and we look forward to sharing your joy when you catch up with yourselves.

I would also like to mention that the measurement for our model of Lightbody comes from looking at the amount of adenosine triphosphate in the cells. We measure Lightbody levels from your physical body's level of mutation. Now Angelic Outreach has gotten several calls from folks declaring that they were in twelfth level Lightbody. We have told them that within this model that can't be so. In this model if you were in twelfth level Lightbody, you wouldn't be able to pick up a telephone because you would be fully in Light and not in this dimension. Now you can have many levels of consciousness and your mind and your consciousness can go many places, but what you are ascending is your physical body and that's why we measure it from there. I knew that if I articulated this model linearly, and in levels, that many of your human egos would involve themselves with, "I'm more evolved than you (or anyone)" games. Please remember that each level is different and essential. No level is "better" than another. Also, as of January 1995, no one on the planet in this parallel reality is in eleventh or twelfth levels of Lightbody.

Finally, we'd like to thank you for being present on the planet at this time. You came here knowing that you would have to go to sleep. You'd have to deny everything that you are, forget everything that you know, and be unrecognizable to yourselves and each other. We have the easy job — we never step away from the Source or experience separation from Spirit. So, we honor you for what you are doing and feel honored to work with you.

— Ariel

What is Lightbody?

All techniques and processes in this book are for Spiritual Light Integration. This is not medical advice. If you are experiencing any of the symptoms mentioned, please see your doctor.

As you probably know, this planet is in a state of ascension. Its frequency is rising at a very rapid rate and it's losing density. Matter, as you know it from the third dimension, is densification of Light. That densification is beginning to drop off and the vibratory rate of each and every one of you, as well as the entire planet, is rising. It's a pretty exciting process.

When you have a process of densification, such as that occurring in your universe, you reach a point when it's gone to maximum separation from the purest forms of Light. At that point of maximum separation, a shift occurs, and the planet begins to reverse its process and start on what we would term a homeward route, i.e. back to the One Point. There are seven to eight million Lightworkers on the planet at this point — what some have called "planetary transition teams." Each one of you is a Lightworker. You are here with special purposes, special skills, and special delights. Many of you are specialists in assisting planets in ascension, having done it thousands and thousands of times.

Each time that a planet ascends, it's a unique process — the process of reunification. And the joy of reunification is expressed differently, depending on how the game was played. This game was one of the greatest possible separation from Spirit you could have. It was very successful.

But the game, as you know it, is now changing. And it began its process of change officially in March 1988. At that point, what we call "activation to first-level Lightbody" occurred for most Lightworkers. That was like a little bell going off in your DNA structure that said, "Yahoo, time to go home!" And it began the process of mutation and change. While this is very joyful most of the time, sometimes it can be a little difficult. But it's a process that all of you have gone through before.

What makes the game interesting is the question, "How should I do it this time? What energies, emotions, and delight will I express in this path of reunification?" What we call the "inbreath and the outbreath" of the Source has occurred many, many times, and this particular inbreath will have its own unique expression and delight, as this planet and all other planets return to the One Point.

This planet is in a state of transition to Light, or a process of ascension. It is a gradual process — you are not matter one day and Light the next day. Everyone is in the process, and many of you are at least halfway.

The Dimensions

First, let me briefly describe the various dimensions or planes of existence in our model. We use a twelve-dimensional model and you, sitting here in a physical body exist in the third dimension: it's matter-based. The fourth dimension is what's called the astral plane: it's basically emotionally-based. Together, these two make up what we call the Lower Creation World. These are the dimensions where the game of separation is carried out. These are the only dimensions in which the illusion of good and evil can be maintained and in which you can feel separated from Spirit and from each other. You've all become quite good at doing that. It's been a very successful game of separation, but now it's time for it to end. So, this planet is in a state of ascension, and is currently vibrating at the lower levels of the astral plane. As part of the ascension process, all of the dimensions will be rolled up into the higher dimensions and will cease to exist.

Because the planet is now vibrating at the level of the mid-astral plane, it's beginning to feel like a dream state, for many of you. You're never quite sure if you are awake or asleep. Continuities are breaking down. There is the feeling that things can change as you hold them in your hand. The pen that you're writing with may become a hammer, and eventually this lack of continuity will no longer bother you, just as it doesn't when you're dreaming. You'll be noticing that your dreamstates are changing, that as you wake up you're not quite sure if you're awake. You will become lucid while you're dreaming, fully conscious in that state. You will be fully self-aware as you move back and forth between different realities, and all of them will feel equally real to you. It won't seem like there is only one true reality, anymore.

The fifth through the ninth dimensions make up the Mid-Creation Realm, in the model that we use. The fifth is the Lightbody dimension, in which you are aware of yourself as a master and a multidimensional being. In the fifth dimension, you are completely spiritually-oriented. Many of you have come in from this plane to be Lightworkers here.

The sixth dimension holds the templates for the DNA patterns of all types of species' creation, including humankind. It's also where the Light languages are stored, and it is made up mostly of color and tone. It is the dimension where consciousness creates through thought, and one of the places where you work during sleep. It can be difficult to get a bead on this, because you're not in a body unless you choose to create one. When you are operating sixth-dimensionally, you are more of an "alive thought." You create through your consciousness, but you don't necessarily have a vehicle for that consciousness.

The seventh dimension is that of pure creativity, pure Light, pure tone, pure geometry, and pure expression. It is a plane of infinite refinement and it is the last plane where you perceive of yourself as "individual."

The eighth is the dimension of group mind or group soul, and is where you would touch base with the vaster part of who you are. It is characterized by loss of sense of the "I." When you travel multidimensionally, this is the plane where you would have the most trouble keeping your consciousness together, because you are pure "we," operating with group goals. So it might seem as though you've gone to sleep or blanked out.

In the model that we use, the ninth dimension is the plane of the collective consciousness of planets, star systems, galaxies, and dimensions. If you visit this dimension, it can be difficult to remain conscious. Once again, it's very difficult to get a sense of "I," because you are so vast that everything is "you." Imagine being the consciousness of a galaxy! Every life-form, every star, planet, and group mind of every species in it is within you.

The tenth through twelfth dimensions make up the Upper Creation Realm. The tenth is the source of the Rays, home of what are called the Elohim. This is where new plans of creation are designed and then sent into the Mid-Creation levels. You can have a sense of "I" at this level, but it won't be at all what you're used to at the third dimension.

The eleventh dimension is that of pre-formed Light — the point before creation and a state of exquisite expectancy, just like the moment before a sneeze or an orgasm. It is the realm of the being known as Metatron, and of Archangels and other Akashics for this Source-system. There are planetary Akashic records and galactic Akashics, as well as the Akashic for an entire Source-system. You are in one Source-system of many. So, we are giving you a description of only one Source-system — this one. If you go to another Source-system, what you will experience will be different. As an Archangel, my home base is the eleventh dimension.

The twelfth dimension is the One Point where all consciousness knows itself to be utterly one with All That Is. There is *no* separation of any kind. If you tap into this level, you know yourself to be completely one with All That Is, with the creator force. If you tap in there, you will never be the same again, because you cannot sustain the same degree of separation if you have experienced complete unity.

Your Bodies

So, in the old world, you have a physical body, and most people's reaction to that physical body is one of it being an enemy, an adversary. After all, it is what you experience karmic limitation through. So most people have this feeling: "If I didn't have a body, I wouldn't be experiencing all this limitation." There can be a total denial that the body itself has a consciousness, and that this consciousness' purpose is to serve you and to serve Spirit. So the physical body walks around most of the time feeling denied and abused, because you say, "Well, I don't want to experience karma through you and therefore I'm not going to pay any attention to what you tell me. I'm not going to feed you what you want to eat. I'm not going to let you play in any way that you want to play." You do all these odd things to your bodies. If you think about it, most of you have a love/hate relationship with your body. "It's too fat, it's too tall, it's too wide, it's too bald, it's too curly, it's too long, it's too short." So, most of you have this sort of relationship with the physical.

You also have something which we call an etheric blueprint. And most of you, if you perceive on an etheric level, perceive this body at about a half-inch away from your skin. It also exists within you. This body holds structures that are seventh-, sixth-, fifth-, and fourth-dimensional. Now, we're going to explain that. We're talking in terms of dimensions. You are currently in the third dimension. The fourth dimension in our model is the astral level. This is where the majority of your karmic patterning is stored within the etheric body. It sets up the motions that go on in the other energy bodies, which bring you karmic experiences. It also works to keep your DNA functioning at limited, survival-based levels by inhibiting the amount of Light your physical body can absorb.

Then you have the fifth-dimensional Lightbody structure (which lies dormant), and in that structure are something we call etheric crystals. These crystals block certain flows and prevent that body from activating too early.

The fifth-dimensional etheric blueprint is made up of an axiotonal meridian system, an axial circulatory system, and spin points through which these systems and structures are connected.

As part of this game of separation, the human axiotonal meridians were cut off from direct connection with the Overself and other star populations. This created brain atrophy, aging, and death. Axiotonal lines are the equivalent of acupuncture meridians that can connect with the Oversoul and resonant star systems.

Through the axiotonal lines, a human body is directly reprogrammed by the Overself into a new body of Light. Axiotonal lines exist independently of any physical body or biological form. They emanate from various star systems and are the means by which the galactic body controls its renewing mechanisms. Picture the Milky Way as the body of a living conscious being. The stars and planets are organs in that body; all the different species on the stars and planets are like cells in the organs of the galactic body, renewing the energies of the organs and cells. Planet Earth and her inhabitants were separated from the galactic body and the Oversoul to play this game of separation, and are now being reconnected.

The axiotonal lines are made of Light and Sound. The functions of the Office of the Christ are necessary to restructure the axiotonal meridians in the human body. Once reconnection has occurred, the Overself transmits the appropriate color/tone frequencies to regenerate the physical body into a Lightbody.

The axiotonal lines lie along the acupuncture meridians and connect into some of them by means of the "spin points." Spin points are small spherical vortexes of electromagnetic energy that feel like they are on the skin surface. There are also spin points in every cell of the body. These cellular points emit Sound and Light frequencies which spin the atoms of the molecules in the cell at a faster rate. Through the increased molecular spin, Light fibers are created which set up a grid for cellular regeneration.

The axial circulatory system was completely vestigial in the human species, due to the axiotonal lines being disconnected so that this game could be played. It is a fifth-dimensional energy system that connects the spin points on the skin surface to every spin point in every cell. It is a model for physical transmutation and it is being renewed now that the axiotonal lines are reconnected. The axial system pulses energy like the circulatory system pulses blood, but the axial system is basically electrical in nature, like the nervous system. The Overself sends energy into the axiotonal line, which then goes into the spin points on the surface of the skin, feeding the physical acupuncture meridians and then the axial system. As the axial system receives energy from the Overself, it recombines color and sound to realign the blood, lymph, endocrine, and nervous systems into the Divine Template, the Adam Kadmon. It also carries the energy from the Overself into the spin points inside the cells. This stimulates the spin points to emit Sound and Light to create a gridwork for the renewed evolution of humankind.

The sixth-dimensional structure holds templates, or patterns, that are set for the formation of matter and Lightbodies. It is where the entire DNA encodement is held. So you have this sixth-dimensional template that determines what is in your DNA and the shape of your physical form. Lightworkers carry bits of genetic material from the various species which live on the 383 ascending planets.

The seventh-dimensional structures are for embodiment of Divinity. They act as an interface between the physical or astral bodies of a given species and its Divine blueprint. The Adam Kadmon is the Divine form from which all sentient species forms emanate; therefore it is inclusive of myriad forms. The seventh-dimensional structures are very flexible, differing from individual to individual. Preset "thresholds" within the structure and within the third- or fourth-dimensional bodies create a ceiling on how much the Oversouls can interface with and embody in any given species.

So, before activation of the bodies to Light, if you were walking around this planet, you were mostly aware of the fourth-dimensional patterning in your bodies.

The next body in this model is what we call the emotional body. The emotional body, the mental body, and the spiritual bodies are made up of double tetrahedrons, if you look at them fifth-dimensionally. They have certain specific rates of spin. In the emotional body, you have all of these wonderful stuck places, and all they are is geometry that happens not to be moving in a coherent fashion. That incoherent motion is caused by the fourth-dimensional structures in the etheric blueprint. So, you sit on emotion — that's part of the karma game. In this game, you are taught to not express. Expressing is dangerous. If you cannot express, you will lock down those wonderful geometries in that field. What happens is you bop along until you run into someone with a complementary "stuck-point." Your little geometries lock and there you are, doing a karma. You're stuck. And you're stuck until it is complete and they get themselves unjammed. You experience this as limitation. You experience this as discomfort. And you experience this as "Why the hell am I here?"

The mental body is also made of geometries. This body's function is to determine your reality. It believes that it's in control. It believes that it is running the show. It isn't, but its whole job is to determine what is "real." It determines how the universe recreates itself in your life. So, by determining what's real, it keeps you stuck in the karma game. There is nothing the mental body hates more than change. Nothing. Because if you change what you're doing now, you may not survive in the future. It keeps maintaining a reality that it thinks will keep you alive, whether it works or not. It doesn't give a flying fig over whether you're happy or satisfied in any way. It is set there to maintain.

The natural state of All That Is is unified within itself. The amount of energy it takes to maintain the illusion of separation is absolutely incredible. It takes so much more energy than to simply let go. That's part of the reason why the mental body was developed to be so strong. The easiest way to maintain the illusion of separation was to have the mental body declare everything it cannot see as "not real." So it screens out all the impulses coming from your Spirit.

The spiritual body (the next one out) is also made of the same double tetrahedrons, and is — for the most part — ignored in a karma game. Its original design is to connect you to your Oversoul, your Christ Oversoul, and to the I AM Presence. Obviously, the spiritual body is underused in a karma game. It just sits out there and those connections are not made.

The spiritual body brings through impulses and information from your own Spirit, which then hit up against a mental body that says, "That's not real." When the emotional body picks up hints from Spirit, instead of trying to express them, it shuts down. And you keep repeating this entire cycle of limitation and separation, because this entire game was based on the illusion of separation from Spirit. That's what it was all about.

Your Chakras

The other things that shift function are your chakra systems. Most of you are aware of chakras. You have a total of fourteen major chakras that exist multidimensionally — seven within your physical body, seven outside your body — plus the Alpha and Omega "chakras." Most people see or feel chakras as radiant, spinning energy sources, but chakras also have a sixth-dimensional internal structure.

Under the karma game, the structure of the seven embodied chakras was deliberately limited so that they could only transduce energy from the astral plane. They were "sealed." With this limited blueprint, a chakra looks like two cones. One of the cones opens out towards the front of the body; the other one opens out towards the back. Where their narrowed points touch in the center of the body, they are "sealed" so that they remain in this configuration. This narrow part in the center tends to be clogged with mental and emotional "debris," causing the spin of the cones to slow down or stop. This starves the acupuncture meridian system of energy and can cause illness or death. This type of chakra structure can only move energy front to back or back to front, and cannot utilize higher-dimensional frequencies.

When the Lightbody process is activated, the "seals" in the center points are broken. The chakra structure gradually opens up from the center until the chakra is spherical in shape. This allows the chakra to radiate energy in all directions and begin to transduce frequencies from the higher dimensions. The body sheds the collected karmic debris and the spherical blueprint makes it impossible for any more to collect. The spheres keep expanding in size, until all the chakras merge as one unified energy field. Each of the upper chakras (the non-embodied chakras) have a different geometric blueprint structure, one that is appropriate for transducing the specific dimensional or Oversoul frequencies associated with the chakra. The eighth and eleventh chakras also contain flat crystalline templates that the galactic axiotonal lines pass through. These templates are used by the Oversoul to modulate the star influences on one's physical body, once one's axiotonal meridians are reconnected. The Oversoul recalibrates the axiotonal lines and the axial circulatory system through the eighth chakra. Therefore, the eighth chakra acts as the "master control" for the mutation of the body's systems and the merging of the energy bodies.

Until recently, the Alpha and Omega "chakras" have been vestigial in the human body type. Even though the Alpha and Omega "chakras" are energy centers, they have a completely different type of blueprint and function than that of the other chakras. They are finely tuned energy regulators for electric, magnetic, and gravitational waves, as well as serving as anchors for the seventh-dimensional etheric blueprint.

The Alpha "chakra" is six to eight inches above and about two inches forward from the center of your head. It connects you to your immortal body of Light in the fifth dimension. The Omega "chakra" is about eight inches below the end of your spine and connects you to the planet as a hologram, as well as to your entire holographic grid of incarnations. Unlike the fourth-dimensional karmic matrix, this is a completely non-karmic type of connection. The eighth chakra is seven to nine inches above the exact center of the head, above the Alpha "chakra." There is a column of Light, about four inches in diameter, that extends from your eighth chakra down through the center of your body, through the embodied chakras, to about eight inches below your feet. This column supports a tube of Light, about one and three-quarters inches in diameter, which runs down the exact center of the entire length of the column.

When the Alpha and Omega "chakras" are open and operating correctly, you will experience something called the Waves of Metatron, moving through the inner column of Light. These magnetic, electric, and gravitational waves oscillate back and forth between the Alpha and Omega "chakras," which regulate the waves' amplitude and frequency. These waves stimulate and support the flow of pranic life force energy in the smaller tube of Light. The Waves of Metatron also assist in coordinating the physical body's mutation to the pre-existing template of your immortal body of Light.

As the embodied chakras open into their spherical structure, grids are laid down which connect the chakras directly into spin points on the skin's surface, thereby connecting the chakras directly into the new axiotonal and axial systems. By connecting the chakra grids into the axiotonal lines, the chakras are hooked up into higher evolutionary, universal resonance grids and wave motions. This assists the chakras and the emotional, mental, and spiritual bodies to merge into one unified energy field. This unified field then receives the Oversoul bodies and moves in synchrony with universal waves and pulses. This whole new system then transmits these waves and pulses through the spin points, into the axial circulatory system, to recalibrate the pulses and flows of bodily fluids.

Now, in a karma game, since you are in a state of separation from Spirit and living in a state of limitation and you're alienated from your physical body, that usually means that you're not in your body. If you are not in your body, you cannot activate the heart chakra.

If you cannot activate your heart chakra, the chakras which are operating predominantly are the base chakra, the navel chakra and the solar plexus chakra. All of your interactions are coming out of instinctive terror, karmic patterning, power, lust, greed, or sheer ego-centered power interactions with people. So you don't get to have a higher interaction until you are fully in your body. And, of course, the upper, non-embodied chakras are not activated at all.

❧ Activation ❧

In March 1988, all of what we call Lightworkers were activated to at least first-level Lightbody on this planet. On April 16, 1989, the entire crystalline structure of matter and every inhabitant on this planet was activated to third-level Lightbody. Now, this is not an optional process; everyone is experiencing this. Lots of people are leaving the planet because they don't want to do this in this lifetime. You can choose to do this process in any lifetime you have ever had, in any parallel reality. So, don't feel that we're losing people. It's OK. They're just not prepared to do it in **this** incarnation.

First Level of Lightbody

So, you have had an activation to the first level of Lightbody. Now when this happened — for most of you — it was as though a lightbulb went off in your DNA: "It's time to go home." That's what it feels like in the body: "It's time to go home." And there's a sense of elation that comes up from the body that's just wonderful. At the same time, the body said: "Time to drop density" and most of you had a very good bout of the "flu." Much of what's going around right now that people are calling the "flu," we call "mutational symptoms." When your body drops density, it will tend to have headaches, vomiting, diarrhea, acne, rashes, anything that is a flu-like symptom — muscle aches, joint aches are very common. And if you remember back to March 1988, there was a "flu" epidemic: it was a Light epidemic!

Current human genetic science has called 99% of the DNA "junk," because "we don't know what it all means." In fact, human DNA holds bits of genetic material from every species on Earth, plus genetic material holographically encoded with the collective experience of all of humanity and the experiences of your holographic grid of incarnations, as well as bits of genetic encoding from the sentient species of 383 ascending planets across five local universes! Your DNA also holds latent encodements for mutating your physical body into a Lightbody.

Only about 7% of the genetic encodements were active before March 1988. Then, in the first level of Lightbody, Spirit activated a series of these latent encodements by infusing a tone/color sequence. These newly activated encodements signalled your body to begin a mutational change in the DNA and a profound alteration in the way your cells metabolize energy.

We measure Lightbody levels by the ability of your cells to metabolize Light. The marker for this new cellular activity is the amount of adenosine triphosphate (ATP) in the cells. Before Lightbody activation, the energy for cellular functioning came from an energy production and storage system which shuttles energy back and forth between adenosine *di*phosphate (ADP) and adenosine *tri*phosphate. ATP is an energy storage compound found in the cells. Within the mitochondria, food is converted into energy for the cells, which is then bound up in the ATP. ATP has a chain of three phosphate groups, which projects out from the molecule. When an ATP molecule loses its outermost phosphate group, it becomes an ADP molecule. The breaking of the chemical bond releases energy for the cell to carry out its functions, such as creating proteins. ADP can again become ATP by picking up some energy and a phosphate group. ATP and ADP lose and gain phosphate groups to release and store energy for cellular functioning. This is a closed system of biological energy, ensuring aging and death. No new energy is gained.

When the Lightbody mutation was activated, a series of latent DNA encodements lit up and began to give new directives to the cells. One of the first instructions was to tell the cells to recognize Light as a new energy source. At first, the cellular consciousness didn't know what to do with this information. As the cells were bathed in Light, the mitochondria (which are very Light sensitive) began to fully absorb this new color/tonal activation and produce lots of ATP, in bursts. The cells had not yet absorbed enough Light to stabilize the phosphate bond, so the ATP broke down very rapidly into ADP, and cellular metabolism was dramatically speeded up. Accumulated toxins, old traumas, and stored thoughts and emotions began to flush from the physical body and created flu-like symptoms.

The physical form in its old manner has separated brain functioning into right and left hemisphere functions. Also, the pineal and pituitary glands are atrophied — about the size of a pea rather than the size of a walnut. On activation, brain chemistry begins to change and to produce new synapses.

Second Level of Lightbody

In the second level, the sixth-dimensional etheric blueprint begins to be flooded with Light and it begins to release the fourth-dimensional structures which tie you into karmic experiences across all lifetimes. As a result, you may have begun to feel a little disoriented, along with having had more bouts of "the flu."

You probably will have found yourself lying in bed, saying "Why am I here?", "Who am I?", and might have gotten an inkling that there was something called "Spirit" in your life. Now we'll also define another term. When we use the term "soul," we are talking about the differentiated part of Spirit that experiences through your physical body. When we talk in terms of Spirit, we are talking about that part of you which is undifferentiated and totally connected to the Source.

So, in the second level of Lightbody, you are releasing fourth-dimensional structures which begin to change the spin in the geometries of your emotional, mental, and spiritual bodies. You are beginning to change very rapidly. Most of what you're experiencing is strictly physical. You may feel very tired.

Third Level of Lightbody

In the third level of Lightbody, your physical senses become outrageously strong. The example we use is that the smell of that old piece of garbage stuck in the garbage disposal is driving you crazy — from upstairs. Everything may seem incredibly tactile. The chair you're sitting on or the clothes you're wearing may be terribly distracting because they feel so sensual. Often, people rediscover the joy of sex in third-level Lightbody. That's why there has been a rise in pregnancies and births since April 1989, when the planet and her population were activated to the third level.

Everything that is happening is very centered in the physical body. It's beginning to open up into what we call a "bio-transducer system." Your body was designed to decode and work with Higher Light energies as well as transmit these energies to the planet. As part of the game of separation, these functions atrophied. The magnification of the physical senses is the first sign of the awakening of your body as a "bio-transducer."

Undifferentiated Light from the Oversoul pours into the fifth-dimensional axiotonal lines. From the axiotonal spin point interfaces on the skin surface, the fifth-dimensional axial circulatory system begins to form. The axial system then extends into and activates the spin points in every cell of the physical body.

Whereas in the first and second levels of Lightbody, the physical body was being bathed in Light, now — in the third level — each cell has Light focused directly into it through the axial system.

The mitochondria usually recognize this Light as "food," and produce more ATP. Because the cell is receiving Light as usable energy, less of the ATP turns into ADP. As the axial system feeds energy from the Oversoul into the cellular spin points, the spin points produce Sound and Light frequencies which change the atomic spin of the cells' molecules, especially in the hydrogen atoms. As the atomic spin in the ATP molecule increases, a new functioning emerges. The three phosphate groups forming the stalk of the ATP molecule begin to act like an antenna for undifferentiated Light, and the symmetrical head of the molecule acts like a prism, breaking down the Light into subtle color spectrums, usable by the dormant DNA encodements.

Before Lightbody was activated, the ribonucleic acid (RNA) in the cells acted as a one-way messenger. It carried directives from the active 7% of the DNA to other parts of the cell for execution, such as what proteins to synthesize. In third-level Lightbody, the RNA became a two-way messenger! Now it took Light, broken down into usable color frequencies by the ATP antenna/prism, back into the DNA strands. The dormant genetic encodements gradually awaken with each successive Lightbody level and give their information to the RNA, which transmits it to the rest of the cell.

It's much like the new CD laser technologies on Earth. An enormous amount of information can be stored on one disk. Imagine that a vast amount of information can be stored in a color range of red and vast amounts of data can be stored in a blue spectrum. A red laser beam is run across the disk and all the red information is now able to be read, but you still know nothing about what is stored in the blue spectrum. You run a blue laser beam over the CD and now all of that data is available. The Light/color frequencies "read" the DNA in much the same way. Until the color spectrum is transmitted, you have no idea what's in there. Each Lightbody level has its own color/tonal signature. In this way, Spirit achieves the gradual mutation of the physical body.

The one-way DNA-to-RNA information transfer and the ATP-ADP energy cycle were closed systems, ensuring entropy. Nothing could change, except to decay. With Lightbody activation, new, fully open systems can develop, making infinite energy and infinite information available to the body. A dialogue between your physical body and Spirit has begun.

In the first two levels of Lightbody, you can still reverse the entire process because the ATP and RNA have not gained this new functioning. At the third level of Lightbody, it is a continuing mutation that you cannot stop. That's why when the indigenous population of this planet and the planet herself were activated, they were activated to the third level of Lightbody: so the process couldn't be messed with, quite simply.

Also, in that activation to the third level of Lightbody, a set point was created between this planet and all the other planets that are ascending out of the physical plane, so that you're all in synch. It isn't just that this planet is ascending; the entire dimension is ascending! And so is the entire astral plane. There will be no more physical and astral planes when this is done. This entire process is something we call an "inbreath" of the Source.

In our model, the Source (the One Point, All That Is, or God) manifests as inbreaths and outbreaths of creativity — very slow outbreaths and very quick inbreaths. A Lightworker once asked us why it takes billions of years to densify a game to this level of separation and yet we're turning the whole game around in twenty years. Imagine that you are the One, and You decide to explore the myriad possible facets of what You are through levels of progressive individuation. It's like stretching a rubber band. As you achieve more and more individuation, the rubber band gets tighter and tighter and tighter. Well, there's a point when it has stretched as far as it can. You have separated the maximum that You can from Your Oneness and the tension is tremendous. So, You turn around and let go of the rubber band — your separateness. What happens? You shoot back to Your Oneness very quickly.

On this planet, you have a game of separation that has now completed every possible permutation of relationship and interaction you can have. Every karmic relationship that you can explore has been explored and when that happens, you begin the "inbreath." This game is over. It's time to go home.

What we term "Lightworkers" are people who are here as transition teams to assist in this process of Light. That's why you're here. Some of you have been here for the entire cycle. Some of you are assisting in setting up this particular game and have decided to stay and see how it would work. If you were to look at time linearly, you're sitting out across linear time and across all parallel times, activating, turning into Light. A planet does not ascend in an instant — it ascends from the moment of its creation. And that's why so many of you took on so many lifetimes here. Others of you are showing up to assist now, and that's OK, too.

Fourth Level of Lightbody

As you transition into the fourth level of Lightbody, you begin to go into what we call the mental stages. This begins a massive change in your brain chemistry and the electromagnetics of your brain. At this point, if you have regulator crystals in your etheric body, they may become very uncomfortable. You may start having cluster headaches, seizures, chest pains, blurry vision, or your hearing may go out.

These crystals keep lines of Light within the fifth-dimensional blueprint from making connections, just like electricity. Chest pains are something you may experience throughout the Lightbody process, because your heart begins to open at deeper and deeper levels. Your entire vision and hearing apparatus begins to alter, as parts of the brain open up. A whole different functioning starts in at that fourth level of Lightbody. The hemispheres of the brain want to begin to start firing across both hemispheres at the same time, and if there is something stopping that, it can feel really yucky. Most people begin to feel some electrical stuff going on in their head. You may literally feel electrical energy running across your scalp or down your spine.

You may have your first taste of non-linear thinking, which can be either delightful or terrifying. You begin to go through a mental shift. The mental body is beginning to say to itself, "Gee whiz. Maybe I'm not running the show."

Usually about the fourth level of Lightbody, someone shows up in your life saying "The prime directive is to follow your Spirit without hesitation," or something similar. Suddenly the mental body gets the idea: "Gee, maybe something else is in control of this because I'm sure not!" And it begins to shift how it views itself and begins to get a little uncertain about what's real and what's not. Your Spirit begins to put through much wider, vaster pictures of reality or patterning through your energy bodies.

In the fourth level, you get the inkling that there is a Spirit. Suddenly, you get impulses from areas you didn't before and you're thinking that maybe you should start following those impulses. Your mental body is screaming: "Wait a minute. What is this?" It starts trying to retain control over the world and it's pretty uncomfortable because it's getting an inkling that everything is changing. Everything it has defined as real is beginning to shift.

You may have flashes of telepathy or clairvoyance. Just about everybody gets empathy right around this time. And once again, the mental body tries to clamp down because it feels like the emotional body is opening and, of course, that's dangerous and it's going to get you killed, according to mental body rules. So the flashes of empathy can be very uncomfortable for people and yet at the same time, it's exhilarating because you feel so much more connection with everything, a sense of "I'm connected to things here. There are people here that maybe I've known before. I know you from somewhere. Gee, you look familiar." And you begin to get an inkling that maybe there's a purpose to your being here.

Fifth Level of Lightbody

At the fifth level of Lightbody, usually the mental body says "Maybe I'll try to follow Spirit. I don't know if I buy it, but maybe I'll try it." And it starts that process of looking for clues.

A person often begins to have some flashes of themselves doing other things. Often, your dream sequencing begins to change. You begin to remember a little more of your dreams. Some people open up to lucid dreaming in the fifth level.

At some points a person can feel like they might be going crazy, because they may be beginning to experience non-linear thought processes. Suddenly, rather than having to look at something in this nice set fashion, they are cognizant of the whole, i.e., non-linear thinking. And then the mental body says, "Wait a minute, I can't control this. Can we survive and do this?" So, it is questioning what is happening: "Is there a Spirit? I think there's a Spirit. I better figure out whether there's a Spirit because otherwise, we're all going to die." You get a lot of the survival patterning coming up out of the mental body. So the mental body begins to shift the way it moves and it begins to drop patterning out.

A part of you is just like a little child saying, "Yeah, we're going to Light. Yeah, we're going to Light." And you're so happy. And then you have the mental body, just an old grump. And you get to see the two halves of yourself: "Wow! I get to make a decision here about what I want to do."

You begin to become aware that you are more than you thought you were. When that happens, the mental body says, "Oh no, we're not!" and slams down, but then it opens up again. So you keep going through this process of feeling like you're opening and closing, opening and closing. It can feel a little manic-depressive. What your Spirit needs you to do is to get your mental body to surrender its control so that you can become an active embodied Spirit on this planet, fully conscious on every dimension.

Also, in the fifth level of Lightbody, you begin to become aware that a lot of your pictures about the way things are aren't yours. You begin to be aware that, "Oh dear, I'm doing that just like my father. My father was picky and I'm acting just like him. Wait a minute, that's not my energy." Or, "My child just knocked over the milk and I'm screaming at her just like my mother screamed at me. That's not my energy. I don't want to be doing this. This is not what I want to be doing here."

You become aware that you contain entire pictures of reality that are not yours. And you begin the mental sorting out process of "Who am I," as different from those around you. Everyone holds, within their energy fields, the entire picture of "the way things are" from their parents, grandparents, siblings, and lovers. The entire picture is updated continuously. As you become aware that these structures are contained in your fields, you can feel very closed in by them.

Because here you are — you can feel all this change going on in your body, all this wonderful stuff, and at the same time, you feel like you are in a glass cage — all this change and you are so contained by these pictures. So you start that sorting out process: "Well, I'll take some of this, I'll take none of that, a little of that and a little of this." And you begin to become more and more aware of your energy. What is truly yours. When you have a thought or a picture about something, you just ask yourself, "Am I just running my father, or is this me?" It can be a little scary to someone, when they first look in the mirror and they say, "Oh no, I really am turning into my mother. I swore I would not turn into my mother." But you find that you get to a point where those pictures of reality begin to shift out of your fields.

Sixth Level of Lightbody

In the sixth level of Lightbody you are actively, consciously shifting reality pictures out of your field. At this time, your Spirit is usually putting you into contact with people who are working with the Lightbody process. Maybe Spirit is throwing books at you off of shelves. Have you had this experience of being in a book store and having books fall at you? You may have those at any time. It's one of the favorite ways for Spirit to say, "Read this." You begin to get other information, other pictures of reality. You begin to take in vaster understandings of your own reality and how you operate in them.

Often, in the fifth and sixth levels, you have experiences of things not being solid. In your meditation, you may look down and sense that your hand is not solid, or you have one of those odd experiences where you put your hand against a wall and you feel the wall give. So you may be having flashes of multidimensionality. You may be having flashes of non-linear thinking and feeling like nothing is real. This can be a real shock for you mental-body types out there who want everything all laid out in nice little lines — suddenly you see the whole picture at once. Then you have to go back and make up how you got there. Some of you experience this extensively. The mental body begins to cognate very differently.

A lot of people leave the planet in sixth level Lightbody, because it's extremely uncomfortable for most of them. "Do I want to be here? Do I want to look at all this stuff? Do I want to be part of this process?" A lot of people opt out. That's okay. They are doing this process in another life. They don't have to do it in all of them. Generally, if we can assist someone to survive the fifth and sixth levels, they're home free. If they choose to not opt out of the planet at that point, they will usually stay and work with the entire process.

Be kind to your fellow human beings. This is a very painful stage because this is the stage where the entire sense of identity is restructured. When you run into people on the street, and many of you will, you may be asked, "What are you doing? You look so wonderful." Give them the information that the planet is going to Light, that we are in an ascension process. "If you want to know more about it, here are some good books you could read. Here are some people you could go see. If you need to talk about it, here is my number." Support those around you.

Usually at the sixth level of Lightbody, you go through a re-evaluative state that is extremely uncomfortable. "Do I want to be here? Do I want to live? Do I want to play?" It can be pretty severe. You hate your job, you hate your life, you hate everybody and everything all at once.

In the sixth level, you find that lots of people begin to leave your life. This is the time when you're likely to change your job, get married, stop being married — all your friends may change, your entire sense of purpose changes and there's a sense of learning to not be afraid of change. If you freeze up, this level can last for up to a year and be very miserable. But most people learn fairly quickly to relax and let everything flow around them.

New people come into your life who are far more in alignment with what you're here to do than you've ever had before. You're all here in work groups — those people you're here to work with. This clearing away of those in your life who are there for karma or out of a sense of obligation can be a little bit scary. But, if you take a deep breath and say "I wish you well and have a nice life. I'll see you next time," you'll find that the people you're here to be with will quickly come into your life. This "amps up" the whole thing and it begins to be fun.

Usually between the sixth and seventh level of Lightbody, you experience what we call a descension of Spirit. This means that a vaster part of who you are in the upper dimensions comes to reside in your body. That shifts everything around.

You feel like you've come through a tunnel. You've come from a place of "Maybe there's a Spirit and maybe I'll try to follow it" to "I know, within every cell of my being, that I am Spirit in action on this planet." And you begin what we call the emotional transition to learning to be the vastness of Spirit. About one-third of the Lightbody structure is now lit up in the etheric blueprint. Many times you may experience yourself as radiating light, which is pretty exciting. Most of the time in the seventh level of Lightbody, people's eyes change. You begin to see a deeper level of Light coming out of people's eyes.

You and those around you are beginning to cognate in a non-linear way and you begin to get flashes of telepathy. You begin to get flashes of communication on levels that you communicate on all the time but are unaware of. You have always been telepathic. You have always been clairvoyant. You've always been multidimensional. But your mental body and brain have been screening it out and away from you. So, the screens are dropping and you begin to recognize what's been there all along. Things begin to feel normal. There's a point where it's no longer a big "A-ah." It's not the lightbulb going off anymore. It's just "I am here. I am. I am fully here, now." You become a delightful dance that you play with your Spirit.

The entire planet and its population appears to be doing a strong re-evaluation. The polarization of energies is happening at more and more heightened levels. It's almost like the volume is being turned up. Planetary polarization is becoming more and more intense. You'll find that those of you who are beginning to live Heaven on Earth, will exist side by side with those who are experiencing Hell on Earth.

I wish to remind you that all beings are vast multidimensional Divine Masters.

We ask that you learn compassion, and compassion is not being co-dependent: "Oh, let me take care of you!" Compassion is being willing to do whatever is necessary to assist someone in taking their next higher step. That occasionally means kicking someone's feet out from under them; that occasionally means being a wake-up call; that occasionally means calling someone on their "stuff"; and it often means loving them for their wholeness, their totality, the parts of them that are awake as well as the parts of them that are asleep. Remember they go into sleep with the first part of the Mission. Honor those who have slept well. Many Lightworkers have a fear of people who are asleep built into them. Begin to dismantle that particular piece of enemy patterning. You will naturally evolve it into a sense of service to Spirit and a service to all life. It will be ecstatic. But understand how difficult this period was and is for many people. Look at the level of re-evaluation, and you'll understand why we call this level the one that determines whether someone will do this process or not. This is the place where a lot of people must bail out or get with the program.

Seventh Level of Lightbody

In the seventh level of Lightbody, you begin to enter the emotional stages of Lightbody: focusing on deeper and deeper levels of opening in the heart chakra. As you open into the heart, a feeling of connection with the planet opens up: that feeling of falling in love with this planet, feeling like "If I don't hug that tree, I just can't make it. I have to hug that tree." There's a playfulness that begins to open up at the seventh level of Lightbody. You become a little more childlike in the way you operate.

At this point, if you've got blocks in the emotional body, they really begin to come up, because as you move toward expressing your divinity and your vastness, anything that blocks that vastness begins to release. Some of it's fun; some of it's not. It depends on how much of a stranglehold the mental body wants to keep. If the mental body is in sync, the release is usually quick and easy.

You may find that you become far more emotional than ever before, and as you move through these levels, you find that your emotions become like a child's: when you're sad, you cry; when you're angry, you yell; when you're happy, you laugh. You express ecstasy. You express whatever emotion is flowing through your emotional body in that moment. You begin to operate in the NOW far more than ever before. You see, in the karma game, your mental body lives in the future: it's always living in "what if"s. The emotional body lives in the past, triggered by what you've experienced before. So, you rarely experience exactly what's happening in front of you. In the seventh level of Lightbody, you begin to experience NOW. Enough synchronization has happened among your fields that you have begun to have long stretches of being fully in the present — and it feels really good.

As the emotional body drops all of its old patterning, it may mean that you have to complete your relationships with a lot of people. Having dropped all those pictures of reality out of the mental body, and now dropping the emotional attachments out of the emotional body means that your relationships with other people begin to change very quickly. In the seventh, eighth, and ninth levels of Lightbody, your personal relationships turn into something we call "transpersonal." That means they are not based on emotional attachment; they become based in whether your Spirit is guiding you to be with that person at any given time. It's a very different way of relating.

By the time someone is in the ninth level of Lightbody, they are usually operating this way most of the time. Sometimes, you may seem "cold" to people, because you don't have the emotional hooks and there is no intensity. "I can't manipulate you. I can't hook into you." People can get very upset. This is a natural part of the Lightbody process, as you shift from being in karmic relations into non-karmic, Spirit-based relationships.

In seventh-level Lightbody, the heart chakra opens to a much deeper functioning than it ever has before. Many people experience chest pains; it's probably not angina. It doesn't feel the same as a heart attack, because it feels like it's in the center of your body, radiating outward. It's an opening of the heart chakra gateway. If you're in a meditative state and you want to go multidimensional, you can go right through your own heart chakra.

On this planet, the heart chakra has a membrane in it, which we call the Gates of Eden. You all know that lovely story about Adam and Eve being cast out of the Gates of Eden, and there is an angel with a flaming sword so that they cannot reenter. What that is is a membrane in the heart chakra that prevents you from going multidimensional. It means that it keeps this game contained. None of the stuff that happens on the physical plane can get above the astral plane, so it can't affect anything else. Part of the way you do that is to close part of the heart chakra, so that you can't have multidimensional experience. That membrane is opened now, in everyone on the planet. The heart chakra shifts its functioning and it begins to open into deeper and deeper levels. You can travel into any dimension through the heart chakra: it is all contained within you. The heart chakra shifts functioning and begins to take predominance over the other chakras.

The way most chakras are portrayed is that they are conical, narrowing in the center, and spinning. Well, they are mutating, too. First they become spherical-shaped and they radiate in all directions at once. Then, if the heart chakra takes predominance, it all begins to open up and the chakra system merges into what we call the unified chakra. It's a unified energy field. It feels wonderful. When you do something like the Unified Chakra meditation, you assist your Lightbody process.

Assisting that chakra merger also assists those energy bodies — the emotional, mental, and spiritual bodies — to begin to merge. They merge into a unified field. In the seventh level of Lightbody, those chakras are kicking into merged states that they haven't been in before. And you begin to become aware that when you have survival fears coming up, or you have blocked emotions, all it means is that these fields have stepped out of unity. It's an illusion, even though it feels real. All you have to do is realign and re-merge the bodies, and the fear drops away.

The chakra unification is really important for your growth into Lightbody, because it allows you to handle any amount of energy (no matter how vast) through the physical form, without any damage: the entire field holds it. You'll have points when you'll tap into a vaster part of yourself and, if your chakras aren't moving in a unified fashion, you will feel as if you've stuck your finger into an electrical outlet. It's like you only have wiring for 20 volts but you just had 400 put through your body. When you utilize the unified chakra, you don't have that happen anymore; you can handle it at all levels.

The pineal and pituitary glands begin to open up in the seventh level of Lightbody, and you may experience a pressure on your forehead or at the back of your head.

When the pituitary gland is functioning at its higher level, you will not age or die. So very often, about seventh-level Lightbody, people start to look really young. Their whole energy changes around their face and lines drop out. The pineal operates in a multidimensional way. One of the things reported is the sensation of an ice pick, of sharp pain right in the top of the head. Most of you have heard of something called the third eye. Well, there is something called the fourth eye, just at the top of your head; it's your multidimensional sight. It's located where the soft spot is, the place that doesn't harden all the way in most of you. For some of you, that eye opens easily; it's just your multidimensional sight and it just does it when it's time. For others of you, it can feel like it's trying to open, but it's hitting up against something. It may be a structure placed within the etheric body. As that's removed, you'll find this eye opens up.

You begin to have these rather odd experiences. You may begin to be aware of yourself in other dimensions or aware of yourself in other bodies on the planet, which is grand fun. We call those concurrents. Most of you have twelve of you, in other bodies in this parallel reality, on this planet right now, living vastly different lives than you may be living now. You become a little more aware of yourself in other bodies. At first when this happens, people think they are remembering past lives, and they might be. But more often they are usually aware of themselves in the same parallel reality. A lot of you have some incarnations in dolphin and whale bodies. So you may have flashes of being in water or a fluidity of motion through and around your body that you've not normally had in a human form. Of course, the dolphins and whales are other individually ensouled species on this planet. They are Lightworkers too. They set up the group mind grids for this planet.

In seventh-level Lightbody, most beings are operating pretty much fourth-dimensionally in their consciousness: "Not only am I going to ascend tomorrow, but I am going to heal this planet. I am single-handedly going to save this planet and all you poor dummies out there. I'm going to do it. I'm going to drag you all to Light. I'm going to protect you from yourself and save you from your karma. And I'm going to save you from the dark forces." Beings in seventh-level Lightbody usually have an identity of being a healer, or an awakener, or a person who saves themselves, others, or the planet. Actually, they are doing karmic monads. It takes a little bit to realize that so many parts of you are still existing in duality. You may be requiring that the planet or people be sick so you can heal them, or lost so you can save them, or asleep so that they can be awakened. It requires that people not be fully functional.

In the seventh level, you are developing the knowing that all beings are vast multidimensional masters. They may be masters who are exploring divinity or they may be masters who are exploring limitation, but they are masters nonetheless. Everyone is doing exactly what they wish to be doing and they are fine. If a person has led a life where they have been constantly protecting and taking care of everyone around them, this is a deeply freeing revelation. Then it becomes okay to simply allow them their process.

This is a time where most beings run an amazing amount of what's called spiritual significance and spiritual ambition. In the physical body, pictures of reality about being completely separate from God are held in deep states of shame or guilt. When people begin to access who they are multidimensionally and they haven't integrated the physical body, they try to deny its pictures of reality. Beings will often adopt spiritual forms and rules. They try to say, wear, and do all the "right" spiritual things, eat all the "right" foods, and suppress or deny any part of themselves or others that doesn't fit their ideals. The mental body is accustomed to following forms and rules. It's trying very hard to find a form for following Spirit.

Spiritual significance is a mental body defense mechanism against feelings of shame and unworthiness held in the physical body. "I'm spiritually advanced (and you're not). I'm one of the 144,000 rainbow warriors (and you're not). I'm going to ascend next Saturday (and you're not). I'm going to heaven (and you're not)." Spiritual significance is by its nature exclusionary.

Spiritual ambition is a mental body defense against feelings of guilt and incompetence held in the physical body. Beings who are immersed in this will often run themselves ragged trying to manipulate other people to get with their program. Everything has to be "the best," "the highest," "the most advanced." Often, a difference of opinion or an implication that they don't know something is taken as an attack on their mastery. It is characterized by a nagging dissatisfaction and placing blame: "I have this wonderful vision and if you would just get with my program, I could carry out my Divine Purpose. It's your fault that I'm not living in heaven on Earth." "Your scarcity pictures are blocking Divine Flow. It's your fault that I'm broke." "Why did you create that in your reality? (Please deny what's going on with you, so I can be comfortable. If you were more spiritually advanced, it wouldn't have happened. So, you only have yourself to blame.)"

Spiritual significance and spiritual ambition are strong ego defenses. As Spirit reveals more and more of what you truly are as divine multidimensional masters, the mental and emotional bodies want to embrace it as personal truth by defining and attaching to it. The physical body is usually oblivious to the revelation or simply doesn't buy it. Everyone runs these defenses at some time in seventh, eighth, and ninth levels.

In seventh-level Lightbody, many people fall into a pattern of spiritual manic-depression. One minute they're declaring, "I'm a divine, multidimensional being!" and the next minute they are proclaiming their worthlessness: "I can't do anything right!" They are bouncing between the feelings of multidimensional Oneness and the feelings of separation held in their physicality. The paradox of being so vast and also being in a finite, matter-based body is nothing short of miraculous. Bouncing between the two extremes is an attempt to resolve the paradox. You cannot. Try holding both poles at once. Allow both to be fully present. Toward the end of seventh-level Lightbody, or at least sometime by ninth-level Lightbody, people begin to understand this process and find living in the center of the paradox ecstatic.

You started with following your Spirit. When you're into the seventh level of Lightbody, there is this sense of catching up. You're beginning to operate from Spirit in your everyday life. You find that you step in and out of survival fears. You have days when you're childlike and love everything and get along fine, and other days when "it's the pits" of fear and survival. You're feeling like there are two of you. You will find, as you progress through these stages of Lightbody, that the duality drops out. You find that "you" spend more and more of your time in a state of ecstasy. And you find you can function in that state.

One of the major fears of the mental body through this transition is "If I become a multidimensional being, I will not be able to function on the physical plane." You find you spend more and more of your time being aware of yourself in other dimensions and other bodies on the planet. It's fine. You can still function in that state; it just takes practice.

You begin to activate. Your whole perception begins to shift and in your meditations, you may experience yourself in other dimensions. You may also experience yourself in other bodies on this planet. You may have flashes of being in simultaneous time, where you are so NOW that you are all "NOW"s at once. This is pretty exciting when it happens, because then you become aware of the probabilities and possibilities of everything that you do. You see all those lines of force heading out from you. You become more aware of your connections with other people and of how deep your connection is with Spirit at any given moment.

We have noticed off and on that in the seventh level of Lightbody, the overarching feeling is, "I am going to ascend tomorrow; I'm out of here." You are being hooked up to parts of yourself that are already in Lightbody, parts of your future self. And what this does is it facilitates you to get your act together. You quickly sort through everything in your life and you really find out what's important to you: "Well, I'm out of here anyway, so I might as well do what I want. I might as well have fun; I might as well do what makes my heart sing."

You learn what makes your heart sing, what it is that you really enjoy. When you shift into eighth level of Lightbody, you find that everything that makes your heart sing is directly related to your Divine Purpose on this planet and that you're part of the Plan. In eighth level of Lightbody, you realize "Gee, I'm not out of here tomorrow.

I'm here for the long haul." You have a deepening sense of purpose and service. You want to do whatever it takes to assist this planet to Light.

Eighth Level of Lightbody

At the eighth level of Lightbody, the pituitary and the pineal gland, generally about the size of a pea, begin to grow and change shape. As they grow, sometimes you will feel pressure in your head. You may or may not have headaches off and on through this process. If you have a really bad mutational headache, understand that the you on the upper dimensions that is assisting you in this mutation cannot feel your physical pain. So, they first thing you want to do is say, "Yo! I hurt. Can we back it off here?" You have to tell yourself on the fifth and sixth dimensions that it is hurting.

Next say, "Please release endorphins." These are a natural brain opiate that allows the pain to ease off. For some of you, you would rather have little headaches for a month and a half. For others of you, you'd rather have a big headache for 24 hours and get it over with. Find out what works for you, because there are points in this process where your brain literally grows. Your brain gets bigger. You may experience cranial expansion. We have seen people entirely change the shape of their skull, particularly as the pituitary and the pineal open and grow. Also, when your pineal is growing, sometimes it feels like someone has their finger between your eyebrows and they're pushing. You also may feel a pushing feeling at the back of your head as the pituitary is growing.

As you transition into the eighth level of Lightbody, there is an activation of what we call the seed crystals. These three small crystals receive Light languages from the upper dimensions. Two of the crystals are located over your eyebrows, directly over the pupils if you are looking straight ahead. The third one is just below your hairline, in line with your nose.

There is also an activation of the recorder cell receiver crystal (on the right side of the head, about one and a half inches above the ear). In the higher dimensions, there is a structure called a recorder cell crystal. It holds vast amounts of information that the soul has gathered over many incarnational cycles on various planets and stars. Periodically, the recorder cell will download parts of the experiential data into the receiver crystal. When this happens, many people feel a tingling, burning, or liquid sensation in the area of the head where the receiver crystal is located. Suddenly, they have all this information and they can't figure out where it has come from.

The eighth, ninth, and tenth chakras activate. The three to five crystalline templates in the eighth chakra realign, so that your energy bodies change their usual motion into spirals of energy. You begin to hook up into multidimensional mind and begin to receive what we call the "languages of Light."

The pituitary and the pineal function together when they are open, causing what is known as the "Arc of the Covenant." It's a rainbow light that arcs over the top of the head, from the fourth eye to the third eye area. That is one of the decoding mechanisms for higher-dimensional language.

Your brain functioning begins to change and you begin to perceive and think in terms of geometries and tones. This can be a little bit unsettling because you usually don't have a translation available. You may feel that you can't talk to people around you because you have no words for what you're experiencing.

It is very common in the eighth level of Lightbody for people to secretly fear that they have Alzheimer's disease. You may have problems remembering what you ate for breakfast or projecting into the future, and this can become quite severe. The other common thing is that you cannot seem to put a sentence together, or when people are talking to you, it's like they are talking in another language. It's a type of audio dyslexia. The big joke about eighth level of Lightbody is: "To gain the 95% of my brain that I haven't used, why did I have to lose the 5% I already had?" All of the pathways in your brain that you are accustomed to using may become non-accessible while entirely new pathways are being created. You may be getting lots of tones in your ears, bands of light, color, geometry, and motion in your head.

You may see flaming Hebrew letters, hieroglyphics, or things that look like equations.

It is a communication from Spirit; it is an encodement. In the early stages, you may have no idea of what's being sent, only that *something* is. When this happens, do the unified chakra technique, unify, and ask for translation facility. You may have to keep asking for quite a while, but that's okay. As you progress through the eighth level of Lightbody, there is a point toward the end, right before you transition to the ninth level, that the translation opens up. All of that stuff that was transmitted from Spirit through this period is suddenly there and accessible on a verbal level.

This is the point of going home. That's the best way we can put it. You are hooking up to your multidimensional mind. The fact that you are a vast multidimensional being is real to you at every level and is undeniable. You become aware of your vastness. Many people bop along through the other stages of Lightbody saying, "Gee, I hope this is real!" It's very wonderful when we see them realize that this process is "real" for them.

Then you become aware that you can be anywhere you want to be, doing anything you want to do. The last vestiges of obligation begin to drop off. Everything you're doing is because Spirit is directing you to. There is no other reason that you ever need. You'll begin to operate without a need for reasons and rationales. You are following Spirit with every breath and every step. You say "I'm doing this because I want to," rather than "I'm doing this because I'm supposed to, or I ought to, or said I would." You begin to communicate with people on a whole new level, a level we call "transpersonal." You interact with someone because your Spirit is guiding you to interact. You talk because the words are there from your Spirit.

In this stage, people often don't know what to do with you, because your fields have changed. All the tetrahedrons they used to be able to hook up with aren't in "hook" position anymore. Those people in your life who want to connect with you through coercion or manipulation or co-dependency drop away pretty fast, because they can't connect with you anymore. You're no longer operating at that level. There's a deeper serenity that begins to flow through you and a heightened, more consistent ecstasy as you remain connected with your Spirit. You're no longer floating in and out so much; you stay in the body. You manifest your multidimensionality through your body.

The other thing that happens in eighth-level Lightbody is that you begin to open up your consciousness, not only through the dimensions, but also across parallels. You begin to be able to coordinate your energy across multi-realities. At first, this can become quite disorienting, but, over time, will become exhilarating!

Whatever you say or do is completely guided by Spirit. This completely shifts the way you relate. It certainly shifts your interpersonal relationships pretty fast. It can bring up a whole lot of fear, fears such as "Will I ever have sex again?" or "Will I ever be able to hold a job?" Sometimes the answer is a big "no."

The eighth level is one of the most transformative levels. Most of you are moving very fast and feel at times as though you're going crazy. You may catch yourself talking in rhyme, unable to talk at all, or talking backwards. The translation will come as you open to the new languages and let them affect your fields and cellular structure. It is literally going into your DNA. Your Spirit is putting through direct encodements at this point. This is also a mutation of the nervous system. All of your nervous system is sort of being "tweaked up" to handle the new levels of information. You may also find that your eyesight becomes kind of blurry, the ringing in your ears becomes so pronounced you have trouble hearing. The nerves in your ears and eyes, and actually your entire sensory apparatus, are being required to process a lot more information than has ever been processed before. So at times there may be brain scrambles. Be patient with yourself and patient with those around you. Keep your humor around you, because there are days when it's very funny. Another thing that is very common in eighth-level Lightbody is heart palpitations or an arrhythmic heartbeat. This is because the internal, fifth-dimensional circulatory system (called the axial system) is coming on line, and your heart may be receiving dual electrical impulses. This goes on until there is a kick-over point, where the axial system and the autonomic nervous system actually merge their functions, and the heart is basically operating from impulses from the axial system. Eighth-level Lightbody is terribly exciting. When 95% of the Lightworkers were in eighth-level Lightbody, they began to hook up into group mind together, and to bring in entirely new programs in service to this planet. It's like cutting a superhighway to Source for the whole species.

Ninth Level of Lightbody

As you transition into the ninth level of Lightbody, the translation opens and you begin to understand tonal languages. It becomes something you can recognize, instead of it just affecting you. Those geometries and patterns that you're working with in your mind become coherent: they are a language. Some of you may experience "hieroglyphics" or "Morse code" — these are all types of Light languages. They are sixth-dimensional. Your Spirit is using these languages to shift the sixth-dimensional structure of your blueprint into a new template for your fifth-dimensional Lightbody.

You are beginning to embody Divinity. The seventh-dimensional threshold may activate, causing lower back or hip pain, and a feeling of density in the pelvic floor. The seventh-dimensional structures are shifting into alignment with your Oversouls. New Alpha/Omega structures are opening around the physical body, allowing more energy to pour in. The fifth- and sixth-dimensional etheric structures are coordinated through the seventh-dimensional alignment with your Oversouls to receive a new Adam Kadmon Divine Image. You may, at this point, experience body shifts: you may find yourself a whole lot taller, or a whole lot thinner, or bigger, or you may grow wings. You may become aware that you have other body types than that of a human. And you begin to integrate non-human identities into the human identity. This is a vast coordination point for all the levels of what you are.

You are translating the languages of light directly and are aware of yourself at other dimensions, in whatever model you care to use. You are aware of the interconnecting crystalline structure that joins everything.

You become far less connected with caring what anybody thinks about you on a personal level. What matters is how you express Spirit *now* with each breath and with each step you take. Who cares what anybody thinks? They'll wake up: they're doing this, too. Remember, this process is not optional; if you're incarnate, you're mutating.

The pituitary gland is opening further and producing more growth hormone. In some women an estrogen imbalance may occur. You may feel exhausted, depressed, and alienated. Sometimes your periods may become irregular, or you may have changes in your flow.

So, as you began the shift to the ninth level of Lightbody, you began a very powerful shift to your multidimensional self. You are making it real and manifest on this planet now: the master that you are. We see you all as masters; everyone is a master. You came to this planet to master the limitations of separation. Great job, guys! Now the game is shifting into who you really are in your vastness. When we look at you, we know every one of you, at every level of your existence. Do you have any idea at all of how much energy it takes to keep you looking this limited and shielded? An enormous amount. Well, you no longer have to pretend. All the holds are off. You have full permission and total support to manifest your divinity.

There is usually a massive descension at the beginning of ninth level of Lightbody and a massive one at the end. Now, in the third, sixth and ninth levels, you go into strong re-evaluation. The ninth level can be one of the most difficult because it's at this point that you begin the final surrender to Spirit. You will discover that you do not control anything on a personal level. You will understand that all you have ever been is a divine instrument. You are "Spirit-in-action." Your Spirit determines the income you have, or the income that you don't have; the direction that your work is taking, or whether you work at all. Spirit designs everything: you are a divine instrument. It is the dissolution of the ego-self. This is the final passage through the gate of awakening.

This can be the most ecstatic experience and at the same time it can be the most painful. For most of you, this is what you have worked for, for lifetimes. Yet, when you come up to that gateway, it can be frightening. The ecstasy that exists on the other side of that gate is beyond description in this language. I'm channeling through this body now, but I live in that state all the time. I am never separated from Source: I *am* Source. That is what is offered to each and every one of you, but it does mean surrender at every level of your being. Ninth level is where that surrender occurs, surrender and ecstasy.

Now, on one level, free will is an absolute reality, but from another level, it is a total illusion. This is what our friends at Earth Mission call the "dis-illusionment." It is a vital part of the Lightbody process because it means the final letting go of the "I-self," as you think of it. As we think of it, your mental, emotional, and spiritual bodies are *strictly* tools for Spirit. They do not have consciousness of their own. It is part of the illusion of separation that ego-self has control. This is our viewpoint, and it's okay if you don't agree. Right now, as most of you are in ninth-level Lightbody, Spirit is beginning to push you up against the gate of awakening. You are already experiencing the dissolving of your identities and your context. Allow it. Surrender to it. It is the resistance that hurts.

Follow your Spirit with every breath and every step. Be that vastness here and you'll be exactly where you need to be, with whom you need to be, doing what you need to do in every NOW-moment. The survival fears drop out: they become unimportant. As you manifest who you really are and what you're here to do, all the nagging little illusions become unimportant and not real. Now, fears may still come up because you're still living in this world, but you're now able to set them aside. In the third, sixth, and ninth levels, you're disconnecting from the consensus reality. You find that when you reconnect, it's painful.

In levels seven, eight, and nine, you find that you're radiating light differently than you ever have. Your eyes appear very clear and different to other people. People will walk up to you and say, "You look so happy." Remember, many people are in terror over surrendering. Say to them, "I follow my Spirit without hesitation. That is why I am filled with ecstasy and joy. I suggest you do the same." That is the easiest thing you can say to them. This will happen.

Some of you may be surrounded by people who are in what we call the "What if ..." syndrome. "What if the poles shift and we go to Pluto?" "What if Denver becomes an oceanfront property?" "What if we're all being controlled by some lizard race that wants to cultivate us for a food supply?" All these wild "what if"s will be floating around you. People will periodically freak out around you. Just stay centered in your Spirit and you'll know exactly what to say in that moment.

At the seventh level, people often feel that they're going to ascend tomorrow: Ashtar is going to come and pick them up in his ship and they're out of here. This is because the energetic links are being set up between the you that's in this body and the you that's in your Lightbody, a you that's a "future self," if you're looking linearly. Because of this, there's a sense of needing to get your life in order. It works. You say everything you've always wanted to say to other people. You do all the stuff you have always wanted to do.

By the eighth level, you know that you're staying and a new sense of purpose begins to fill you. You get that you're here and that you're here with something to do, and it becomes a joy. In the eighth level, you quit bopping in and out of your body. We see a lot of Lightworkers tap in multidimensionally, but they don't come all the way into their body. So they flip back and forth. In the eighth level, you come into your body. You will feel more centered than ever, more calm than ever before. You now know that you're not crazy because you're so centered and grounded. You become what has been termed "humanity exalted," as you bring more of your vastness here. By the ninth level, you've brought so much of your vastness here that you've become terribly noticeable.

In the eighth level of Lightbody, your upper chakras are open and functioning. The vestigial spiritual body is now merged with your mental and emotional bodies into a unified field. The eighth chakra's templates are put in order and your fields begin to operate in a different fashion. You hook up with your Oversoul. There's a sense of being connected with Spirit all the time.

As your ninth and tenth chakras open further and you open the eleventh and twelfth chakras, you hook up with the Christ Oversoul and you begin to operate from the Christ level of your being here on the planet. At first, you may step in and out of this and it may feel a little uncomfortable as you go from being Divine Love, Will, and Truth to being a "poor bumbling idiot" again. This soon settles down. Sometime after you go through the Gate of Awakening, you begin to operate from the Christ level all of the time. Some of you have chosen to stay working at the Christ level: that will be your path for here. For some of you, you will begin the hook up to the I AM presence. If you begin to operate from that level of Godhood sometime in the tenth or eleventh level of Lightbody, it will be pretty hard to look human. Pretty hot stuff!

At the ninth level of Lightbody, you're moving into states of being that you have never been in before, experiencing the being state of your own truth, experiencing the being state of your unconditional love, and experiencing the being state of your Light and power. It is called the Threefold Flame and it exists in the heart of everyone. It is a flame that resonates at all dimensions. Most people are usually strong in one component of it.

At the end of the ninth level, you begin a descension — usually quite massive. You've gone through all the ego surrender and this descension is extremely transformative: you may begin to emit Light.

The last three levels of Lightbody are what we call the "spiritual levels." This is where your fields are completely unified, your chakras are open up to the fourteenth chakra. Your fields are now merged, and you are fully hooked into the Christ Oversoul at every level of your being. You have the hookups to your I AM presence.

Tenth Level of Lightbody

In the tenth level, you begin to manifest avatar abilities. That means that you can be exactly where you want, when you want. Teleportation, apportation, and manifestation come in at this level of Lightbody, because you are fully conscious of being one with the

Source and being everything. When you are All That Is, what is not you? You *are* the universe, recreating itself according to your pictures of reality. At the tenth level of Lightbody, you finish the hookups and operate from your vastness, from what we call your Godself. You feel connected with everything. There is not a leaf that falls on this planet that you're not aware of, because you are the planetary consciousness. We want you to understand here that this means that this level of perception is all the way into the deepest part of the human consciousness, all the way into the human genetic consciousness. All of this must be integrated, all the way back to the physical. No one is going to be out flying around the ethers now. You need to bring it all back here.

So, what begins to happen as you hook up with the Oversouls is that those double tetrahedrons have exchanged sides, and you are now operating in a unified field. The geometries begin to move in a double helix. Now in a karma game, you only have two-strand DNA, but in Lightbody you have a three-strand (or more) DNA. So, your body forms a fifth-dimensional strand in the center. You begin to build what we call the "Merkabah vehicle" within your energy structures. "Merkabah" means "chariot" in Hebrew.

The Merkabah is a crystalline Light structure that allows you to pass through space, time, and dimensions, completely in your totality. The Merkabah has a consciousness of its own. You may begin to work with it to travel to other Source-systems. From our perspective, going to Lightbody is only a part of a much larger process. We see all planes and dimensions merging back into the Source for this universe, which then merges with other Source-systems, and so on, back to the One. This is a vast, vast program.

In our viewpoint, there is nothing more beautiful or magnificent than the Divine expressions that you will bring forth on your return. For some of you, that return is to this Source-system. For others, it is a return to a different Source-system and you're here to set up the connections for when they all merge. Some of you are just here to move the planet to Lightbody. Others of you will take over from there, shifting the planet to its next realm, and its next, and its next. We deal with the ascension of whole dimensional systems.

You construct this crystalline Light structure out of your own fields, with the assistance of your Spirit. Now we talk about three different axes with different functions: the Angelic function, the Space Brotherhood or Extraterrestrial function, and the Ascended Master function. These fit together. At the time of ascension, the Space Brotherhood will hook together all the Merkabah vehicles they are building in their own fields, to link around the planet, forming the planetary Lightbody — literally building the vehicle for this planet to ascend. Planet Earth will be taken from the third dimension and the dimension will be collapsed.

The Ascended Master axis will act as directors and navigators. They are here to work with the coordinates for taking this solar system out of this area to a multi-star system. They act as navigators.

Many of the Angelics will go into Lightbody, but others will return to pure energy form. As incarnate Angelics, our energy is the "fuel" for this process.

At the tenth level of Lightbody, you begin to work consciously according to your axis. All of you have all the DNA encodements to do all of these functions. It's just a matter of which part of the process your Spirit wishes you to play with this time.

No one of these axes is "more important" or "better" or "more advanced" than another. Play your part fully.

Eleventh Level of Lightbody

You have built the structure of your Merkabah and you begin to shift into the eleventh level of Lightbody. This is where you decide whether to stay in Lightbody and ascend with the planet, whether you will ascend ahead of the planet and act as advance crew, or whether you will go to pure energy form. This is decided in the eleventh level of Lightbody, when you are hooked up to your upper-dimensional Merkabah vehicle through the axiotonal lines.

The axiotonal lines are part of your embodied Lightbody structure but they also connect you with other star systems and universes. These lines of Light lie along the physical acupuncture meridians and connect to your physical body through something called "spin points." Your Lightbody structure is made up of many lines of Light, intersecting in beautiful geometries. In the course of your mutation, a whole new fifth-dimensional circulatory system was built. Cellular regeneration was accomplished through the axiotonal spin points and you were restructured at the molecular level. Your Spirit has created and strengthened these structures throughout all the levels of Lightbody, preparing your physical body to receive the greater Merkabah.

In the eleventh level of Lightbody, all of these structures are firmly in place and fully activated.

You may have noticed that time is speeding up. It speeds up to the point where it becomes simultaneous. So, you will find yourself kicking in and out of feeling that you're everywhere at once and that you're in simultaneity and then in the time line. You'll get used to stepping back and forth. By the time most of the people on this planet are in the eleventh level of Lightbody, this planet will no longer be in linear time. It will be in simultaneity. You are going to have a lot of fun, because that's when you'll see that "past lives" are a joke: you have lives and they all have resonances.

Every time that you choose Light in any one of the parallels, it affects every single life you have ever had. Ever! That's how powerful it is. One person choosing Light in one lifetime affects the whole planet across time and across all parallels. There are seven to eight million Lightworkers incarnate in this parallel alone. How much effect do you guys think you have? Just what do you think you can do? Anything you want, as long as you follow Spirit.

You are operating fully from your God-self and there is *no* separation. Remember when, in the lower levels, you were following Spirit for all you were worth? Well, you've caught up! So, you have a few headaches on the way and you get the flu, but now it's the payoff!

What you love to do more than anything in the world is your key to manifesting your part in the Divine Plan. Many of you are here with very special skills and perceptivities to assist the planet. You may be a specialist in intergalactic diplomacy, new family structures, new forms of government, or how to equitably allocate food and other resources on a global scale. Creating new types of community living, new rituals for an awakened spirituality, new Light-based technologies, or new expressions through the arts may be what makes your heart sing.

In the eleventh level of Lightbody, you are manifesting your vision of Heaven on Earth and expressing the ecstasy of your Spirit.

Twelfth Level of Lightbody

At the twelfth level, you act on your decision about what to do. That may be hooking up with other people around the planet or all kinds of things. There are many structures that have to come into place for this planet's final ascension: different councils, new governments, all kinds of things. And you're doing it all right now just by being here. Remember, you are working in simultaneity and you simply become more conscious of it. And you're doing it now. It has already happened, so it *will* happen. A planet ascends from the moment of its creation. Nothing will be lost. The entire planetary history is recorded in the Akashic, so you don't need the memory in your body.

You see, every time you make a choice that isn't in the will of your Spirit, Spirit's choice will always occur, but a parallel reality is spun off to hold the other choice. So, there are quadrillion, quadrillion, zillions of these parallel realities. But as all you guys, sprinkled across the time line, awaken and follow Spirit, all those parallels pull back together. You are now living in a constant merging of all those parallels. So, there's a point when all those parallels have merged, and there's only the path of Spirit from the moment of its creation. There never *was* a karma game except in the records. But not in you: you don't have to carry it with you. You don't carry it in your body, you don't carry it in your mind, you don't carry it in your heart. Pretty exciting stuff! This is how you ascend a planet. You reweave it. Each of those NOW-points is the fabric of what you would call space and time. From our perspective, we see lines of force that come down into each NOW-point, across all the parallels, like "grappling hooks." The dimension gets pulled up across time.

So, as you shift from eleventh to twelfth level Lightbody, this is the final activation of the Divine Plan for planet Earth. This planet goes to Light, shifts out of this dimension and is brought into a multistar system. Everyone is in Lightbody, and follows their Spirit in total sovereignty and total mastery. Then the whole way back is the expression of the return, at every level of your identity and at every level of your being, as you return and experience your Source.

Questions and Answers

Q. What are some of the other mutational symptoms?

A. There's often a point where food no longer tastes like food to you. You can feel hungry all the time and when you eat, your body doesn't register that it's gotten any nourishment. This is because enough of your Lightbody has become activated that you also need Light as a nutrient. There's an easy trick for this. It sounds crazy, but it works like a charm. Take both hands, palms out towards the sun, and make a triangle with thumbs touching to form the base and your forefingers touching to form the sides and the apex. This acts as an antenna and prism for the Light behind the light. Try this for about fifteen minutes. You will feel your body drink in the Light and then you will feel full.

Also, please eat whatever your body wants you to eat. Throw out the rulebooks. You're here to follow Spirit, not spiritual rules. If you're a vegetarian and your body wants a two-pound steak, please eat it. If you hate sprouts but your body wants them, do it. You may feel very directed to drink alcohol, particularly beer, because it has certain components that your body needs to assist it to mutate. Throw out all the "should"s and "ought to"s around what's OK to eat, because you may find yourself eating some really strange things — like spinach with cinnamon.

You'll find that your sleeping patterns become terribly erratic. You may jump from two hours' sleep a day to twelve, and back again.

You may also wake up tired. Remember that you're a vast multi-dimensional being and are working hard in the sleep state. As you open more and more to being aware of yourself in other realms, your physical body gets tired, as though it's doing the work. So, say to yourself "Please tighten up the veil," or "I need a night off."

Remember that you're in control of how fast your Lightbody process moves. The more Light you breathe in, the faster you move this process. Doing the Unified Chakra technique is a very simple basic technique that allows you to build your Lightbody because it allows your chakra system to function as it will in Lightbody and it gently assists your energy bodies to move into a merged state. We suggest that you do this several times a day until you get used to it. Then you can say, "Unify," and you unify in an instant. You will get so that you are naturally in this state. Then when you step out of it, you will find that it feels weird to you. If you find that the outside world is too crazy, simply say, "Unify." If you find that you're picking up too much energy from outside, it's because your chakras and energy bodies are not unified.

The other thing you can do is call forth the energy of Grace in your life. The Divine energy of Grace is the most powerful tool you have on this planet. Grace has enveloped planet Earth and the energy is available any time you need it. Grace Elohim is a very personable being and will talk to you anytime you like. Grace is the Elohim of the silver ray and the energy is visible as sparkly iridescent snow. It looks like fairy dust. So, if you see that around you, you know that Grace is with you.

Grace is the Divine force which allows you to make a complete break with the past in each NOW moment. We urge you sincerely: please do not process your "stuff" or try to "fix" yourself. The universe recreates itself around your pictures of reality, absolutely and impersonally. If you hold a picture of reality that there's something wrong with you or that you need to be fixed, the universe will recreate around this ad nauseam. You'll process stuff from this lifetime, every other lifetime you've ever had, and then you'll start on other planets, and then you'll process the planet itself! Please stop. The force of

Grace is on this planet so that this is unnecessary. Please use it; it is your greatest asset.

Use the force of Grace in every aspect of your life. You can Grace your car. If the car's screwing up, call out, "Grace, engine please!" We call Grace the "divine lubricant. " Merlin calls her "Cosmic Crisco." There's a reason for this. Remember those tetrahedrons in your field that get stuck in karmic patterns? If you're locked down with someone and you call on the energy of Grace, this iridescent snow falls down on those tetrahedrons and immediately unlocks them. You can use Grace on everything and Grace is delighted to help you in any way possible — after all, that's her Divine Expression. If you catch yourself processing, please stop and call Grace.

One of the patterns we've seen over and over on this planet is: "If only I could fix 'X' in my life, then I could ascend or go to Light." Well, I've got news for you. As long as you're trying to fix yourself, you're not going anywhere. You are now completely who you are: a vast, multidimensional master in the various stages of Awake and Awakening. There is nothing to fix. It is simply a matter of opening, of awakening, of remembering, and of expressing. So, that's the Ariel lecture. We've been known to beg people to stop doing this. We see so many of you Lightworkers struggling and getting bogged down in everything imaginable. It's totally unnecessary and you don't have time: this planet's moving way too fast for you to process your karma and limitations. Karma is just the illusion of a karma game, and you're leaving that behind.

There is a difference between Gracing something and living in denial. This is not a call to deny different parts of your reality. When you have accessed different parts of the physical body's consciousness or the human genetic consciousness, you are going to have a lot of things (like shame, guilt, fear, and despair) pour out of the body. We need to clear the human genetic consciousness. Processing this will take you forever, because you would process each lifetime separately — each human experience held in the collective human consciousness separately — and you would be constantly dwelling in the past. Grace is always NOW. If you're constantly participating with your Spirit in the NOW and Spirit leads you into the human genetic consciousness, you'll express from the physical body's realities. This is still under the force of Grace; it allows you to just let it go. Express it and move on. Processing keeps you constantly in the past, analyzing and extrapolating into the future. You are never NOW. Call in Grace.

We're talking to you as though the Lightbody process is linear; it is not linear. From our perspective, it is a totally non-linear process. You each have a unique tonal signature, the tone that you are. Lightbody is like a chord. So, if you're sitting at, say, the seventh level, you may have a resonance with, say, your third-level self, so you can be having the flu-like symptoms. You can also have resonance with your ninth-level self, so you begin to hear tonals and see geometries. So, although the Lightbody process has an overall pattern, it is also an experiment that each of you is playing with. You will each do this in your own unique fashion, as you express your divinity. So, we find it pretty exciting and say, "Oh, that's a nice twist. What an interesting thing to put in!"

We strongly feel that transitioning a planet to Light is "high-velocity fun." That's why we do it. We're hoping that soon you will feel that way, too. You've all done this thousands of times before and it's what you do for a good time. Figuring out how you will do it this time is fun. The melody of Lightbody as it plays through you is uniquely yours; that's what makes it so exciting. Every time you take a body type to Light, the experience is completely new. For every planet that goes to Light, exactly what happens depends on the density, the species, and the overall collective consciousness of the planet. The planet doesn't always go to Light, even though its inhabitants may. What makes planet Earth particularly special is that the planet herself is going to Light. That's why there's so much focus on your planet: to assist the planet in this process. That was the promise made to the planetary consciousness when she agreed to be the stage for this karma game.

Right now, there's a major pattern being cleared from the planet, what we call "enemy patterning." In September 1989, the planet released her enemy pattern toward humanity. This means that your planet no longer feels that she must be vindictive to her human population. This heads off many of the foreseen catastrophes on this planet. Even when there are natural disasters — earthquakes, volcanoes, floods — the loss of life will usually be minimal. The destruction of property can be massive, however — a signal to disconnect from that stuff.

There's another thing you can work with. There are points in the Lightbody process where your brain function shifts and you may get headaches. You can ease these by assisting the opening of the pineal and pituitary glands — this is a natural thing that has to happen. In a meditative state, close your eyes and focus your attention right between your eyebrows. It may give you a slight headache and it may take several times, but at some point, you will see a bright flash of light as the pineal kicks over to its new function. For the pituitary, focus your eyes and attention "backwards" into your brain until you see a flash of light. That tells you that your pituitary has kicked over. This will usually ease off the headaches and assist the growth of the pineal and the pituitary glands.

What determines the level of your Lightbody activation is a tonal color sequence. The entire Lightbody process can be expressed in tonal, color, and geometric patterns. You may sense these in meditation, as your Spirit works with your energy bodies. When you listen to toning, some of it will feel good. That's for you. Some of it may not feel good. That's for other people.

Q. Will parallels ascend, too?

A. Free will within a karma game means that you can choose to do something that is not in accordance with the will of your Spirit. Whenever this happens, a parallel reality is spun off which follows what Spirit wanted. This happens every time you make a choice which differs from the choice of Spirit.

As you awaken and begin to follow Spirit, no new parallels are created, and those that were created from your earlier choices are being pulled back and merged. You are living in constant, daily merging of thousands of parallels on this planet. When all these parallels have merged, all you have left is the reality that reflects the path of Spirit from the dawn of creation. There never was, therefore, a karma game.

From our perspective, each NOW-point makes up the fabric of everything, what you call "space and time." From our perspective, we see lines of force entering each NOW-point across all parallels. They are like "grappling hooks" into the third dimension, to be used to pull the dimension "up" into a higher dimension, across time.

You will begin to sense yourself across time and also at this NOW-point in the timeline. By the time most people are at the eleventh level of Lightbody, this plane will no longer be in linear time. You will exist in simultaneity and see the joke about "past lives." All your lives resonate with each other across time and space. When any one of your personalities chooses Light, it affects every other, across all time and parallels. This in turn affects everyone that all these personalities come into contact with. So, just one person choosing to follow Spirit affects the entire history of planet Earth.

There are seven to eight million Lightworkers in this parallel. Just think what we can all do. Anything! As long as you follow Spirit, there is nothing you cannot do.

Q. How does the planetary process differ from ours?

A. The planet was activated to third-level Lightbody on April 16, 1989. She went into seventh-level in January 1993, entered eighth-level on May 30th, 1994, and entered ninth on October 15, 1994. You can see that the entire Divine Plan is speeding up dramatically. Earth is dumping whole reality pictures. Have you noticed all the recent retrospective programs on TV and in the newspapers: "Let's dig through the Second World War." These historical perspectives have to do with the planet releasing and clearing pictures of reality from the consensus. She is dropping whole packages of experience that have been drummed into her throughout the course of the karma game. The other thing you are going to feel is a sense of incredible impendingness on the planet. There is a constant sense that something is about to happen. Depending on where your orientation is, this can be very stressful or it can seem comforting. "Well, everything is moving along." The polarization is increasing. The planet herself feels like she is going into the classic, spiritual manic-depressive swing. "Oh, I'm turning into a star!" and, "We're going to blow up!"

The planet is requiring that people absolutely drop their enemy patterning. So, all of a sudden, you have a wave of anti-Semitism in Europe. It won't last because there's no enemy patterning to sustain it. It's an expression, more than an action. You'll become aware of how international events have a different feel because they are more of an expression, than an action. Creating a war and sustaining it are actions, whereas expressing hatred is not. Once the hatred is expressed, it usually dies out because there's no underlying etheric blueprint to fuel it. All enemy patterning is being released from the planetary structure and out of everyone. Every "us and them" pattern in everyone's field is up for release.

All kinds of new ideas are coming into the mass consciousness. There are Lightworkers everywhere. How many of you watched *Alien Nation?* It did a lot of prep work. A lot of things are coming into the mass consciousness to allow new ways of thinking, living, and relating. We like the Apple Computer slogan: "Your parents gave you the world; give your children the universe." There's all the work that *Star Trek: The Next Generation* and *Deep Space Nine* have done to teach people about the nature of multiple realities and the nature of time and space as it relates to consciousness. This has been very valuable. They have covered the delicate diplomacy necessary to invite a planet into the galactic community in "First Contact." In "Transfiguration," a being turns into a Lightbody on the helm of the starship Enterprise.

You are going to notice a lot of encodement showing up in music. The "Rave" scene is very powerful. It allows a meeting of people to link consciousness and raise energy for the planet; celebration moves through their bodies. At the same time, there are messages of hate in other types of music. The polarization continues.

The overall feeling on this planet right now is, "What the hell's going on?" So, we ask you to be kind, because as the old pictures drop out, it's scary. The planet herself has a lot of fear coming up.

We ask that you "ground up" rather than down into the planet. The planet is in the middle of a mutation and you grounding into her upsets her. She doesn't need to have to stabilize you right now. She's hard pressed to stabilize herself. In fact, what you can do is to help stabilize her by grounding up into the vastness of your Spirit and then acting as a pole for that energy. This allows the planet to be supported from her own vastness.

Q. What is a "descension"?

A. Descension occurs when a higher aspect of your Spirit comes to reside in your bodies. Now usually you've been channeling this higher aspect first, tapping into a larger part of your vastness. Descensions happen all along this process of mutation. It can be as gentle as a sweet revelatory experience, just being a "bliss ninny" for a few days, or it can be totally disorienting. It may make you question who you are, why you're here, and what you're doing.

A big thing that can happen in a major descension is that your very identity can get blown out the window. The more rigid your ideas about who you are, the more difficult a descension can be. If your systems are more open, it's just "Well, who am I today?" and "The reality for today is ..."

The easier a descension is, the less jarring it is. You have all experienced at least one because it's a natural part of the process. You generally have a descension as you go into levels three, six, and nine, and they vary. Some people think that they're walk-ins, but they're not. A descension can be so dramatic that it looks like a walk-in. We're seeing this happen a lot more because people are having more intense descensions.

Q. Are we affecting the planet's mutation?

A. Of course. Now remember that the universe recreates itself according to your picture of reality. If your picture is that the planet is polluted and being destroyed, then guess what happens: you will have a polluted, destroyed planet. If your picture is that it's a beautiful, self-cleansing planet that sustains its occupants in a most exquisite manner, that's what you'll get. So we ask that you focus on what is beautiful and positive. Running fear about the ozone layer will not help. It'll only make the hole bigger. The hole was designed to be there, anyway, to allow divine forces and rays more access into here.

You can do all kinds of things to help the planet — you can plant trees, you can clean up garbage — without running fear or guilt. Fear can render you immobile. Transform these feelings into a sense of serving the planet. Learn to be a Divine Gardener. Sow a few seeds of Love, tend the new growths of Truth, and reap the manifest fruits of Divine Will.

Q. Was there some angelic event that coincided with the full manifestation of Grace's energy?

A. There have been lots of events. Basically, Grace's energy came around the planet as part of the planetary gridwork in September 1989. Gateways will open up every month from here on in, and you'll get used to it. These are ways for you to access different energies, different technologies, different information and different aspects of your own Spirit. For each one of you and the planet herself, all the hookups are being made to the "you" that's already in Lightbody.

If you don't resist a gateway and let the energy flow through you, it's quite wonderful. If you resist changes, the energy jams in your field. We have noticed here that humans have a real proclivity for living in the future, and they seem to have a liking for event-orientation. One of the problems we've noticed in quite a few groups on the planet is this constant looking forward to the future opening of some gate or another. We would say gates are opening all the time, and it's much more powerful to be NOW and in the present with your Spirit. Those who have been very focused in opening this or that gate at some future point have often missed all the miracles in the NOW moment.

Q. How does the Lightbody process affect animals?

A. A lot of species are choosing to leave the planet right now because the devic consciousness does not wish to retain its particular body type in Lightbody. It wants something different. Now, it's all right to love and care for other species, but remember that all consciousness knows what's going on.

For most species, their bodies are not experiencing mutational symptoms. They are mutating naturally. They don't need to unify their fields like you do because they never split them up. The only species having any trouble is the domestic dog. Cats are fine; their function is actually to help this process. They are excellent channels and the entire feline hive soul has agreed to help humans to ascend, so they are very good to have around. Let them sleep with you if they want to.

Dogs and cats have polarized into holding the poles of the old and new worlds respectively. Dogs are absorbing a lot of the energy being released and cats are bringing in new energies. Dogs seem to be having increased parasite problems, so they need more attention than before. Do the "Invocation to Water" over their food and water bowls.

Q. The axiotonal lines are a natural property of a balanced energy field. By what dynamic do these lines assist in manifestation?

A. It is Spirit that manifests them. You have a hookup into the higher grid systems. Through the spin points, the axiotonal lines in your body hook you up into the crystalline grid systems that exist through every dimension. So, when Spirit wants to manifest instantaneously, those lines light up inter-dimensionally.

In the templates of the eighth chakra, the lines have to line up in exact formation with the crystalline grid. The axiotonal lines hook up through the eighth chakra and go off into different star system grids in both this universe and other Source-system universes. Spirit activates those lines to manifest more of its own vastness through the body, which in turn activates more lines, which allows more Spirit to enter, and so on.

Now, when you get this grid system set up, there's an activation at the eleventh chakra, the gateway to the I AM presence. When the templates are aligned and hooked up to the grids, then you have the manifestation of all god-level abilities. But to do this, you must go through the Christ Oversoul; otherwise you burn your body up.

As you pass through the eighth-level of Lightbody, you have opened to the languages of Light and are beginning to decode them. When you don't understand something, simply open to your Spirit and allow tones to come through your body. This will decode the knowledge held deep within your field. So, just let the tones come through. The sound is coming from the upper dimensions and your body is being used as an instrument. You don't have to do it: Spirit does the work.

Q. What does a high-pitched whistling in the ears mean?

A. It's probably an upper-dimensional being trying to get in touch with you. Go really quiet, say "I am open to receive," and let it come in. You may get tones, words, or melodies.

The Council of Ein Soph has brought in the vow break to speed up mutational clearing. It will remove all etheric crystals. Share it with your friends.

⋘ AWAKEN VOW BREAK ⋙

I now rescind any and all vows that I have taken to experience the illusion of unconsciousness. As Lightbearer of my genetic lineage, I break these vows for myself and all of my ancestors.

I declare these vows null and void in this incarnation, and all incarnations across time and space, parallel realities, parallel universes, alternate realities, alternate universes, all planetary systems, all Source systems, all dimensions, and the Void.

I ask for the release of all crystals, devices, thoughtforms, emotions, matrices, veils, cellular memory, pictures of reality, genetic limitation, and death. NOW!

Under the Law of Grace and by the Decree of Victory!

By the Decree of Victory! By the Decree of Victory!

As Spirit wills, I ask for Awakening! As Spirit wills, we are Awake!

In the beginning, I AM THAT I AM!

B'resheet, Ehyeh Asher Ehyeh!

"Help! I'm Mutating!": What You Can Do

All techniques and processes in this book are for Spiritual Light Integration. This is not medical advice. If you are experiencing any of the symptoms mentioned, please see your doctor.

A few of these symptoms must be handled by an etheric surgeon, but most you can take care of yourself. By your request, we have added suggestions for which specific Angelic Outreach Potion to use with each symptom. The potion "Magnificence" helps most of them. No matter what kind of mutational symptoms you are experiencing, we suggest that you do four things first:

1) "The Unified Chakra" with the "Invocation to Light"

2) Spiritual Hygiene (see below)

3) Ground multidimensionally. Imagine a thick line of Light beginning at the Omega chakra (eight inches below your spine), extending upwards through your spine and on upwards into the eighth through eleventh chakras, and up into the fourteenth chakra. Ground into the vastness of your Spirit, not into the planet: she's mutating, too. Allow your Spirit to stabilize you. Run seven to twelve lines of Light downward from the point of the Omega chakra, opening around your feet like a cone. You are not grounding into the Earth. You're stabilizing yourself across the parallel realities of the planetary hologram.

4) If the first three have not helped, ask for assistance from your Spirit and your multidimensional friends. You must ask for help or we can't assist you.

Spiritual Hygiene

Whenever you are dropping density of any kind, this technique helps. Do it several times a day if necessary. Visualize the violet flame of transmutation and the silver ray of Grace mixing together to form a beautiful iridescent violet. Then see it pouring into your physical body and filling it. Then bring it through the emotional, mental, and spiritual bodies separately. Also, place sea salt and invoke the rays into your bath water. Wash your clothes and bed-linens with a handful of sea salt, to remove energetic residue. Because you do most of your clearing in your sleep, call in these rays to transmute the old energies as you make your bed. You'll feel so much better. (Universal Detox, Home Sweet Home Enviro-pack)

The Triple Grid

Keeping your space energetically clean is essential — not only because you are transmuting and dropping density, but because everyone on the planet is transmuting also. You are affected by the energies in at least a half-mile radius around you. The triple grid technique is extremely versatile for creating an energetically clean and stable living, working, or driving environment. It's based on the principle of "ask and it shall be given." It's important to be specific in what you ask for.

This technique requests specific groups to do their particular functions. The Legions of Michael are good at infusing energies into a structure and maintaining the structure itself. The Destroyer Force Angels act like a cosmic charcoal filtration system. They create the space for Light to emerge into its next highest level. These beings create Divine potential and expansion of the Light and should not be confused with the Dark Forces, who create condensation of the Light. Circle Security is a branch of the Intergalactic Federation of Planets and Stars. Their job is to set up, keep clear, and maintain inter-dimensional and inter-universal communication grids.

In the triple grid technique, you ask the specific group to set up their level of the grid, designating the geometric shape, size, and location. Spherical grids are the most stable and easy to maintain, so we suggest working with this geometry for most everyday applications (such as around your home, car, or workplace). You will want to renew the grid weekly or when you notice the energy getting funky.

"Legions of Michael: grid level one, spherical, my house. Destroyer Force Angels: grid level two, spherical, my house. Circle Security: grid level three, spherical, my house."

"Destroyer Force Angels, please spin your grid, spinning out astral entities, stray electromagnetic frequencies, fear, disharmony, anger, adverse astrological influences, expectation, frustration, viruses, fungus, bacteria, worry, astral distortions, miscommunication, sadness, enemy patterning, scarcity, loneliness and spin out anything that hasn't been mentioned in this or any other language, but which you know needs to leave the space at this time." (These are just a few suggestions. Fill in whatever is needed, according to your situation.)

When the clearing feels complete, continue with: "Reverse spin, same stuff." When that feels complete, end with "Stop spin. Thank you."

"Legions of Michael, infuse your grid with the energies of Grace, Faith, Hope, Peace, Purity, Liberty, Harmony, and Victory Elohim. Infuse with love, intimacy, the Unified Chakra, centeredness, clarity, full connection with Spirit, tolerance, clear communication, health, wealth, following Spirit without hesitation, mastery, sovereignty, living Heaven, and anything else I haven't mentioned in this or any other language, but which you know needs to be in the space at this time. Please seal grid. Thank you." (Again, more suggestions. Fill in whatever you need, according to your situation.)

"Circle Security, realign grids to harmonize with upper-dimensional gridworks. Release all distortions and parasites on the grids. Infuse frequencies for clearer communication with Spirit. Seal grid. Thank you."

Grids for your home: We used a possible home grid in the above example. When setting up a home grid, look for what energies in your environment may be adversely affecting you and what energies you need to support you on a daily basis.

Are you in the flight path of your local airport? "Spin out microwave and radar transmissions." Are you fighting with your partner or housemate a lot? "Spin out karmic monads, anger, resentment, miscommunication, referencing the past, obsolete telepathic images, astral entities ... ." "Infuse clear communication, compassion, mastery, sovereignty, intimacy, transpersonal positioning, honesty, love ... ."

Do you live in an apartment complex with noisy, fighting, impoverished neighbors? "Spin out hatred, violence, astral entities, enemy patterning, scarcity, struggle, hopelessness, stress, other people's karma, inconsideration, fear ... ." "Infuse harmony, Divine provision, peace, clarity, gentleness, honor ... ."

Are you heavily mutating and clearing? "Spin out density, obsolete pictures of reality, struggle, resistance, fatigue, obsolete genetic encodements ... ." "Infuse peace, hope, connection to Spirit, surrender, Grace and Purity Elohim, require of me whatever it takes ... ."

Ask the Destroyer forces to spin the grid in both directions continuously. The grid will remain spinning until you ask them to stop. This will help you and you environment to not accumulate what you are releasing.

Grids for your car: Parallel merger disorientation and mutational weirdness seem to be amplified when people are driving their cars. Often, they don't even know where they are or where they are going. Obviously, this can be dangerous. We suggest always gridding your car and to renew the grid every time you leave your home. Many people have found it helpful to hang a quartz crystal from the rear view mirror and to infuse the grids into the crystal. It acts as a reminder to renew the grids. Just put your hand around the crystal and say, "Renew grids." Here are some suggestions on what to ask for:

Place a spherical grid around the car and ask the Destroyer forces to "Spin out spaciness, disorientation, frustration, parallel bleedthrough, adverse astrological influences, other people's karma ... ." "Infuse clarity, zen-like serenity, excellent mechanical workings, a stable reality bubble ... ." You can also ask the Legions of Michael to "tractor beam" you to your destination. **Do not infuse invisibility**! People will hit your car.

Grids for your workplace: We want to emphasize that the Triple Grid cannot be used to manipulate other people. It sets an environment where certain energies are more difficult to access and other energies are more easily available. If someone really wants to be a pain, they can; they'll just have to work a little harder. You are setting a space for higher possibilities. In your workplace, "Spin out competition, ego, manipulation of others, self-manipulation, secrecy, enemy patterning, miscommunication, dishonoring, rabid individualism, astral entities, struggle, frustration, dissatisfaction, fear, scarcity, deceit, resentment, obsolete telepathic images, impatience ... ." "Infuse honesty, integrity, vision, fulfillment, mastery, sovereignty, competence, easy co-creation, patience, the Unified Chakra, joy, harmony, humor ... ."

The Triple Grid can be done around a location without you being physically there. Try doing it around the mall, the courthouse, the grocery store, or the post office, before you get there. Perhaps it would be fun to set up and maintain this grid around Congress, the White House, the Pentagon, or the IRS. Remember that it cannot be used to manipulate others; it just makes particular energies more or less easily available.

This is a very versatile technique. We have given you the everyday applications. The spherical geometry is very stable and easy to maintain. Live in it all the time and it will be easier to live Heaven on Earth.

Headaches

This is the second most common mutational complaint. We'll break it down by type:

Sharp chronic pain in head, neck, or shoulders: Probably etheric crystals — get them out! Contact an etheric surgeon trained in this technique.

Cranial expansion: If you're getting lumps, bumps, and pressure in your skull, your brain is probably growing. Reach up with your hands and pull the cranial plates apart. This usually does the trick but if not, find someone who does cranial-sacral bodywork.

Pressure between the eyebrows: This one feels like someone has their finger between your eyebrows and is pushing. That's exactly what you do for it. Take your finger and press there for a few moments. Usually, it eases right up. This is the pineal growing. This technique also works for pressure at the upper back of the skull (pituitary growth) and pressure on the top of the skull, center back (the fourth eye).

Severe headache at base of the skull: This is what we call an "under construction" headache. Most people are conditioned to contract their body and energy bodies when they feel severe pain. In this case, if you do that it will increase the pain dramatically. Take your hands and place them over your ears. Now, imagine that as you move your hands away from your body, you are also pushing your energy bodies out and away from your head. It sounds silly, but it often works.

Severe mutational headaches that nothing has helped:

1) Inform the "you" in the fifth or sixth dimension, who is directing this work, that what is being done hurts. The "you" in Lightbody cannot feel your physical pain, so, tell yourself to back it off.

2) Say "Please release endorphins!" These are natural brain opiates. Usually you will feel an immediate release and easing of the pain.

3) Buy some dioptase. This mineral has dark green crystals on a matrix base. We have found it works wonders.

4) Potions good for all mutational headaches: Mystical Articulation and Divine Expression. They boost the mutational headache very quickly and it seems to help a great deal.

Flu-like symptoms: This is the most common complaint because, as you're dropping density, if you don't or can't transmute it, it's got to come out somehow. (Try Magnificence, Subatomic Tonic, and Universal Detox.)

Nausea and Vomiting: Often people who have a lot of stored fear in their bodies get this. Often there is a lot of mucous in your body as you are releasing fear. Say the "Invocation to Water" over your food and drink. If this doesn't help, let yourself vomit. You should feel better quickly. Another thing that may cause nausea is if your energy bodies are spinning too fast. It's like motion sickness. If you put your hands out and tell your fields to slow down, they'll slow. Deliberately slow down your fields. If you are clearing things from the human genetic consciousness in your body, you may have a lot of nausea, and you find yourself vomiting energy. (Use Pathcutter if you are clearing genetics.) This is pretty common. There is also a vent in the sternum that you may get a lot of pressure in. If you think of it as the aperture of a camera, and open it up and kind of spray energy out of your body, it seems to really help. It's the same with the headaches. There is also another one of these vent points at the back of the neck in the middle. If you get a lot of pressure buildup in the head, if you sort of open that up like a camera aperture, it triggers like a fire hydrant and it will often release a lot of pressure in the neck and shoulders.

Diarrhea: We've noticed that people with lots of stored rage tend to get diarrhea. Once again use the "Invocation to Water." You may just have to get used to it, because some people get the runs every time they bring more Light into their bodies.

Muscle Aches and Joint Aches: People with this one usually have lots of stored resistance. This is also very common after a "walk-in" or a strong descension. It can be a rejection reaction at the cellular level. Sometimes it looks like rheumatoid arthritis. Take "Omega 3" fish oil capsules. It seems to lubricate the body. Also imagine that you are lying in an ocean of Light with your head toward the shore. As the waves wash over you, they bring Light into your body. As the waves ebb, they pull out the resistance. (Surrender, Universal Detox, Ecstasy)

Fevers and Sweats: Many folks get this one without the rest of the flu symptoms. Sometimes the fever is very high. Your skin may get quite red. Often, a person's energy bodies are vibrating out of phase with the physical body. You have two ways to approach it:

1) Lower the vibrations of your fields by slowing the spin or imagining them growing heavier.

2) Deliberately try to increase the vibration of your body by trying to make the fever higher. Either way, you should feel a "click" as they go back into phase and the fever should drop immediately. Most people have found making yourself hotter helps. It is easier to do than making yourself cooler.

Tiredness: There are many causes for this. You may be in re-evaluation or working very hard while asleep. In this case, honor the energy drop and rest. Also, if it continues, ask your Spirit for a night off. Notice if your body is doing a lot of releasing. You may need to do a physical de-tox to help your body release density. (Universal Detox, Fire of Purpose)

Other Physical Symptoms

Vibrating while meditating or on awakening: This is a very natural part of the Lightbody process, but is often quite alarming when it starts. It simply means that your vibration is rising. Relax. Enjoy it.

Pain in the exact center of sternum: This is usually the heart chakra opening to a new level. Breathe and call the Silver Ray of Grace into the heart. Then deliberately open your heart chakra. Keep breathing and opening it until the pain subsides. The heart chakra is the multi-dimensional gateway. It may be like a rusty door and may need the lubrication to open. (Alignment, Ecstasy, Love Potion #9)

Pain in the lower back and hips: If you are in eighth- or ninth-level Lightbody, or you are a walk-in, the pain may be caused by seventh-dimensional Divinity thresholds maxing out. See your etheric surgeon. (E3, Subatomic Tonic, Ecstasy, Heavenly Body)

Arms and hands tingling or falling asleep: This sometimes happens for up to four months. Often this is the laying in of Lightbody structures for etheric healing or surgical abilities. Usually this only occurs in Lightworkers who have this as part of their Divine Purpose. We have also seen a lot of these type of nervous system mutations in eighth-level Lightbody, as the nervous system is being required to handle a lot more Lightbody impulses. If you find your hands or feet going to sleep while you are using them, it is time to do an adjustment in the brain. The pineal gland emits tonal and electromagnetic frequencies that help regulate the electrical pulses in the autonomic nervous system, as well as the pulse of the spinal fluids in all sorts of different rhythms in the body. If for some reason the pulse coming from the pineal gland to the base of the skull into the spine is disrupted in some way, it will cause problems in the nervous system where you may even lose your grip. You may have deep leg jerks as you are trying to go off to sleep. It feels almost like the sheaths of the nerves are trying to be pushed backwards. This can be very uncomfortable. If you put your finger in between your eyebrows, you're pressing on what's called the Ajna center, which is the center which connects to your pineal gland in your brain. Take your other hand and put your finger at the very base of your skull, in the middle. Focus your attention inwards to the center of your brain. What you're going to notice if you are having this nervous system problem is a band of Light, going from the center of the brain to the brain stem, that looks like lightning or like electricity. Start to breathe into it and slow that down until it looks like a laser, bluish-white in color, and about the thickness of a pencil. Once you have got that smoothed out, you begin to pulse the Light. Your Spirit will adjust the pulses to the rhythm that you need, and you will feel your entire body and nervous system relax. Keep this up until you feel fully relaxed. Usually takes a minute or so. (E3, Service One-on-One, Mystical Articulation, Merkabah)

Changes in food habits: You may find you crave some very strange food combinations. Your physical body may need various nutrients in different proportions than ever before. Remember, it's changing at the cellular level. So, throw away your rulebook on diet. Another common experience is feeling hungry or unsatisfied no matter what you eat or in what quantity. Your body is beginning to need Light as a nutrient. First, say the Invocation to Water over everything that you eat or drink. Secondly, go outside and raise the palms of your hands to the sun. Make a triangle with your fingers. Your thumbs form the base and your index fingers form the apex. You're making an energetic prism. Ask for the Light behind your visible light spectrum. Feel it pour in through your palms. After ten to twenty minutes, you'll feel "full," like you've had a good meal. (Heavenly Body, Ecstasy)

Sensory and Perceptual Changes: As you progress in your Lightbody, you go through many changes in how you experience the world. Your senses become more acute and open into the psychic gifts that lie behind them. Also, your multidimensional perception opens up. Here are some common symptoms:

Excessive Sensory Input: Sometimes, one or all of your physical senses suddenly amplify. If this is disturbing, focus on one sense and extend it, gently shutting down all the others. This usually brings the senses back into balance. (Divine Expression, Magnificence, Gifts of the Holy Spirit)

Ungrounded or spacey: Ground multidimensionally. Also, it's helpful if you focus your attention fully on your feet. Try to feel the texture of what your feet are resting on. This brings you more into your body. (Fire of Purpose, E3)

Low-level anxiety, dizziness, and clumsiness: The brain is opening in its perceptions across multi-parallels. The body is beginning to sense that perhaps it could exist in more than one reality at a time. If you find that focusing on your feet isn't working, run a grounding cord from your Omega chakra, eight inches below your spine, up your spine, up into the upper chakras, grounding into your vastness, into Spirit. Run seven to twelve lines of Light downward from the point of the Omega chakra, opening around your feet like a cone. You're not grounding into the Earth. You're stabilizing yourself across the parallel realities of the planetary hologram. To your physical body, opening perception across parallels is like being in a reality earthquake. Put yourself in a doorway and hold on to the door jambs. Your body's instinctive response will usually calm right down. This usually seems to help, even in the worst cases. (Serenity, Mastery, Planetary Service, Divine Mother, Divine Expression)

Objects appear to move, melt, or shimmer: This is a common perception as you move into multidimensional sight. You may be beginning to sense the atomic motion within everything, parallel realities, energy flows in the room, or the beginning of "far-seeing" clairvoyance. If this is unsettling to you, remember that your physical body exists "NOW," in this parallel of third-dimensional reality, and you can use it to re-center your consciousness. Simply extend any physical sense, except your sight, and your body will bring you fully back into your usual reality. Also, focusing on your feet, as in the previous paragraph, helps greatly. (Mystical Articulation, Subatomic Tonic, Magical Visions, Love Potion #9)

Hazy Vision: If you open your eyes after a deep meditation, sometimes the room appears hazy. We have seen people virtually blinded. This means that you are between physical sight and clairvoyant or multidimensional sight. Your vision is neither here nor there. To adjust it, try yawning. Yawning is one way that people shift their bodies and consciousness through different energy frequencies. You can consciously use yawning to shift levels of perceptivity. Close your eyes and yawn, with the intent to make your vision third-dimensional and bring it back here. Or close your eyes and yawn with the intent to shift your sight into other psychic or dimensional levels. Your optic nerve is being required to handle a lot of impulses that it has never had before. Blurry vision is very common, especially in eighth-level Lightbody. If you find that you can't find any comfortable distance where your eyes will focus, we suggest that you **not** go out and get eyeglasses. Generally, within a weeks' time, you won't be able to see again. Your physical sight is very linked to the perceptions of the mental body. As new perceptions are coming in through your brain and through the spiritual body, it's very natural that some of the physical sight turns off as the mental body becomes less predominant. It will come back. It may take a few months, but it will usually come back. (Mystical Articulation, Subatomic Tonic, Magical Visions, Love Potion #9)

Audio Dyslexia: Very common in eighth-level Lightbody. When you listen to someone speak and you can hear the words, but your brain can't seem to make sense of them, it is called "audio dyslexia." Your brain functioning is becoming non-linear. The translation faculty from non-linear thought to linear language may not be on line yet. There are levels of Lightbody where it briefly seems like some people are talking in a foreign language, but you know they are not. This can be scary, because the mental body may send out panic signals and fears about going crazy. You are becoming very sensitive to people's energy. On this planet, what most people say verbally is totally at odds with what they say energetically. Most people don't know that they are lying or not being genuine. You are becoming so sensitive to someone's energy that you can no longer decode their verbal lies. The audio dyslexia is a brief stage while building Universal Mind translation facility and the ability to sense truth in yourself or others. Take a breath, laugh, and wait for further instructions. (Mystical Articulation, Transpersonal Transformation)

Hearing beeps, tones, music, or electronic "Morse code": It may be tinnitus or it may be a Higher Light transmission. We suggest that you relax and simply let the signal come through. Don't worry about understanding it; the translation facility comes over time. (Mystical Articulation, Surrender, Yod, Gifts of the Holy Spirit)

Memory Loss: This is a natural part of Lightbody. As you begin to live more and more in the "NOW," you lose the ability to reference to the past. This could be an inability to recall karmic patterning and relationships or simply to remember what you had for breakfast. There are many people living with the secret fear that maybe they're in the beginning stages of Alzheimer's disease. A very few may actually have the disease but the vast majority are simply living more "NOW." This break with referencing to the past can be very freeing. Clutching the past fosters the fear of change. You realize how much of your energy is tied up with preserving the past, reminiscing, chewing over "what might have been," or holding on to the way it's always been. Some people are also finding it very hard to project into the future. This, too may be unsettling, because you may miss appointments and such. The old world couldn't function without dwelling in the past, projecting into the future, and living by a clock, if not a stopwatch. In the new world that is emerging, people will live by their Spirit, delighting in the "NOW." As you become fully NOW, you literally become "in the world, not *of* the world." You live in a separate world from other beings. (Alignment, Mystical Articulation, Surrender, Yod)

Spiritual significance, spiritual ambition, spiritual manic-depression: Just about everyone goes through these at some time in their Lightbody process, usually at the seventh, eighth, and ninth levels. They manifest from trying to deny or run away from guilt, shame, survival patterns, and feelings of separation held in the physical body. Spiritual significance and spiritual ambition are ego defenses and, unfortunately, the person rarely knows (or admits) that they're running them. (Mastery, Transpersonal Transformation, Alignment, Planetary Service, Quantum Wealth, Surrender, Magical Visions, Love Potion #9)

Blowing lightbulbs and fuzzing electronics: At many points in the Lightbody process, you may find that you are buying an awful lot of lightbulbs. You'll notice that they tend to burn out or flicker when you are next to them. Your television may ghost or snow when you walk by or are merely in the room with it. Your speakers may "static" when you are near them. These little annoyances are caused by changes in your electromagnetic body, your auric field. There are several times in the Lightbody process when the electromagnetic body stretches. Sorry, there's nothing you can do for this one that we know about, except try to align your energy with your objects. With the electronic object off, try to merge your energy fields with the object. It is very normal to have some problems with electromagnetic frequencies. You may be much more sensitive to them than you have been before. You may feel radar. You may feel the electromagnetic waves. You may feel things coming off your television. Try the technique of merging your energy with it. (E-3, Subatomic Tonic, Yod).

THE POTIONS

Many times we've heard Lightworkers exclaim "I wish you could put that energy/entity/quality/ability in a bottle!" So we did. We listened to your requests, looked at the planetary energies impacting you now and in the recent future,* and created these "potions" to be of assistance.

In the past, these potions have included gem, flower, rare gas, and starlight elixirs and essences, in specific proportions. We infused each potion with its appropriate higher-dimensional qualities. The main purpose of these ingredients was to ground and buffer the higher frequencies for the physical body.

On May 30th, 1994, a dramatic shift occurred in the Divine Plan for planet Earth. The timetable for ascension was moved up and, due to this change, we feel it is appropriate to take the potions into pure frequency. We will no longer use the essences and elixirs to create a bridge and soften the energies. Your bodies are now prepared to absorb the higher-dimensional frequencies directly.

These potions are made with pure distilled water and infused by various members of the Council of Ein Soph. They are more intense than the old recipes and we think you'll love them even more.

> — Of the Source in service to the Source,
> Ariel Elohim for the Council of Ein Soph ("the Crew")

*"recent future" is a phrase Ariel uses to express non-linear time.

> **All of the potions described here are for spiritual use only.
> These are not medicines and no medical use is suggested.**

Alignment

This potion is for aligning every part of you to the One Probability, Spirit, the Earth and humanity. Polaria, Victory, and Harmony Elohim add their energy to this one.

Divine Expression

This potion assists in opening all parts of yourself to the creativity and expression of Spirit, especially toning. Some folks have found it very helpful for easing all kinds of anxiety and fear. Coronis in a bottle.

Divine Mother

Helps access the female frequencies of divinity. Allows nurturance of the body. Carries the energies of comfort, compassion, and nurturing. Helps with feelings of "Cosmic homesickness." This potion is infused by representatives of the Office of Divine Mother: Isis, Mother Mary, Quan Yin, Krzani, and TaMa.

Ecstasy

Opens the capacities of all of the bodies to Divine Ecstasy. It assists the fifth-dimensional, sixth-dimensional, and seventh-dimensional structures to fully interface, trinitizes all polarities, and helps the Kundalini to awaken. Several folks infuse this potion: Isis, Osiris, Polaria, Harmony and Grace Elohim.

E-3 (Essential Evolutionary Encodements)

This potion assists in the integration of multi-species, multi-universal encodements in the DNA. These genetic encodements have already been activated and the multi-universal orientations are beginning to open and manifest. E-3 assists you to integrate extraterrestrial perceptivities and orientations into your human-ness (and, on a vaster scale, into the hologram for life on planet Earth). It allows your mental body to follow Spirit with ease, open its closed systems, and integrate a vaster sense of identity. It fosters a sense of interconnectedness within the universe, and an awareness of yourself in other species on other ascending planets, within and outside of the Love-universe. This allows you to recognize what is essentially "you," beyond the human cultural context. It softens human-centrism and xenophobia, allowing you to access new brain functions and non-human perceptivities and skills. You become a coordination point for the ascension across multiple universal systems, multiple planets, multiple species types, and truly manifest your essential nature through your human form. Infused by the entire Council of Ein Soph.

Fire of Purpose

For accessing and manifesting your piece of the Divine Plan with clarity, focus, and joy. Aru Kiri in a bottle.

Gifts of the Holy Spirit

Prepares the bodies for reception of the gifts of the Holy Spirit. Assists in accessing the Christ level of the Oversoul and manifesting it here. Acts as a bridging frequency into the I AM. Infused by the Holy Spirit Shekhina.

Group Synergy

It enhances evolutionary synergies and grids. Adds clear focus and alignment to group goals and vision. This bottle is infused with the Christ Consciousness.

Heavenly Body

Designed to help you bring your vision of your perfect body into physicality. Heavenly Body is helpful for anyone who wants to recreate their body in a greater state of health, change their body type or weight, bring new motions, skills, or grace into their body. Heavenly Body will rapidly orient you to what exactly is keeping your body in any given shape or movement, and help you manifest thought into form. Great for dancers, martial artists, shape-shifters, athletes, etc. Infused by the ZeOr.

Home Sweet Home Enviro-pack

Everybody needs an energetically clean, secure and supportive home. The Enviro-pack is created in three parts. The first part, "Cleanse" is designed to clear out old thoughtforms, emotions, astral residue, boogies and generally old energy. The second part, "Seal," seals the space after you've cleansed it, and is designed to maintain your environment as a supportive haven for who you are as a Master. It will help you maintain harmony and unity among your bodies and clear communication with Spirit. The third part is Tachi's own blend of sacred salt. Use this for sealing the doors and windows in your home. This will help keep astral influences and other negative energies out of your living space. The Enviro-pack comes in its own handy-dandy pouch with instructions. It's infused by Purity Elohim, Uriel, and Aru Kiri.

Love Potion # 9

Assists in opening the heart chakra into deeper and deeper levels. Helps dissolve heart chakra armoring, thereby relieving much chest and upper back pain. Expands capacities for experiencing and expressing unconditional Love. Infused by Michael Elohim and the collective Golden Angels. Use liberally.

Magical Visions

Opens the sight and vision of the Magical Child. Assists you to quickly parallax your "reality" into a perspective of magic, miracles, and play. Opens you to experience the beauty and wonder in the High Astral Plane. The fairy and elfin kingdoms are assisting our ascension into the fourth dimension; therefore, their representatives have helped to infuse this potion: Arianna, Pan, Lightning Bolt, Skorm, Alia na Morigan, El Veron, The Merlin, and Hope Elohim.

Magnificence

For integration of new frequencies into all of the bodies. This potion eases all mutational and descension symptoms, and allows the body to delight in becoming Light. Quan Yin and Polaria zap this one.

Mastery

This is for manifesting fifth-dimensional identity and vision. Living as the Masters we are all the time and co-creating Heaven on Earth is what it's all about. Ariel and Serapis infuse this one.

Merkabah

Opens, balances, and evens out the spins of all Merkabah geometries. Helps you understand the Merkabah functions. Aids focus and pranic breathing. Assists in fully conscious contact with Spirit. This one is infused by Melchizedek, Michael, Uriel, and Metatron.

Mystical Articulation

Bio-transducer booster for accessing and translating languages of Light. Opens up the conscious mind into multidimensional perceptions. Particularly good for people who can't remember or don't get much when they meditate. Also great for relieving mutational headaches and the effects of having low endorphin production. Helpful for all eighth-level lightbody symptoms. Merlin and Metatron formula.

Pathcutter (formerly Phoenix)

This is a cellular release formula. It eases the expression and release of emotions, density, survival patterning, and karma matrices held in and around the physical body. Use very sparingly and under the direction of Spirit. Intense, but it helps a lot. Purity Elohim infuses this potion.

Planetary Service

This potion is created for people whose design is to work with the planet, planetary grids, land masses, or anything vast. It specifically helps to stop your Lightbody wiring from frying or power surging. It assists you to smoothly bring energies and multidimensional perceptions all the way into the physical body, for more effective Lightwork. As it assists your ability to shift consciousness, it also contains elements to soften spiritual significance, cut spiritual ambition, and maintain compassion for others. Eases cognitive dissonance between fifth-dimensional orientations and third-dimensional manifestations. The ZeOr/Quan Yin/Uraeus medical team infuse this potion.

Quantum Wealth

Also known as IMF, or Interdimensional Monetary Flow. This formula is designed to help integrate at all levels that Spirit is the provider of all resources. Aids you to surrender into quantum wealth. Yeah! This potion has a synergy of Aru Kiri, Victory and Faith Elohim.

Serenity

This potion is created under the auspices of Peace and Victory Elohim. It is designed to help you stay centered and calm in the midst of any type of extreme change, be it personal, mutational, or planetary. It eases transformational shock and trauma. Serenity cuts through fear and the tendency to focus on negative or destructive possibilities. It assists you in seeing the perfection of the Divine Plan in all things, and living Heaven on Earth as your Spirit is creating it around you.

Service One-on-One

Designed for people who do one-on-one work. This potion acts like a tonic for the body's wiring: it keeps the axiotonals open and flowing smoothly for doing hands-on work. It keeps your body balanced with whatever frequencies are coming through in service to your client, and it has elements designed to assist you in being able to empathize and perceive clearly without taking on your client's energy. It strengthens diagnostic and counseling abilities. It contains ingredients to ease karmic monads (healer/healed, enabler/enabled, savior/saved, guru/disciple). It helps you interact with your clients transpersonally and to maintain a fifth-dimensional perspective. Infused by Quan Yin and Adama Rex.

Subatomic Tonic

This one is for molecular integration of a new octave of Spirit. I asked for this potion to assist in the awakening and integration of teleportation, apportation, and translocation, as well as the manifestation of the Gifts of the Holy Spirit. Take this one very sparingly and under the direction of Spirit. This potion is infused by the Holy Spirit Shekhina.

Surrender

This potion assists you to go through the Gate of Awakening by surrendering to your Spirit. It helps collapse closed systems, ego defense structures, denial, and resistance. The entire Council of Ein Soph infuses this one.

Transpersonal Transformation

This elixir assists the physical and emotional bodies to shift from personal to transpersonal relationships. It's especially helpful when dealing with lovers and relatives. Grace Elohim and El Veron infuse their energies.

Universal Detox

Designed under the auspices of Grace and Purity Elohim. It allows the bodies to let go of resistance to change, cuts addiction, brings up vitality, helps you feel nurtured, balances yin/yang, promotes change without denial, and fosters a new vision of health. It clears toxins to the spiritual, mental, and emotional bodies, such as destructive thoughts and emotions, E.L.F. waves, microwaves, boogies, cords, vows, past decisions about health, process addiction, 4-D distortions, and other people's pictures. It clears toxic residues from the etheric blueprints. Universal Detox should be used very sparingly, and in conjunction with a good physical detoxification program.

Yod

Carries the energies of completion, purification, and mobilization. Taking this potion is somewhat like tuning up your car and placing it in neutral — revved up and ready to go. This potion is designed for Phase I: YOD, P.H.O.E.N.Y.X. O.F. Y.A.H. Program. K'or Takh and the Takh Group infuse this potion.

All of the potions described here are for spiritual use only. These are not medicines and no medical use is suggested.

✒ INVOCATIONS ✒

— *Introduction* —

Greetings Lightworkers,

We have brought these Invocations through to assist you in this incarnation on planet Earth. There are seven to eight million Lightworkers embodied at this time, to assist in this planet's ascension to the Light dimensions.

These Invocations are designed to support you in building your Light Body, embodying Spirit, healing and balancing your bodies, and walking the Path of Joy.

The Unified Chakra technique is most helpful if done many times a day until it becomes natural. It builds your Light Body, unifies your bodies with Spirit, and allows you to live your life with maximum perceptivity and minimum stress.

The "Invocation to Light" is a true joy to those who use it daily. It gently raises your vibration as it assists you in opening to higher Light frequencies. It is a declaration of your intent as a Lightworker.

The "Invocation to Water" is basically used over food and drink to shift its vibration to a higher level. It can also be used over your bath, shower, pool, hot tub, gasoline, paints, etc. Most people use it as a grace at meals.

The Invocations to the Rays have many uses: healing for yourself or others, opening into higher dimensions, accessing information and energies, protection, and transformation. We suggest that you become familiar with these emanations of Light. Also, we advise you to combine the Silver Ray of Grace with any Ray you are visualizing, allowing it to become iridescent and sparkling!

The Invocations of Qualities can be used along with the Rays. They correspond to some aspect of the Emanation. They can also be used alone, when you want to foster a special quality in yourself or your space.

These Invocations are encoded phrases. That means that there are layers of energy placed in each word. Therefore, we advise that you not change the words.

We thank you for your presence on the planet at this time. Your service and dedication to the Light is beautiful to behold.

Ask, and all will be given to assist you. We love you and we are always with you.

Of the Source in Service to the Source,
— Archangel Ariel

⋙ INVOCATION TO THE UNIFIED CHAKRA ⋘

I breathe in Light
Through the center of my heart,
Opening my heart
Into a beautiful ball of Light,
Allowing myself to expand.

I breathe in Light
Through the center of my heart,
Allowing the Light to expand,
Encompassing my throat chakra
And my solar plexus chakra
In one unified field of Light
Within, through, and around my body.

I breathe in Light
Through the center of my heart,
Allowing the Light to expand,
Encompassing my brow chakra
And my navel chakra
In one unified field of Light
Within, through, and around my body.

I breathe in Light
Through the center of my heart,
Allowing the Light to expand,
Encompassing my crown chakra
And my base chakra
In one unified field of Light
Within, through, and around my body.

I breathe in Light
Through the center of my heart,
Allowing the Light to expand,
Encompassing my Alpha chakra
(Eight inches above my head)
And my Omega chakra
(Eight inches below my spine)
In one unified field of Light
Within, through, and around my body.
I allow the Wave of Metatron
To move between these two points.
I AM a unity of Light.

I breathe in Light
Through the center of my heart,
Allowing the Light to expand,
Encompassing my eighth chakra
(Above my head)
And my upper thighs
In one unified field of Light
Within, through, and around my body.
I allow my emotional body to merge
With my physical body.
I AM a unity of Light.

I breathe in Light
Through the center of my heart,
Allowing the Light to expand,
Encompassing my ninth chakra
(Above my head)
And my lower thighs
In one unified field of Light
Within, through, and around my body.
I allow my mental body to merge
With my physical body.
I AM a unity of Light.

I breathe in Light
Through the center of my heart,
Allowing the Light to expand,
Encompassing my tenth chakra
(Above my head)
And to my knees
In one unified field of Light
Within, through, and around my body.
I allow my spiritual body to merge
With my physical body,
Forming the unified field.
I AM a unity of Light.

I breathe in Light
Through the center of my heart,
Allowing the Light to expand,
Encompassing my eleventh chakra
(Above my head)
And my upper calves
In one unified field of Light
Within, through, and around my body.
I allow the Oversoul to merge
With the unified field.
I AM a unity of Light.

I breathe in Light
Through the center of my heart,
Allowing the Light to expand,
Encompassing my twelfth chakra
(Above my head)
And my lower calves
In one unified field of Light
Within, through, and around my body.
I allow the Christ Oversoul to merge
With the unified field.
I AM a unity of Light.

I breathe in Light
Through the center of my heart,
Allowing the Light to expand,
Encompassing my thirteenth chakra
(Above my head)
And my feet
In one unified field of Light
Within, through, and around my body.
I allow the I AM Oversoul to merge
With the unified field.
I AM a unity of Light.

I breathe in Light
Through the center of my heart,
Allowing the Light to expand,
Encompassing my fourteenth chakra
(Above my head)
And to below my feet
In one unified field of Light
Within, through, and around my body.
I allow the Source's Presence to move
Throughout the unified field.
I AM a unity of Light.

I breathe in Light
Through the center of my heart.
I ask that
The highest level of my Spirit
Radiate forth
From the center of my heart,
Filling this unified field completely.
I radiate forth throughout this day.
I AM a unity of Spirit.

⋙ INVOCATION TO LIGHT ⋘

I live within the Light.
I love within the Light.
I laugh within the Light.

I AM sustained and nourished
By the Light.
I joyously serve the Light.

For I AM the Light.
I AM the Light.
I AM the Light.

I AM. I AM. I AM.

⋙ INVOCATION TO WATER ⋘

I take this, the Water of Life,
I declare it the Water of Light.
As I bring it within my body,
It allows my body to glow.
I take this, the Water of Light,
I declare it the Water of God.
I AM a Master in all that I AM.

⤜ INVOCATION TO CLARITY ⤛

I stand within the Infinite NOW;
All roads are open to me.

I love within the Infinite NOW;
All paths are clear to me.

I laugh within the Infinite NOW;
All ways are known to me.

Within the Infinite NOW lies all Power.
Within the Infinite NOW lies all Love.
Within the Infinite NOW lies all clarity.

I act within the flow of Spirit,
Acting, loving, knowing
All That Is.

⋙ INVOCATION TO UNITY ⋘

I AM a Christed Being.
I AM in unity with Spirit.

I AM a Christed Being.
I AM in unity with All That Is.
The Light of my own Being
Shines upon my path.

I AM a Christed Being.
I AM in unity with All That Will Be.
I hold the shining Light of the Source
Within my heart.

I walk in unity with Spirit.
I laugh in unity with the Source.
I love in unity with my fellow beings.

I AM a Christed Being.
I AM a bridge between Heaven and Earth.

◈ INVOCATION TO THE RED RAY ◈

I call upon the Elohim
Of the Ruby Red Ray,
To pour your Light through my body.

I call upon the Elohim
Of the Ruby Red Ray,
To pour the Strength of the Source
Through every cell of my body,
To re-create my body in Light.

May the Ruby Light
Heal all cellular damage,
Release all stress and pain,
Calm all fear of change.

My body is whole in the Light.
My being is calm in the Light.
I have the strength of the Source.

◈ INVOCATION TO TRANQUILITY ◈

I go within
And open the petals of the Crystal Lotus

I go within,
And as the Lotus blooms,
My mind, my body, and emotions quiet.

As my consciousness steps
Into the center of the Lotus,
I become tranquil with who I AM.
I flow with the serenity of Spirit.

As I sit within the Lotus,
I know the Buddha that is Myself.

⋙ INVOCATION TO THE ORANGE RAY ⋘

I call upon the Elohim
Of the Carnelian Ray,
To pour the Vitality of God
Through my body.

I call upon the Orange Ray,
To awaken my Divine Creativity.

I call upon the Orange Ray,
To deepen my Love and connection
To the planet.

I AM a Master of flow and change,
I feel the beauty of all of Creation.

⋙ INVOCATION TO CREATIVITY ⋘

I bubble with Divine Expression.
The spark of creativity
Is the spark of Life.
I sculpt realities like fine clay.

I AM the Master artisan of my Life,
I create Visions of the planet in Light
And, behold, the Light is there.

I paint portraits of kind persons
And, behold, more Love is in the world.

I sing of the movement of Spirit
And, behold, I AM soaring.

INVOCATION TO THE YELLOW RAY

I call upon the Elohim
Of the Topaz Ray,
To pour Divine Realization
Through my body.

Through the Yellow Ray
I awaken my Divine Purpose.

I call upon the Yellow Ray,
To strengthen my sense of service
To the Source's Vision.

I call upon the Topaz Ray,
To soften my ego,
That I may surrender to Spirit.

INVOCATION TO AWAKENING

I call the child that I AM
To take my hand and teach me Joy.

I call the child that I AM
To show me the delight of discovery
In all the worlds that I AM.

I take my hand and dance
With the patterns of the Galaxies.
I open my heart and sing
With the patterns of Mastery.

I AM the child that I AM
And I awaken all that I can be.
I awaken I AM.

⪻ INVOCATION TO THE GREEN RAY ⪼

I call upon the Elohim
Of the Emerald Green Ray,
To pour abundance through my body.

I call upon the Elohim
Of the Emerald Green Ray,
To connect me with my Divine Flow.
As is above, so is below.

I call upon the Green Ray
To strengthen
The opening of my heart, completely.

I call upon the Emerald Ray
To assist my creation of abundance.
As is above, so is below,
All is Love, All is Flow.

⪻ INVOCATION TO DIVINE FLOW ⪼

I AM the Universe, re-creating myself.
I AM the Universe flowing
To myself, through myself, from myself,
Creating all I see.

I AM the Divine Flow of All That Is.
Abundant is my motion.
I AM the Universe, re-creating myself
To flow abundance.

❧ INVOCATION TO THE BLUE RAY ❧

I call upon the Elohim
Of the Sapphire Blue Ray,
To pour the Light of Sacred Translation
Through my body.

I call upon the Elohim
Of the Sapphire Ray,
To pour Divine Truth
Through my body,
That I may speak the Truth
Of who I AM.

I call upon the Sapphire Blue Ray
To assist me in communicating Love,
And my translation of light to Light.
I call upon the Elohim
Of the Sapphire Blue Ray,
To sweeten my voice so that all
Will hear the Truth of God.

❧ INVOCATION TO LAUGHTER ❧

Some say that laughter is the best medicine.
Some say that laughter is the antidote to sin.

Some say that laughter is a waste of good time.
I tell you laughter is fully Divine.

This planet has a bunch of serious folks,
They just don't get The Cosmic Joke.

And some spend their lives in hot pursuit
Of what they call a Cosmic Truth.

But I heard a joke in the Heavens above ...
Laughter is Truth —

And the punch line is Love.

⤜ INVOCATION TO THE INDIGO RAY ⤛

I call upon the Elohim
Of the Indigo Ray,
To awaken and strengthen my third and fourth eyes,
For I now choose to See.

I call upon the Elohim of the Star Sapphire Ray,
To awaken the Star
That holds the memories of who I AM.

I call upon the Elohim of the Indigo Ray,
To activate the recorder cell
That I may remember and understand.

⤜ INVOCATION TO THE UNIVERSE ⤛

I AM the Universe.
I AM the spin and swirl of galaxies.
I AM the movement of planets in their orbits.
I AM a comet in the night sky.

I AM a human being
Moving with the flow of Spirit.
I AM an atom
Containing All That Is.

I AM the Universe,
Laughing as I dance.

I AM Life.

⋘ INVOCATION TO THE VIOLET RAY ⋘

I call upon the Elohim
Of the Violet Ray,
To pour Divine Transmutation
Through all that I AM.

I call upon the Amethyst Ray
To transform every cell,
Every atom of my bodies
Into Higher Light.

I call upon the Violet Flame
To burn within my soul
And release all veils that separate me
From Spirit.

I call upon the Violet Flame
To burn away my illusions,
To burn away my resistances,
And transmute my fear to Love.

⋘ INVOCATION OF THE KEEPERS OF THE ⋙ FLAME

I AM a Keeper of the Flame.
I carry it forth
Into every part of this world.

I AM a Keeper of the Flame.
I carry it forth
Into every part of my being.

I hold the Flame of God high
So that all may see the shining Light
Of the Divine Plan.

I AM a Keeper of the Flame
And I carry it forth into many worlds,
So that all may know the Light
And carry it onward.

⤳ INVOCATION TO THE GOLD RAY ⤶

I call upon the Elohim of the Gold Ray
To pour Divine Wisdom into my consciousness.

I call upon the Elohim of the Gold Ray
To reveal the Weights and Measures,
The Balance and Proportions
Of the Universe.

I call upon the Elohim of the Gold Ray
To illuminate my mind,
So it will grow peaceful
With Understanding.

May I be wise in my actions,
Balanced in my emotions,
Peaceful in my mind.

⤳ INVOCATION TO MASTERY ⤶

I AM a Master,
Dancing through dimensions.

I AM a Master of possibilities,
Weaving the tomorrows into NOW.

I AM a Master of balance,
Skipping on the tightrope of Life.

I AM a Master
Whose strength is compassion.

I AM a Master
Who plays with infinity.

I AM a Master
Who tickles the stars.

⪻ INVOCATION TO THE SILVER RAY ⪼

I call upon the Elohim of the Silver Ray
To pour Divine Grace through my bodies.

I call upon the Elohim of the Silver Ray
To release all karmic patterns,
To release all pockets of resentment,
That I may know Joy.

I call upon the Elohim of Grace
To fill my being with forgiveness,
To fill my life with gratitude,
And fill my heart with celebration.

I call upon the Elohim of the Silver Ray
To release my bindings of pettiness,
To break the yoke of hatred,
And free my soul.

I call upon the Elohim of Grace
To fill me with the Joy of Living —
NOW.

⪻ INVOCATION TO JOY ⪼

I have a tickle in my toes
That makes me dance down the street.
I have a giggle in my belly
That makes me hug all I see.
I have a fountain in my heart
That splashes love on the world.
I know the Joy of Spirit
So I laugh in my soul.
I have Joy in living
So I celebrate the Light.

⋙INVOCATION TO THE COPPER RAY⋘

I call upon the Elohim of the Copper Ray
To show me the Divine Blueprint of Life.

I call upon the Elohim of the Copper Ray
To show me the patterns
Of my existence.

I ask that the Copper Ray
Connect and sustain all the primary rays
Through my bodies.

I call upon the Elohim of the Copper Ray
To lead me in the spiral dance,
So that I may ascend to Light.

⟨⟩ INVOCATION TO THE SPIRAL DANCE ⟨⟩

From my center I call the spiral.
I spin. I glow.

From the center, I grow the spiral
In the home of my soul.

I expand my soul and set it to spin.
In my body, the dance begins.

The spiral grows, its apex in the heart.
It surrounds my body, the vibration starts.

From the Highest Spirit to the soul,
As is above, so is below.

Another spiral, from the Christ,
Created from a Higher Light,
Matches the other with perfect spin
And brings the apex deep within.

Where they touch, a flame, so bright,
Pulls my body into Light.

For it is the Christ within
That puts the galaxies to spin.

In the Light I AM entranced,
Let us lead the spiral dance.

✥ INVOCATION TO THE TURQUOISE RAY ✥

I call upon the Elohim of the Turquoise Ray
To lead me through the Ocean
Of Divine Consciousness.

I call upon the Turquoise Ray
To connect me with all my incarnations.

I call upon the Turquoise Ray
To connect me with all my manifestations.

I AM one with the Greater Consciousness.
I AM Divine Connection,
We dive into the Light and Laugh.

✥ INVOCATION TO FLIGHT ✥

I feel the tingling in my back.
I feel the weight in my shoulders.
I feel the spreading of my wings.

Preparing to fly,
I hear the call of the wind.
I smell the freedom of the skies.
I touch the edge of wonder,
As I begin to lift.

I love the feel of soaring.
I know the thrill of diving.
I light the sky with brilliance,
As I kiss the face of God.

⋙ INVOCATION TO THE PINK RAY ⋘

I call upon the Elohim of the Pink Ray
To pour forth Divine Unity.

I call upon the Elohim of the Pink Ray
To assist me in accepting
My Christ Self.

I call upon the Elohim of the Pink Ray
To pour Divine Love through my bodies.

May the Love of the Christ
Flow through me.
May the Unity of Spirit
Work through me.

I AM a Christed Being.
I AM in Unity with the Source.

⋙ INVOCATION TO SERVICE ⋘

I ask in the Name of the Christ,
That I be sustained in the Light.

I ask in the Name of God,
That I be guided and assisted
In my service to the One.

I ask in the Name of the Source,
That the Holy Spirit Shekhina
Fill me with Her Gifts,
That I may serve more fully.

I ask in the Name Yod-Hey-Vav-Hey,
That I may serve the Light
In this world.

⋙ INVOCATION TO THE RAY OF RAPTURE ⋘

I call upon the Elohim
Of the Ray of Rapture
To pour your Light around my bodies.

I call upon the Ray of Rapture
To assist me in building
My vehicle of Light.

I call upon the Elohim of Rapture
To connect me to the I AM Presence.

I call upon the Elohim of Rapture
To merge me with my Source.

The closest description of the color of this Ray is gold, copper, bronzish honey. Imagine the combined color of all the Rays right before they merge to White. Also, the Ray of Rapture is often experienced as much thicker than the other Rays, much like honey.

⋙ INVOCATION TO THE I AM PRESENCE ⋘

Ehyah Asher Ehyah.
I AM THAT I AM.
I call upon the Fellowships of Light,
I call upon the Guardians of Light,
I call upon the Angels of Light,

To assist me as I AM
To be who I AM
Linking me to I AM.

Ehyah Asher Ehyah.
I AM THAT I AM.

❧ INVOCATION TO THE WHITE RAY ❧

I call upon the Elohim of the White Ray
To pour the full crystalline
Light of the Source
Through every part of my being.

I call upon the Elohim of the White Ray
To activate the crystal templates
Of my bodies.

I ask that I be attuned
To the fullness of the White Ray,
So that I may be fulfilled.

I call upon the Elohim of the White Ray
To fill me with the Light of God.

⪻ INVOCATION TO KIDDUSH HA-SHEM ⪼

Blessed is Yod-Hey-Vav-Hey.
Kodosh! Kodosh! Kodosh!
Holy! Holy! Holy!

King of the Universes,
You who set the Divine Order,
May You set the order of my life
According to Your Will.

Blessed is Yod-Hey-Vav-Hey.
Kodosh! Kodosh! Kodosh! Adonai Tsebayot.
Infinite Light.
Infinite Love.
Infinite Truth.

Lord God of Hosts,
May Your Glory cover the Earth.
May your Light sustain the Earth
As It sustains the Heavens.

Holy! Holy! Holy!
Is the Lord God of Hosts.
May the Earth be covered in your Glory.
In this world and the World to Come.

Kodosh! Kodosh! Kodosh!
Adonai Tsebayot.
Maloch Kol Ha-aretz K'vodoh!
Lay-olam Vo-ed.

Amen. Amen. Amen. Amen.

⊰⊱ THE CLARION CALL ⊰⊱

Parallel merges,
Magnetic surges.
Time collapses,
Straining synapses.
Nothing is wrong —
Bring it on!

Bodies are hurting
From encodements bursting.
Resistance depleted;
Works almost completed.
These changes are strong —
Bring it on!

Physical bodies' communion
Is genetic reunion.
With codes of Infinity
For embodied Divinity.
Our bodies are coming along —
Bring it on!

Mental delusions and
Shattered illusions.
Go through the Gate:
Awakening waits.
Surrender, go on —
Bring it on!

To shift realities
Into Divine Normalities,
It's very effective
To parallax perspective.
For what do you long?
Bring it on!

From transpersonal knowing
Attachments are going.

Emotional upheaval,
Then Spirit is revealed.
The love for the One —
Bring it on!

Open the heart to jubilation,
Open the mind to revelation.
Open the body, open the Soul
To Beloved Spirit's goal.
The mission's nearly done —
Bring it on!

Mystical missions
Need magical visions.
Hearts open and wild
Frees the Magical Child.
We're dancing towards Home —
Bring it on!

Our ecstatic birthright filled
With Grace and de-Light
Is heaven styled
Through the Magical Child.
Touch the new dawn —
Bring it on!

Won't you join in the fun?
Everybody can come
To the Universal Celebration
Of humanity's graduation.
Join in Victory's song —
Bring it on!

Old worlds are ending,
Universes ascending.
Merkabahs' spinning
This world's new beginning.
Call of the One —
Bring it on!

Merkabah merges,
True Love surges.
Space/time collapses,
Spirit enrapts us.
The flight of the One —
Bring it on!

⤳ AMEN ⤳

I AM a temple of the Light. Amen.
I AM a guardian of the Sacred Arc of the Covenant.
I carry the Laws of God within my heart.
I step between the veils.
I speak with my Source.
Amen.

I AM a temple of the Light. Amen.
I shine forth the letters of the Holy Name from my brow.
I AM a guardian of the Threefold Flame of the Ein Soph.
I AM a priest within the temple of my spirit.
Amen.

I AM a temple of the Light. Amen.
I AM a guardian of the Sacred Arc of the Covenant.
I shine forth the flame of the letters to the world,
So that all may be a temple of the Light,
Keepers of the covenant.

I AM a temple of the Light. Amen.
I AM a guardian of the Sacred Arc of the Covenant.
Amen. Amen. Amen. Amen.

SOURCES

To order potions, contact Alchemical Creations: call them at (303) 322-0508, or write to them at P.O. Box 31645, Aurora, CO 80041-1645. Catalog $1.

To order from the complete line of our books and tapes, contact "Wings Around the Planet": call them at (303) 733-8183, or write to them at 303 S. Broadway, Suite B-333, Denver, CO 80209. Catalog $1.

Oughten House Publications (the publisher of this book) also distributes some of our tape sets. To contact Oughten House, call (510) 447-2332. P.O. Box 2008, Livermore, CA 94551-2008. Free catalog.

For information on workshops, Lightbody Mutational Services, or private appointments with Tashira Tachi-ren, contact Angelic Outreach/P.H.O.E.N.Y.X. O.F. Y.A.H: call them at (303) 634-4293, or write them at P.O. Box 101133, Denver, CO 80250-1133. After June 1, 1996, call them at (503) 321-5111 and get their new address. Beginning April 1, 1996, you may access their Web Home Page at www.net1comm.com/ao.

About the Publisher and Logo

The name "Oughten" was revealed to the publisher fifteen years ago, after three weeks of meditation and contemplation. The combined effect of the letters carries a vibratory signature, signifying humanity's ascension on a planetary level.

The logo represents a new world rising from its former condition. The planet ascends from the darker to the lighter. Our experience of a dark and mysterious universe becomes transmuted by our planet's rising consciousness — glorious and spiritual. The grace of God transmutes the dross of the past into gold, as we leave all behind and ascend into the millennium.

Publisher's Comment

Our mission and purpose is to publish ascension books and complementary material for all peoples and all children worldwide.

We currently serve over fifty authors, musicians, and artists. Many of our authors channel such energies as Sananda, Ashtar, Archangel Michael, St. Germain, Archangel Ariel, Serapis, Mother Mary, and Kwan Yin. Some work closely with the Elohim and the angelic realms. They need your support to get their channeled messages to all nations. Oughten House Publications welcomes your interest and petitions your overall support and association in this important endeavor.

We urge you to share the information with your friends, and to join our network of spiritually-oriented people. Our financial proceeds are recycled into producing new ascension books and expanding our distribution worldwide. If you have the means to contribute or invest in this process, then please contact us.

OUGHTEN HOUSE PUBLICATIONS

Our imprint includes books in a variety of fields and disciplines which emphasize our relationship to the rising planetary consciousness. Literature which relates to the ascension process, personal growth, and our relationship to extraterrestrials is our primary focus. We are also developing a line of beautifully illustrated children's books, which deal with all aspects of spirituality. The list that follows is only a sample of our current offerings. To obtain a complete catalog, contact us at the address shown at the back of this book.

Ascension Books & Books for the Rising Planetary Consciousness

The Crystal Stair: A Guide to the Ascension, by Eric Klein. A collection of channeled teachings received from Lord Sananda (Jesus) and other Masters, describing the personal and planetary ascension process now actively occurring on our planet.
— ISBN 1-880666-06-5, $12.95

The Inner Door: Channeled Discourses from the Ascended Masters on Self-Mastery and Ascension, by Eric Klein. In these two volumes, intended as a sequel to *The Crystal Stair*, the Masters address the challenges of the journey to ascension.
Volume One: ISBN 1-880666-03-0, $14.50
Volume Two: ISBN 1-880666-16-2, $14.50

Jewels on the Path: Transformational Teachings of the Ascended Masters, by Eric Klein. In this book, the ideas and themes introduced in Klein's earlier books are clarified and refined. The reader is brought up to date on what exactly the ascension process consists of and how to be a more active participant in it. Current topics are also discussed. This is the best one yet! — ISBN 1-880666-48-0, $14.95

An Ascension Handbook, by Tony Stubbs. A practical presentation which describes the ascension process in detail and includes several exercises to help you integrate it into your daily life. Topics include energy and matter; divine expression; love, power, and truth; breaking old patterns; aligning with Spirit; and life after ascension. A best-seller! — ISBN 1-880666-08-1, $12.95

What Is Lightbody? Archangel Ariel, channeled by Tashira Tachi-ren. Offers a twelve-level model for the ascension process, leading to the attainment of our Light Body. Recommended in *An Ascension Handbook*, this book gives many invocations, procedures, and potions to assist us on our journey home. Related tapes available.
— ISBN 1-880666-25-1, $12.95

The Extraterrestrial Vision: Channeled Teachings from Theodore, channeled by Gina Lake. The mid-causal group entity, Theodore, tells us what we need to know about our extraterrestrial heritage and how to prepare for direct contact with those civilizations which will soon be appearing in our midst. — ISBN 1-880666-19-7, $13.50

Lady From Atlantis, by Robert V. Gerard. Shar Dae, the future empress of Atlantis, is suddenly transported onto a rain-soaked beach in modern-day America. There she meets her twin flame and discovers her mission: to warn the people of planet Earth to mend their ways before Mother Earth takes matters in her own hands!
— ISBN 1-880666-21-9, $12.95

Intuition by Design, by Victor R. Beasley, Ph.D. A boxed set of 36 IQ (Intution Quotient) Cards contain consciousness-changing geometrics on one side and a transfomative verse on the other. The companion book tells you the many ways to use the cards in all aspects of your life. An incredible gift to yourself or someone you love. — ISBN 1-880666-22-7, $21.95

Angels of the Rays, by Mary Johanna. This book contains portraits of, information about, and messages from twelve different angels who are here to help us in our ascension process. Includes twelve removable full-color Angel Cards and directions for their use. — ISBN 1-880666-34-0, $18.95

Navigating the '90s, by Deborah Soucek. Down-to-earth, practical ways to help yourself make the personal shifts in awareness and behavior required by these accelerated times. Loving and succinct observations and exercises through which we can reclaim our true selves and shed the "programming" of our past.
— ISBN 1-880666-47-2, $13.95

My Ascension Journal, by Nicole Christine. Transform yourself and your life by using the journaling methods given in this book. Includes several real-life examples from the author's own journals, plus many blank pages on which to write your own ascension story. This quality-bound edition will become a treasured keepsake to be re-read over and over again. — ISBN 1-880666-18-9, $24.95

Bridge Into Light: Your Connection to Spiritual Guidance, by Pam and Fred Cameron. Lovingly offers many step-by-step exercises on how to meditate and how to channel, and gives ways to invoke the protection and assistance of the Masters. Companion tape available.
— ISBN 1-880666-07-3, $11.95

Transformational Tools

We offer an ever-expanding selection of transformational tools to assist you in your journey back to mastery. These include books and tapes, with such titles as *Intuition by Design*, *Heart Initiation*, *Ascending From the Center*, *Ascension: Beginner's Manual*, *The Thymus Chakra Handbook*, *Parallel Realities*, *The Feminine Aspect of God*, *Ascension Merkabah*, *Soul Alignment*, Joshua Stone's books on ascension, and several series of tapes by authors such as Tashira Tachi-ren, Solara, August Stahr, and Crea. Hear the voices and experience the energies of our authors, on companion tapes to *Bridge Into Light* and *The Extraterrestrial Vision*. We also have products such as Ascension Cards to help you focus on your ascension process as it unfolds in your life. For more information on these and other titles in this category, please call or write for our free catalog.

Children's Books and Tapes

Books and tapes in this category include titles such as *Nature Walk, Mary's Lullaby, Song of Gothar, Bear Essentials of Love,* and the "Little Angel" book series. Although primarily intended for children and adults who interact with children, they speak to the "child" within us all.

Music Tapes

We carry many titles of spiritually-based music, including both vocal and instrumental types, by artists such as Richard Shulman, Omashar, Stefan Jedland, and Michael Hammer. Create your own "ascension chamber" whenever you play them — at home or wherever your journey takes you. For a listing of available titles, call or write for our free catalog. You may reach us at the location listed on page 143.

ATTENTION: BUSINESSES AND SCHOOLS!

OUGHTEN HOUSE books are available at quantity discounts with bulk purchases for educational, business, or sales promotional use. For details, please contact the publisher at the address on page 143.

READER NETWORKING AND MAILING LIST

The ascension process presents itself as a new reality for many of us on planet Earth. Many Starseeds and Lightworkers seek to know more. Thousands of people worldwide are reaching out to find others of like mind and to network with them. The newly formed Oughten House Foundation stands ready to serve you all.

You have the opportunity to become a member, stay informed, and be on our networking mailing list. Call or write to us for more information. We will do our best to keep you and your network of friends up to date with ascension-related literature, materials, author tours, workshops, and channelings.

NOTE: If you have a network database or small mailing list you would like to share, please send it along!

 *Announcing ...*

Oughten House Foundation, Inc. has recently been created as a publishing, educational, and networking organization. The purpose of the Foundation is to serve all those who seek personal, social, and spiritual empowerment. Our goal is to reach out to 560 million people worldwide. The Foundation has a non-profit (501(c)(3)) status and seeks members and other fund-raising affiliations. Programs for all age groups will be offered.

An integral part of our mission involves the development of a global network to support the dissemination of information, especially through organized community groups. Information related to membership and program services is available upon request. Please contact Oughten House Publications, or call (510) 447-2332.

CATALOG REQUESTS & BOOK ORDERS

Catalogs will gladly be sent upon request. For catalogs to be sent outside of the USA, please send $3.00 for postage and handling. Book orders must be prepaid: check, money order, international coupon, VISA, MasterCard, Discover Card, and American Express accepted. Include UPS shipping and handling as follows (no P.O. boxes for UPS):

UPS Domestic Shipping and Handling:

ORDER TOTAL	GROUND	3-DAY	2-DAY	NEXT DAY
$00.01 to $10.00	$ 4.50	$ 6.00	$ 8.25	$16.00
$10.01 to $30.00	$ 5.75	$ 7.25	$10.00	$19.50
$30.01 to $50.00	$ 7.00	$ 8.25	$11.25	$21.00
$50.01 to $70.00	$ 8.50	$10.25	$12.50	$25.00
$70.01 to $100.00	$10.50	$13.00	$14.50	$27.50
$100.01 to $150.00*	$12.50	$15.75	$17.50	$35.00

*All orders over $150.00 need to call for a shipping estimate
*HI, AK, PR orders are shipped Priority Mail or Book Rate
*All continental US orders shipped UPS unless requested otherwise
*Allow 48 hours to process all regular orders

INTERNATIONAL ORDERS:

Charges include actual shipping costs for international Air or Surface Printed Matter, plus an additional $4.00 handling fee.

If paying by check or money order, please use US funds, through a US bank or an International Money Order, payable to Oughten House Publications. Allow approximately 6 weeks for international delivery and 10 working days for US delivery. (Note: Book prices, shipping, and handling charges are subject to change.)

To place your order or get our free catalog by phone, call our Toll-Free Orders Hot Line: (888) ORDER- IT (888/673-3748)

If you are not ready to order, but need more information, call us at (510) 447-2332. For mail or fax orders, send to:

OUGHTEN HOUSE PUBLICATIONS
P.O. Box 2008
Livermore • California • 94551-2008 • USA
Fax (510) 447-2376
e-mail: oughten@rest.com

New York Times and *USA TODAY* Bestselling Author

SHERRYL WOODS

WITH CHEF TEDDI WOHLFORD

The
SWEET
MAGNOLIAS
Cookbook

150 FAVORITE SOUTHERN RECIPES

The Sweet Magnolias Cookbook

ISBN-13: 978-0-373-89260-0

Library of Congress Cataloging-in-Publication Data

Woods, Sherryl.
    The sweet magnolias cookbook: 150 favorite Southern recipes /
     Sherryl Woods with Chef Teddi Wohlford.
    p. cm.
    ISBN 978-0-373-89260-0

    1. Cooking, American--Southern style. 2. Cookbooks. I. Wohlford, Teddi. II. Title.
TX715.2.S68W665 2012
641.5975--dc23

2011049668

www.Harlequin.com

Printed in U.S.A.

SWEET MAGNOLIAS BOOKS
by SHERRYL WOODS

Stealing Home

A Slice of Heaven

Feels Like Family

Welcome to Serenity

Home in Carolina

Sweet Tea at Sunrise

Honeysuckle Summer

Midnight Promises

Catching Fireflies

Where Azaleas Bloom

CONTENTS

1   SWEET MAGNOLIAS MARGARITA NIGHTS
(& OTHER COCKTAILS AND MUNCHIES!)

2   SULLIVAN'S RESTAURANT SPECIALTIES OF THE HOUSE

3 SERENITY FARMERS' MARKET

4 SUNDAY BRUNCH AT SULLIVAN'S

5 MAMA CRUZ'S RECIPE FILE

6

CHEF ERIK'S DECADENT DESSERTS

7

THE CORNER SPA'S LOW-CAL HEALTHY SELECTIONS

INTRODUCTION

Throughout the Sweet Magnolias books—ten of them to date—food plays an important role. Southern food. Grits and gravy. Fried chicken. Red velvet cake. Peach cobbler. Bread pudding. Oh, my! I can gain ten pounds just writing about these things. As for eating them, it's best I not go there, at least on a regular basis. Moderation, that's the key. I try to remember that in real life, if not in my fictional world of Serenity, South Carolina.

The talk of food is particularly prominent in *A Slice of Heaven*, Dana Sue's story centered around Sullivan's—her regional success story, a restaurant known for putting a new spin on traditional Southern dishes. But food—and drink—also come into play at the infamous margarita nights held by the group of old friends who call themselves the Sweet Magnolias, at the café in The Corner Spa where less caloric offerings are available and in the many backyard get-togethers of the Sweet Magnolias and their families. These Southern gals are, you see—like the friends you have in your community or neighborhood—always ready to share a meal and have some fun.

As for myself, I have an interesting relationship with food: I love to eat! A little too much, perhaps. I also love to write about food. I guess I must be good at inventing things because the funny thing is, I've never really considered myself much of a cook.

While growing up, I didn't show much interest in learning to cook (I was too busy reading!), but by the time I was in my early teens, I was the default cook in my family. My working mother hated to cook. My dad enjoyed it, but he also worked. If I expected dinner at a reasonable hour, I figured out that I had to make it, so I set out to learn a few basics. I managed to get food on the table most of the time. At least until the night my parents arrived home to find me standing in the yard in tears and cradling my hand, which I'd managed to sear with hot grease, probably while attempting to fry chicken. That gave my mother pause. In the end, though, I kept cooking. Nothing fancy, mind you. No baking pies or cakes. No exotic, complicated dishes. Just get-it-over-with meals that were edible.

Once I was out and on my own, my repertoire expanded. I was, after all, trying to impress a date from time to time. I recall the first Thanksgiving dinner I made for friends. I had to call my dad, the grand master of the Thanksgiving meal in our household, to figure out what on earth I was supposed to do with the turkey. He also coached me through our family's traditional dressing and how to perfect our favorite sweet potatoes with marshmallows.

These days I do more writing about cooking than actual cooking, but I still like to get into the kitchen and try to impress some of my friends. It seems that a lot of them have taken cooking classes or belong to some gourmet club that hosts fancy monthly dinner parties. I'm traumatized every time I invite them to dinner, wondering how they're going to react to my dishes. My proudest moment came a few days after I'd grilled grouper and served it with a mango-papaya chutney I'd made from scratch. A friend reported having a similar dish at a fancy restaurant we all love and said, "Yours was better!" So, apparently I do have my moments of culinary triumph.

Then one day I was busy writing away—no doubt creating dishes on the page but not in the kitchen—when my publisher suggested that it might be nice to have a cookbook reflecting all the many occasions on which food plays a comforting or celebratory role for the Sweet Magnolias. While I was still trying to wrap my mind around the thought (how would I ever write a cookbook?), along came an out-of-the-blue e-mail from a reader named Teddi Wohlford.

Teddi said she loved the Sweet Magnolias books, then added that she identified particularly with Dana Sue because she, too, is a Southern chef. She was also, as it turned out, the answer to my prayers. Teddi cooks! She caters! She's published a couple of Southern cookbooks of her own! Well, you can see how this might be a match made in publishing heaven.

Since the Sweet Magnolias series began, many of you have asked about recipes for some of the dishes mentioned. Here they are, along with many, many more created by Teddi, who (like Dana Sue) has put a new spin on many traditional Southern dishes and kicked 'em up a notch. I have worked my way through these incredible recipes and developed a whole new relationship with my treadmill along the way. But trust me, it's been worth it. I hope you enjoy them as much as I do!

Sherryl Woods

Helen's Lethal Margaritas—Page 3
C'mon, Baby, Light My Fire Chicken Wings—Page 10

SWEET MAGNOLIAS MARGARITA NIGHTS

Hey, y'all. I'm Dana Sue Sullivan, one of the three original Sweet Magnolias, and I'll be your guide through these pages. I'll tell you a little about myself, a lot about Serenity, South Carolina, and a few secrets I'm probably supposed to be keeping to myself.

I'd like to believe the task was turned over to me because, as the owner of Sullivan's, I'm the best cook, but the truth is everyone else in Serenity is so darn busy. Or suddenly claims to be. You know how it goes.

Here's a little background on the Sweet Magnolias to start. Three of us—Helen Decatur-Whitney, Maddie Maddox and I—have been best friends since we met on the playground at Serenity Elementary School, which at the time was the only elementary school in town. Now there are two. That's how small Serenity is, which can be both a blessing and a curse. Neighbors around here sure do have a way of getting in your business. I think they like to look at it as part of the small-town Southern charm, though personally I'm a lot fonder of some of our other traditions.

At any rate, I won't say just how long ago it was when the three of us started calling ourselves the Sweet Magnolias, but I spotted my first gray hair the other day. That alone was almost traumatic enough to call for a margarita night.

You see, that's what margarita nights are all about: friends getting together to support one another in a crisis, no matter how large or small. Helen, Maddie and I have faced our share of crises over the years, I can tell you that. Divorces, controversy, serious problems with our kids. We sometimes joke that Helen became a lawyer just because she knew we'd all eventually land in so much hot water!

Whenever there's trouble for any one of us—or for any of the many women we've welcomed into the fold in recent years—the first thing we do is call for a margarita night. It used to be that these get-togethers were impromptu, but now that there are so many of us and our schedules are so crazy, we have to plan for them. Either way, planned or spontaneous, I'm not sure what we'd do without these occasions when we can let off steam.

It's not about Helen's Lethal Margaritas, not really. Nor is it about my Killer Guacamole, though it is to die for, if I do say so myself. It's about friends supporting friends through tough times. It's about finding laughter through the tears, about giving advice—whether it's wanted or not. We can even manage to keep our opinions to ourselves from time to time if that's requested, though I assure you, it's not our first choice.

Now that some of us are getting a little older (my daughter and her friends are now Sweet Magnolias, for goodness' sake, as is Helen's mother, Flo, much to Helen's dismay), we've added some more substantial food to these gatherings. Those C'mon, Baby, Light My Fire Chicken Wings are just one of the recent additions. You'll find more ideas here for fleshing out a menu that can even be put together at a moment's notice.

But, like I said, it's not about the drinks. Or the food. Those are incidental to the camaraderie. All it really takes to achieve the perfect margarita night is getting a group of women together to make the burden of your troubles a little lighter. No matter what you're facing, don't you find it's always a little easier when you're surrounded by friends? I sure do.

Helen's Lethal Margaritas

1 (6-ounce) can frozen limeade concentrate

¾ cup tequila

¼ cup triple sec or Grand Marnier

2 tablespoons agave nectar or honey

Okay, y'all, it doesn't get much easier than this—and sooo delish!

Fill the container of a blender with 4 cups of ice. Add all ingredients. Secure lid on blender, and blend until smooth. Pour into 4 salt-rimmed margarita glasses, or simply pass straws to your best friends and let everyone gather around.

SERVES 4

Note: Agave nectar comes from the same plant that tequila is made from. You can find it in most grocery stores today or in health food or nutrition stores. It makes a really authentic margarita!

STRAWBERRY MARGARITAS—substitute 12 ounces of frozen strawberries for 2 cups of the ice in the recipe.

MANGO MARGARITAS (Dana Sue's favorite!)—substitute 12 ounces of frozen mango chunks for 2 cups of the ice in the recipe.

Dana Sue's Killer Chunky Guacamole

3 ripe avocados

Zest and juice of 1 lime

½ cup diced ripe (firm) tomato

⅓ cup finely diced purple onion

¼ cup minced fresh cilantro

4 garlic cloves, minced

2 jalapeño peppers

Sea salt to taste

1. Using a sharp knife, cut avocados in half, lengthwise. Remove and reserve pit from each avocado. Carefully scoop out avocado from the peel, then dice into small to medium chunks.

2. Combine avocado with lime zest and juice in a medium mixing bowl. Stir gently.

3. Add tomato, onion, cilantro and garlic.

4. As far as the jalapeño goes, you decide whether you want this guacamole fiery hot, mild or somewhere in between. For the hot stuff, leave in all the seeds and ribs of the peppers. For the less brave, remove all the seeds. And for wimps, you'll want to remove all the seeds *and* the ribs of the peppers.

5. Season to taste with sea salt. Stir gently to blend, trying not to mash the avocado.

6. Place the avocado pits in the bowl with the guacamole, then cover the bowl tightly with plastic food wrap. Refrigerate up to 1 day before serving.

TO SERVE

Remove the pits. Serve with fresh, crisp tortilla chips and your favorite salsa. Of course, margaritas are a must!

MAKES 3½–4 CUPS, depending on the size of the avocados.

Magnolia Blossom Cocktail

1 jigger vanilla vodka

1 jigger half-and-half

2 tablespoons vanilla-infused simple syrup

¼ teaspoon orange flower water

4–6 ounces chilled lemon-lime soda

½ teaspoon grated lemon zest

In a tall glass filled with ice, add first 4 ingredients. Add lemon-lime soda to near top of glass. Stir gently. Add grated lemon zest on top of cocktail.

MAKES 1 COCKTAIL

Note: Make your own simple syrup for cocktails rather than purchasing it at a gourmet market. Simply combine 1 cup water and 1 cup granulated sugar in a small saucepan. Bring to a boil, stirring to dissolve the sugar. Remove from heat, and let cool to room temperature. (Stir in 1 teaspoon vanilla for a vanilla-infused simple syrup.) Store any unused simple syrup in the refrigerator for use within a week or so. You can also freeze the syrup to extend the life for up to 2 months.

Snow Cream Martinis

1½ cups vanilla vodka

½ cup white chocolate liqueur

½ cup sweetened condensed milk

3 cups chipped ice or small ice cubes

Combine all ingredients in a blender. Process until almost smooth.

SERVES 6

Note: This festive cocktail tastes like a winter wonderland!

Mint Juleps

3 loosely packed cups washed fresh mint leaves

4 cups boiling water

¾ cup sugar

2 cups Maker's Mark whiskey

GARNISH (OPTIONAL)
Mint sprigs

1. Fill a large glass bowl with mint leaves. Reserve a few for garnish.
2. Pour boiling water over the mint. Cover with plastic wrap, and let steep until mixture reaches room temperature. Strain mint liquid, and discard leaves.
3. Add sugar to mint liquid, and stir to dissolve. Add whiskey.
4. Bottle as desired, then cork or seal bottles.
5. Refrigerate up to 6 months. Serve over crushed ice with a sprig of mint for garnish.

MAKES 6 CUPS

Note from Dana Sue: I admit that I miss the (time-consuming) ceremony and cherished tradition of making individual mint juleps—crushing the mint, stirring the sugar until it dissolves, adding bourbon, then pouring over crushed ice—but I adore the ease of this recipe version! I almost always have the mixture on hand during the hot summer.

Citrus Bourbon Slushy

8 cups water, divided

1 family-size tea bag or 4 regular-size tea bags

1 packed cup light brown sugar

1 (12-ounce) can frozen orange juice concentrate, thawed

1 (12-ounce) can frozen lemonade concentrate, thawed

1 (6-ounce) can frozen limeade concentrate, thawed

2 cups bourbon

1. Bring 2 cups water to a boil. Add tea bag(s). Let steep 5 minutes only. Lift tea bag(s) from water after steeping, then discard.

2. Add brown sugar. Stir to dissolve.

3. Add remaining ingredients, and stir to blend.

4. Cover, and freeze 2–4 hours until slushy, stirring several times with a fork while freezing.

MAKES ALMOST 1 GALLON

Note: This drink is almost as refreshing served over crushed ice instead of freezing. Dilute with lemon-lime or club soda if you prefer a less potent cocktail.

Fire & Ice Pickles

2 (32-ounce) jars
nonrefrigerated pickle slices

4 cups granulated sugar

2 tablespoons Tabasco sauce

1 teaspoon crushed red
pepper flakes

4 minced garlic cloves

① Combine all ingredients, and mix well.

② Cover, and let stand at room temperature 3–4 hours, stirring
occasionally.

③ Divide into 4 (1-pint) canning jars. Seal tightly.

④ Refrigerate up to 1 month.

MAKES 4 PINTS

*Note: Best if made at least 1 week before eating to allow
flavors to develop.*

C'mon, Baby, Light My Fire Chicken Wings

WINGS

30 chicken wings

1 envelope dry ranch dressing mix

1 cup flour

1 quart canola or vegetable oil

SAUCE

½ cup butter

3 packed tablespoons light brown sugar

½ cup mild hot sauce, such as Texas Pete Hot Sauce or Frank's RedHot Sauce

2 tablespoons apple cider vinegar

½ teaspoon garlic powder

½ teaspoon crushed red pepper flakes

WINGS

1. Snip off wing tips from chicken wings, then cut wings into two sections (at the joint). Blot chicken wings dry using paper towels.

2. Place ranch dressing mix and flour in a zip-top gallon-size bag. Shake to blend.

3. Add wings (10 at a time) to bag. Seal shut, shake to coat lightly. Place coated wings on a plastic-lined baking sheet.

4. Repeat with remaining wings.

5. Refrigerate at least 30 minutes, or up to 1 day before frying.

6. When ready to fry, heat oil in deep fryer or Dutch oven until temperature reaches 375°F.

7. Fry wings in batches, cooking each batch 8–10 minutes.

8. Transfer wings from fryer to a plate lined with paper towels.

9. Repeat with remaining wings.

10. Place cooked wings in large bowl or pan, covering loosely with foil while preparing more. Make the sauce while the wings are cooking.

SAUCE

In a small saucepan, melt the butter and brown sugar. When brown sugar has dissolved, whisk in the hot sauce and vinegar. Add remaining ingredients, and whisk until well blended.

TO SERVE

When all wings are fried, drizzle with sauce. Stir to coat well. The longer the wings sit in the sauce, the hotter they get. (For milder wings, remove from sauce after 15 minutes.)

SERVES 4–12 (you know what I mean!)

Note: This Sweet Magnolia recipe will remind you of buffalo wings, but down South, we gotta make it just a little something special. Gild the magnolia by serving with our blue cheese dressing (see page 13) and some celery sticks —to help cut the heat!

Cheddar Blossoms

2 cups (8 ounces) grated sharp cheddar cheese, room temperature

½ cup butter, room temperature

1¼ cups all-purpose flour

½ teaspoon sea salt

¼–½ teaspoon ground cayenne pepper (you decide!)

Poppy seeds

1. Preheat oven to 350°F.
2. Combine cheddar and butter in a medium mixing bowl. Blend well.
3. Whisk together flour, salt and cayenne pepper. Add to cheese and butter mixture. Blend well.
4. Fill the barrel of a cookie press with dough. Choose the five-petal flower disc, and secure onto the end of the cookie press.
5. Press cheddar blossoms onto ungreased cookie sheets, spacing 1" apart. (If dough is too firm, it will not press out easily. Microwave the dough briefly to soften, if necessary.)
6. Sprinkle some poppy seeds in the center of each blossom.
7. Bake 1 pan at a time in center of oven 20–25 minutes, until golden brown.
8. Immediately remove cheddar blossoms from cookie sheet, and transfer to cooling rack to cool completely.
9. Store in an airtight container at room temperature up to 2 weeks. Alternately, cover tightly, and freeze up to 4 months.

MAKES ABOUT 80

Note: No Southern affair (whether plain or fancy) would be complete without cheese straws. This is the Sweet Magnolia version of cheese straws—making them just a bit more special with the addition of poppy seeds in the center of each darling little blossom. These are a yummy treat and greatly enjoyed at any cocktail buffet, wedding reception or simply with a glass of red wine.

Blue Cheese Dressing
(with cognac)

1½ cups mayonnaise

1 cup heavy whipping cream

½ cup white wine vinegar

2 tablespoons cognac

4 ounces blue cheese crumbles, divided

Sea salt and freshly ground black pepper to taste

In a blender or food processor, combine first four ingredients with half of the blue cheese crumbles. Blend until smooth. Stir in remaining blue cheese, and season with salt and pepper. Cover, and refrigerate up to 1 month.

MAKES 3 CUPS

Note: This drop-dead fabulous blue cheese dressing is a favorite of Sullivan's Restaurant patrons. On Margarita Nights, you can find the Sweet Magnolias feasting on chicken wings and celery sticks—being dunked first in this dressing.

Cheddar Corn Muffins—Page 22
Lowcountry She-Crab Soup—Page 25

SULLIVAN'S RESTAURANT SPECIALTIES OF THE HOUSE

I'd like to say that Sullivan's was always my dream, but the truth is until my husband, Ronnie, and I split up, I hadn't put much thought into opening up my own restaurant. I was content to cook for anyone who'd hire me, though I have to say that most of the menu offerings at Serenity's mom-and-pop places didn't present much of a challenge. This has always been a fried chicken, potato salad and greens kind of town.

Now, as a born and bred South Carolinian, I like Southern cooking as much as anyone, but I just can't seem to keep myself from putting a little spin on the traditional dishes from time to time. I'd accumulated an entire file box of recipes over time, trying them out on Ronnie and my daughter, Annie, and the Sweet Magnolias every chance I got.

When I found out Ronnie had cheated on me—and about two seconds after I'd chased him off with a cast-iron skillet—I decided the time had come to do something exciting and challenging just for me. With encouragement from my best pals, Maddie and Helen, I put together the business plan for Sullivan's, a restaurant dedicated to putting some zip into regional specialties. Though I'm real proud of our fancy decor, the perfectly pressed linen tablecloths and napkins I insisted on and the painting by our world-renowned local botanical artist Paula Vreeland (Maddie's mom) in our foyer, it's the food that brings customers from all over the state.

Yes, that's right. They come from all over. Oh, I had plenty of doubters, folks around here who said I'd never make a success of an upscale restaurant without being in Charleston or Columbia. But guess what? I proved them wrong. The glowing reviews started coming in from the big newspapers and regional magazines—and so did the customers.

By the time Ronnie and I reconciled, I was a whole lot stronger than I'd been when we first fell in love way back in high school—and a successful restaurant owner to boot! By then I didn't need a man in my life, but the pitiful truth is I sure did want this particular man. You know how that goes. Some things just never change. When the right man comes along, it's hard to get him out of your system, even after he's made a mistake the size of Ronnie's. Sometimes you just have to take a leap of faith that the apologies and the commitment are sincere.

Now I wouldn't share my trade secrets with just anyone, but folks keep asking about certain dishes, like my catfish with its spicy cornmeal coating or the peachy grilled chicken in a spicy peanut sauce. See what I mean? These are not the same old same old.

There are a lot more recipes here, straight off the Sullivan's menu. Pretty soon you'll be just like me, taking something ordinary, adding a dash of this and a teaspoonful of that and kicking all your cooking up a notch. But if you get any ideas about opening your own restaurant, promise you'll steer clear of Serenity. There's only room for one gourmet restaurant in this town, and Sullivan's has filled that niche. At least I like to think it has.

Toasted Pecan & Red Pepper Jam

8 (½-pint) canning jars, lids and screw-on bands

2 cups (about 8 ounces) pecan halves

1 green bell pepper, seeded, finely chopped

1 red bell pepper, seeded, finely chopped

6–8 jalapeño peppers, seeded (if desired), finely chopped

1½ cups apple cider vinegar

1 tablespoon butter

6½ cups sugar

1 (3-ounce) pouch liquid fruit pectin

1. Place jars, lids and bands in a large pot. Fill with hot water. Bring to a boil over high heat, and boil at least 5 minutes.

2. Scatter pecan halves on a rimmed baking sheet. Bake at 350°F about 10 minutes, just until nuts begin to smell toasted. Remove from oven, and let cool. Using a serrated knife, coarsely chop pecans.

3. Place peppers in a 1½–2 gallon saucepan or Dutch oven. Add vinegar and butter. Stir in sugar and pecans. Cook mixture over high heat, stirring often. Bring mixture to a full rolling boil that cannot be stirred down.

4. Stir in pectin. Return to a boil, and boil exactly 1 minute, stirring constantly. Remove from heat. Skim off any foam with a metal spoon.

5. Ladle immediately into prepared jars, filling to within ¼" of tops. Wipe jar rims clean. Cover with two-piece lids. Screw bands securely.

6. Place jars on elevated rack in canner. Lower rack into canner. Water must cover jars by 1–2". Add boiling water, if necessary.

7. Cover, and bring water to a gentle boil. Process 10 minutes in boiling water bath.

8. Remove jars, place upright on towel to cool 30 minutes, then turn jars upside down.

9. Alternate jars upright, then upside down for the first 2 hours of cooling to help suspend pecans and peppers in jam. Cool completely.

10. After jars cool, check seals by pressing middle of lids with finger. If lid springs back, lid is not sealed, and refrigeration is necessary. Properly sealed jars can be stored at room temperature up to 2 years.

Note: Enjoy with grilled poultry, pork or most seafood. Super yummy served with cream cheese and crackers for a speedy appetizer. Also makes a great bread-and-butter gift.

Garlic Toast Rounds

1 French baguette, cut into ¼" slices Garlic & herb seasoning

½ cup extra virgin olive oil

1. Preheat oven to 300°F.

2. Brush one side of each piece of bread with olive oil. Lightly sprinkle with garlic & herb seasoning.

3. Bake 30–40 minutes, until rounds are golden and completely dried out.

4. Remove from oven, and transfer to cooling rack. Allow to cool thoroughly before storing airtight up to 2 weeks.

MAKES ABOUT 60 PIECES

Note: Serve these delicious petite toasts with appetizers of almost any variety. These are great with savory dips and fondues as well as alongside salads and soups.

Bacon & Swiss Appetizer Cheesecake

CRUST
1½ cups finely crushed
Ritz crackers

¼ cup melted butter

FILLING
2 (8-ounce) packages
cream cheese, softened

2 eggs

2 cups grated Swiss cheese

10 slices bacon,
cooked, crumbled

½ teaspoon dried basil

¼ teaspoon dried
marjoram

¼ teaspoon dried thyme

⅛ teaspoon freshly
grated nutmeg

Salt and pepper to taste

TOPPING
1 cup sour cream

3 slices bacon, cooked, crumbled

¼ cup chopped green onions

SERVE WITH:
Crackers

Toast rounds or points

CRUST
① Preheat oven to 325°F.
② Stir together cracker crumbs and butter.
③ Press into the bottom of a 9" springform pan.
④ Bake 15 minutes. While crust is baking, prepare filling.

FILLING
① Combine all ingredients, and beat well with an electric mixer.
② Spread filling over baked crust.
③ Bake 30 minutes.
④ Remove from oven, and place on cooling rack.

TOPPING
While the cheesecake is still warm, top with sour cream, and spread evenly over entire surface. Allow it to come to room temperature. Top with crumbled bacon and green onions. Cover, and refrigerate until ready to serve (within 3 days).

TO SERVE
Loosen cheesecake from pan by running a knife around the edge, then release spring, and remove cheesecake along with the bottom of the pan from the walls. Serve in small wedges with an assortment of crackers or homemade toast rounds or points.

SERVES 16–20

Shrimp, Crab & Swiss Appetizer Cheesecake

1½ cups finely crushed Ritz crackers

2 cups (8 ounces) grated Swiss cheese, divided

¼ cup butter, melted

3 (8-ounce) packages cream cheese, softened

3 large eggs

1 tablespoon OLD BAY Seasoning

½ teaspoon cayenne pepper

8 ounces fresh lump crabmeat, picked through

8 ounces cooked, squeezed dry salad-size shrimp

8 ounces sour cream, room temperature

1 chopped bunch green onions

CRUST

1. Preheat oven to 350°F.
2. Spray the inside of a 9" springform pan completely with cooking spray.
3. Combine cracker crumbs, 2 ounces (½ cup) of the grated Swiss and melted butter. Press firmly in bottom of prepared pan.
4. Bake 15 minutes. While crust is baking, prepare filling.

FILLING

1. Combine cream cheese, eggs, OLD BAY Seasoning and cayenne. Beat until smooth.
2. Stir in crabmeat, shrimp and remaining 6 ounces of grated Swiss cheese.
3. Pour onto baked crust. Using a spatula, level filling.
4. Bake 45 minutes.
5. Let cool in pan on cooling rack 10 minutes. (You may need to run a thin knife around inside of pan if filling has stuck to pan.)
6. Release spring, and carefully remove springform wall from cheesecake.
7. Evenly spread sour cream over top of cheesecake. Cool to room temperature.
8. Sprinkle top with green onions. Cover, and refrigerate up to 2 days before serving.

SERVES 16

Cheddar Corn Muffins

2⅔ cups corn muffin mix
(see next recipe)*

1 (14½-ounce) can whole-kernel corn,
drained

6 ounces grated cheddar cheese

1 cup sour cream

2 eggs, beaten

1. Preheat oven to 400°F.

2. Grease a standard-size 12-cup muffin tin.

3. In a large mixing bowl, combine first 3 ingredients.

4. In a separate small bowl, blend together sour cream and eggs. Stir into dry mixture.

5. Divide batter among muffin cups. Let rest at room temperature 5–10 minutes.

6. Bake 18–20 minutes, until tester inserted in center comes out clean, and center of muffin springs back when touched.

7. Let muffins cool in pan 2–3 minutes. Remove from pan, and transfer to cooling rack. Serve warm.

MAKES 12

Note: These muffins are such a breeze to make and absolutely delicious served with almost any soup, stew or chili.

*If you choose not to make your own corn muffin mix, you can use 2 (8½-ounce) packages of store-bought corn muffin mix.

Corn Muffin Mix

4¾ cups all-purpose flour

4 cups yellow cornmeal

1 cup sugar

4 tablespoons baking powder

2 tablespoons salt

1 cup all-vegetable shortening

Combine all ingredients, and blend well using either a food processor or handheld pastry blender. Freeze in an airtight freezer bag for use within 6 months.

MAKES ABOUT 10 CUPS

Navy Bean Soup

1 pound dried navy beans

8 cups chicken broth or stock

1 (28-ounce) can diced tomatoes

2 cups medium-diced yellow onions

8 ounces deli ham, cubed small

1 cup thinly sliced celery

2 bay leaves

2 tablespoons Worcestershire sauce

1 tablespoon soy sauce

1 tablespoon minced garlic

¼ teaspoon freshly grated nutmeg

Salt and freshly ground black pepper to taste

GARNISH (OPTIONAL)
½ cup minced fresh parsley

1. Place dried beans in a colander, and flush with running water. Sort through beans, and remove any bits of debris.
2. Place rinsed beans in a Dutch oven. Fill pot with water, covering beans by several inches. Soak at least 8 hours.
3. Drain beans, and return to the pot. Add chicken broth and all remaining ingredients except for salt, pepper and parsley.
4. Bring soup to a boil, and boil gently 1 hour.
5. Reduce heat to simmer. Cover pot with lid, and simmer 3 hours, until beans are tender.
6. Season with salt and pepper. Garnish with parsley just before serving.

SERVES 6–8

Note: Pair this hearty and healthy soup with a piece of cornbread or a warm yeast roll and butter. A crisp garden salad is the ideal accompaniment.

Lowcountry She-Crab Soup

1 cup finely diced Vidalia onion (or other sweet yellow onion)

1 cup finely diced celery

¾ cup (1½ sticks) butter

¾ cup all-purpose flour

6 cups chicken stock

2 (10-ounce) bottles clam juice

½ teaspoon ground mace

1 tablespoon OLD BAY Seasoning

1 teaspoon white pepper

2 cups heavy whipping cream

2 tablespoons dry sherry

2 tablespoons cognac (or brandy)

1 pound fresh lump crabmeat, picked through

1 tablespoon crab roe (optional)*

1. In a large saucepan or small Dutch oven, sauté onion and celery in butter over medium-high heat, cooking until vegetables are tender.

2. Add flour, and cook 2–3 minutes, stirring constantly.

3. While whisking, pour in chicken stock and clam juice. Season soup with mace, OLD BAY Seasoning and white pepper.

4. Lower heat to simmer, and cook at least 15 minutes.

5. Stir in cream, sherry and cognac. Heat through for about 5 minutes.

6. Add crabmeat and roe. Stir gently but thoroughly to blend—you don't want to break up that beautiful crabmeat.

SERVES 6–8

*I get my crab roe from my trusted seafood purveyor because it's a hard-to-come-by item. You can make the soup without the crab roe (and it still tastes fabulous without it), but it wouldn't be she-crab soup. I've heard that if you're unable to find crab roe, you can substitute a finely chopped, hard-cooked egg.

Gullah Peanut & Sweet Potato Soup

¼ cup butter

½ cup chopped onion

½ cup chopped celery

6 cups peeled, coarsely grated sweet potato (about 2 pounds)

8 cups chicken stock or broth

1 cup smooth peanut butter

Salt and freshly ground black pepper to taste

GARNISH (OPTIONAL)
Chopped roasted, salted peanuts

1. In a large soup pot, melt butter over medium heat. Add onion, celery and sweet potatoes. Sauté until onion and celery are soft but not browned, about 5 minutes.

2. Add stock or broth, and bring to a boil.

3. Reduce heat to low. Cover, and simmer until sweet potatoes are very tender, about 30 minutes.

4. Remove from heat, and let cool slightly.

5. Working in batches, puree in a blender or food processor.

6. Return to saucepan, and whisk in peanut butter until mixture is smooth and heated through; do not boil.

7. Season to taste with salt and pepper. Ladle into soup bowls, and garnish with chopped peanuts.

SERVES 6–8

Sherried Mushroom Soup

2 tablespoons butter

1 medium onion

1 pound cleaned, sliced mushrooms

¼ cup minced fresh parsley

1 garlic clove, minced

1 tablespoon minced fresh thyme
or 1 teaspoon dried

3 cups chicken broth or stock

4 cups half-and-half

2 cups heavy whipping cream

1 tablespoon sugar

1 teaspoon salt

¼ teaspoon freshly ground black pepper

3 tablespoons cornstarch

½ cup golden sherry

1. In a Dutch oven over medium-high heat, sauté first 6 ingredients until softened.

2. Add chicken stock, half-and-half and whipping cream. Bring to a boil over medium heat.

3. Reduce heat, and season with sugar, salt and pepper.

4. Dissolve cornstarch in sherry. Add to soup, stirring constantly until thickened.

SERVES 6

Note: Creamy, rich and delicious, this is an elegant soup. Drastically lower the fat and calories by using fat-free half-and-half or milk.

Baby Greens with Pears, Blue Cheese & Toasted Walnut Vinaigrette

1½ cups walnut halves

VINAIGRETTE

½ cup sherry vinegar or white wine vinegar

2 tablespoons orange marmalade

1 tablespoon Dijon mustard

1 tablespoon fresh thyme leaves
or 1 teaspoon dried

1 cup canola or vegetable oil

½ cup walnut oil

Salt and freshly ground black pepper to taste

SALAD

12 cups mixed baby greens

½ red onion, sliced paper-thin

3 medium pears, quartered, cored,
thinly sliced

4 ounces blue cheese crumbles

⅔ cup sweetened, dried cranberries
(such as Craisins)

8 thin, crispy gingersnap cookies,
broken into pieces

Preheat oven to 350°F. Place walnut halves on a baking sheet, and bake 10–12 minutes, just until nuts begin to smell toasty. Remove from oven, and let cool to room temperature. Using a serrated knife, coarsely chop walnuts.

VINAIGRETTE

1. In a blender or food processor, combine vinegar, marmalade, mustard and thyme.
2. With machine running, add oils through the top of the machine in a thin, steady stream.
3. Season to taste with salt and pepper.
4. Add ½ cup toasted walnut pieces. Process briefly.

SALAD

On each of 6 salad plates (or 1 large salad platter), arrange the baby greens. Top the salad greens with the remaining 1 cup walnut halves, onion, pears, blue cheese, cranberries and gingersnaps. Drizzle with the vinaigrette.

SERVES 6

Note: This is one our favorite recipes for a tasty and elegant composed salad. All the flavors work so well together, and it's so pretty to serve!

Citrus Salmon with Crunchy Crumb Topping

6 boneless, skinless salmon fillets, about 6 ounces each

Salt and freshly ground black pepper to taste

MARINADE
¾ cup orange marmalade

¾ cup Worcestershire sauce for chicken

½ cup orange juice

Grated zest and juice of 1 lemon

Grated zest and juice of 1 lime

2 tablespoons coarse-grain Dijon mustard

2 tablespoons dried, minced onion

1 teaspoon ground ginger

CRUMB TOPPING
½ cup coarsely crushed gingersnap cookies

½ cup coarsely crushed croutons

MARINADE
1. Combine all marinade ingredients in blender or food processor. Blend until almost smooth.
2. Arrange salmon in a single layer in a gallon-size zip-top plastic bag.
3. Pour ⅔ of the marinade over salmon. (The remaining marinade will be used as a finishing sauce.)
4. Refrigerate 8–24 hours, turning bag over several times.

SALMON
1. Remove salmon from marinade, and pat dry.
2. Sprinkle with salt and freshly ground black pepper.
3. Cook according to your preference, whether broiling, pan-searing in a skillet or grilling over hot coals.
4. Serve cooked salmon with remaining marinade drizzled over top.

CRUMB TOPPING
Mix ingredients together. Sprinkle salmon liberally with crumb topping just before serving.

SERVES 6

Sea Bass with Vegetables & Herbs en Papillote

6 pieces (16" × 12") baking parchment

6 (8-ounce) pieces boned, skinned sea bass

Sea salt

Freshly ground black pepper

⅓ cup finely minced fresh tarragon or 2 tablespoons dried

2 medium yellow crookneck squash, very thinly sliced

2 medium zucchini squash, very thinly sliced

3 peeled medium carrots, cut into match sticks

3 peeled shallots, sliced paper-thin

1 pound asparagus (tough ends trimmed, discarded; spears cut in half)

4 ounces melted black truffle butter or ½ cup black truffle oil

SIDE (OPTIONAL)
Basmati or Carolina Gold Rice*

1. Preheat oven to 425°F.

2. Place a piece of sea bass in the center of each piece of baking parchment. Sprinkle each with sea salt, pepper and tarragon.

3. Divide all vegetables equally in layers on top of the fish. Sprinkle again with sea salt and pepper.

4. Drizzle the melted truffle butter (or oil) over the vegetables.

5. Assemble the parchment packets: Gather the two long sides of parchment to the center. Make a ½" fold, and roll down 2 or 3 times, creasing each fold to make a tight seal. Fold both sides of each end toward a center point, creasing to seal. Fold each end snugly under the packet.

6. Place 3 packets on each of 2 rimmed, foil-lined baking sheets. Bake 20 minutes.

7. Remove from oven, and let stand 5 minutes before transferring packets to individual serving plates.

8. Serve hot, letting each diner open own packet. Serve alongside hot, steamed basmati or Carolina Gold Rice to catch all those fabulous juices.

SERVES 6

CONTINUES →

Note: En papillote always refers to food prepared in packets. Baking parchment paper is traditional to the French method of preparation, although some people prefer to use aluminum foil. Each diner gets his or her own little package to be opened at the table just before dining. Who doesn't like having their own little present to open?!

*Carolina Gold Rice, a long grain rice, is an heirloom grain—a trendy ingredient first grown in the Lowcountry regions of South Carolina and Georgia in the late 1600s. Although it is a bit pricey, it is sought out by serious foodies for its delicious taste and enticing aroma. The gold in the name refers not to the color but to the economic stronghold that this lucrative staple maintained. It is available in grocery stores and gourmet kitchen shops in the Lowcountry of South Carolina and online at www.ansonmills.com.

Herb Cheese Spread

2 (8-ounce) packages cream cheese, softened

1 cup butter, softened

2 garlic cloves, minced

1 teaspoon salt

½ teaspoon dried oregano

½ teaspoon dried basil

½ teaspoon dried dill weed

½ teaspoon dried lemon & pepper seasoning

½ teaspoon freshly ground black pepper

¼ teaspoon dried marjoram

¼ teaspoon dried thyme

1 tablespoon honey

In a medium mixing bowl, combine cream cheese and butter. Beat until light and fluffy. Add remaining ingredients, and blend well. Cover, and refrigerate up to 1 week, or freeze up to 2 months.

MAKES ABOUT 4 CUPS

Note: This creamy, dreamy appetizer spread is terrific! I just keep finding ways to use it. It's delicious spread on crackers and savory breads. It's also a perfect partner for hot pasta, a steamy baked potato or steamed vegetables. At Sullivan's Restaurant, we serve it with our bread baskets.

Bourbon & Brown Sugar Grilled Salmon with Tropical Fruit Salsa

4 (6-ounce) boned, skinned salmon fillets

MARINADE
¼ packed cup brown sugar

¼ cup soy sauce

¼ cup bourbon

Juice and zest of 1 orange

2 teaspoons minced fresh gingerroot

2 teaspoons minced fresh garlic

¼ teaspoon freshly ground black pepper

SALSA
1½ cups small-diced fresh golden (extra sweet) pineapple

1 peeled, small-diced kiwi

½ peeled, small-diced fresh mango

½ cup chopped green onions

1 fresh jalapeño pepper (seeds and ribs removed if milder heat is preferred)

¼ cup seasoned rice vinegar

1 tablespoon sugar

Salt and freshly ground black pepper to taste

GARNISH (OPTIONAL)
Chopped fresh cilantro

MARINADE
Place salmon in a single layer in a glass container of suitable size or in a large zip-top food storage bag. Combine all marinade ingredients, and stir to dissolve sugar. Pour marinade over salmon fillets; cover, and refrigerate 1–8 hours, turning salmon several times. Prepare salsa while salmon is marinating.

SALSA
Combine all salsa ingredients, and toss gently but thoroughly. Cover, and leave at room temperature 1–8 hours before serving with the grilled salmon.

SALMON
1. After marinating, discard marinade, and pat salmon dry between paper towels.
2. Heat grill until very hot. Coat food rack with a nonstick grilling spray.
3. Place salmon fillets on food rack. Cook several minutes until cooked almost halfway through.
4. Carefully turn salmon over, and continue to cook just until desired degree of doneness. (Please, do not overcook!)
5. Transfer salmon to a serving platter, and serve topped with the room-temperature tropical fruit salsa. Garnish with cilantro.

SERVES 4

Sweet & Tangy
Tomato-Basil Vinaigrette

½ cup canned, crushed tomatoes

½ cup balsamic vinegar

¼ cup minced fresh basil leaves

½ cup freshly grated Parmesan cheese

2 tablespoons sugar

1 teaspoon salt

1 teaspoon freshly ground black pepper

1 cup extra-virgin olive oil

In a blender or food processor, blend together all ingredients except the olive oil. With the machine running, add the oil in a thin, steady stream.

MAKES ABOUT 2½ CUPS

Note: This recipe is best if made several hours or up to 3 days before serving. Serve over fresh salad greens or as a pasta salad dressing.

Shrimp Scampi Linguine

1 cup freshly grated Parmesan cheese

1 pound linguine

SHRIMP

1 tablespoon cornstarch

¼ cup golden sherry

2 pounds large, raw, peeled, deveined shrimp

SAUCE

1 cup (2 sticks) butter

2 tablespoons Dijon mustard

1 teaspoon freshly grated lemon zest

1 tablespoon freshly squeezed lemon juice

¼ cup minced shallots

2 tablespoons minced fresh garlic

½ teaspoon crushed red pepper flakes

¼ cup minced fresh parsley

SHRIMP

Preheat oven to 450°F. Place cornstarch in a medium mixing bowl. Whisk in sherry to dissolve cornstarch. Add shrimp, and stir to coat in cornstarch mixture. Let stand while preparing the sauce.

SAUCE

1. In a small saucepan over medium-high heat, combine the first 7 ingredients. Stirring constantly, cook until butter melts and sauce develops. Remove from heat.
2. Stir in parsley. Arrange shrimp in a 13" × 9" × 2" baking pan or suitable casserole dish.
3. Pour sauce evenly over shrimp. Bake 10 minutes.
4. Remove from oven, and sprinkle with Parmesan cheese. Return to the oven for another 5 minutes.
5. Serve shrimp and sauce hot over freshly cooked linguine.

SERVES 6

Panfried Catfish with Spicy Cornmeal Coating

1 cup vegetable or canola oil

CATFISH SOAK
2 cups buttermilk

½ teaspoon ground cayenne pepper

4 catfish fillets (6 ounces each)

CORNMEAL COATING
1 cup all-purpose flour

½ cup cornmeal

1 tablespoon Cajun and Creole seasoning

1 tablespoon garlic salt

1 tablespoon freshly grated lemon zest

½–1 teaspoon ground cayenne pepper
(you decide!)

WET MIXTURE
3 eggs, beaten

3 tablespoons freshly squeezed
lemon juice

CATFISH SOAK

In a medium mixing bowl, whisk together the buttermilk and cayenne pepper. Add catfish fillets, making sure each comes into contact with the soaking liquid. Refrigerate 4–12 hours. Remove catfish from soaking liquid, and pat dry between paper towels. Discard the soaking liquid.

CONTINUES →

CORNMEAL COATING

Combine all ingredients in a gallon-size zip-top food storage bag. Secure shut, and shake to blend. Set aside.

WET MIXTURE

In a shallow dish, whisk together the eggs and lemon juice.

BREADING PROCEDURE

Once you have dried off the catfish fillets after their buttermilk soak, you can proceed. The proper breading technique (for all frying) is a dry-wet-dry method. Dredge the catfish fillets, one at a time, into the spicy cornmeal coating, then the egg mixture, then back to the spicy cornmeal coating (dry, wet, dry).

FRYING

1. Heat oil in a large skillet over medium-high heat to 370°F. (Check the temperature with a thermometer if you have one.) You will know when the oil is hot enough to fry if you drop a tiny bit of breading into the hot oil and it sizzles furiously. The oil should be hot but not smoking.

2. Carefully lower the catfish into the skillet, frying two fillets at a time. The thickness of the fillets determines the cooking time. Total frying time is approximately 7–8 minutes, turning once halfway through frying.

3. Remove from skillet, and let drain on wadded paper towels.

4. Repeat with remaining fillets.

SERVES 4

Note: Catfish can be quite strong tasting. The buttermilk soak helps lessen that strong (sometimes offensive) flavor. This buttermilk soak also works nicely with wild game and fowl. It also helps tenderize the meat some.

Pan-Seared Trout
with Browned Butter & Lemon Sauce

SAUCE

½ cup butter

1 lemon

1 teaspoon coarsely ground black pepper

TROUT

4 boneless rainbow trout fillets
(5–6 ounces each)

Salt and freshly ground black pepper

4 sprigs fresh rosemary

1 lemon, very thinly sliced

SAUCE

1. Place butter in a small saucepan. Bring to a boil over medium heat. Continue to boil, stirring often, until nutty smelling and amber colored. Remove from heat.

2. Using a vegetable peeler, remove the lemon zest (colored part of the peel). Add lemon zest to the browned butter.

3. Juice the lemon, removing the seeds. Add lemon juice and pepper to the browned butter sauce. Cover sauce to keep warm while you prepare the fish.

4. Just before serving, remove the lemon zest, and discard.

TROUT

1. Rinse trout fillets, and pat dry between paper towels, skin-side up. Season fish with salt and freshly ground black pepper.

2. Place a sprig of rosemary on each fillet. Place 2 slices of lemon on top of each rosemary sprig.

3. Heat a large skillet over medium-high heat. Spray pan lightly with nonstick cooking spray. Place 2 pieces of trout on skillet, flesh side up. Cook 3 minutes.

4. Carefully turn over with the lemon slices coming in direct contact with the skillet. Cook 2 minutes more.

5. Transfer to serving plates or platter, covering loosely with foil to keep warm while you prepare the other two trout fillets. Drizzle each serving with browned butter & lemon sauce.

SERVES 4

Peachy Grilled Chicken with Spicy Peanut Sauce

CHICKEN

24 chicken tenders

1 (8-ounce) bottle teriyaki marinade

4 large, peeled fresh peaches, each cut into 12 wedges

24 bamboo skewers, soaked in water several hours

SAUCE

1½ cups hot water

½ cup crunchy peanut butter

1 teaspoon minced garlic

1 teaspoon ground ginger

Tabasco sauce to taste

Salt to taste

CHICKEN

1. Place chicken tenders in a zip-top bag. Add teriyaki marinade, and marinate according to package directions.

2. Remove tenders from marinade, and discard marinade. Pat chicken dry, using paper towels.

3. Secure one end of chicken tender onto pointed end of skewer. Add peach slice to the skewer, then bring the chicken tender around and over the peach slice, securing chicken again on the skewer. Slide another peach slice onto the skewer and wrap peach slice with the remainder of the chicken tender, securing end of chicken on skewer in "S" fashion.

4. Repeat process with remaining peaches and chicken. Prepare sauce before grilling chicken.

5. Heat grill.

SAUCE

In a small saucepan, combine ingredients. Cook over medium heat, whisking constantly until thoroughly heated and thickened. Do not allow to boil. Keep warm while grilling chicken.

GRILLING

Grill chicken over hot coals several minutes, turning once, until the chicken is no longer transparent. Serve hot or warm with peanut sauce.

SERVES 12 as an appetizer or 6 as a main course.

Honey Grilled Pork Tenderloin with Peach Salsa

SALSA

3 cups peeled, chopped peaches

¼ cup minced fresh parsley

2 jalapeño peppers, seeded, finely chopped

2 tablespoons fresh lime juice

1 tablespoon sugar

1 tablespoon seasoned rice vinegar

1 teaspoon salt

PORK

2 pork tenderloins (1¼ pounds each)

⅓ cup soy sauce

½ teaspoon ground ginger

5 fresh garlic cloves, minced

2 tablespoons brown sugar

¼ cup honey

1 tablespoon dark sesame oil

3 tablespoons vegetable oil

SALSA

Combine all ingredients, stirring well. Cover, and refrigerate several hours or overnight. Bring to room temperature prior to serving over grilled pork tenderloin.

PORK

1. Butterfly tenderloins by making a lengthwise cut in each, cutting to within ¼" of other side. Place in a large zip-top bag.

2. Combine soy sauce, ginger and garlic in a small bowl. Pour over tenderloins. Seal bag, and refrigerate at least 3 hours (or overnight), turning occasionally.

3. Remove tenderloins, and discard marinade.

4. Combine brown sugar, honey and oils in a small saucepan. Cook over low heat, stirring constantly until the sugar dissolves. Set aside.

5. Heat grill; coals should be moderately hot. If using a gas grill, heat to medium.

6. Place tenderloins on a greased rack, and brush with the honey mixture. Grill 20 minutes, turning once and basting frequently, until meat thermometer inserted into the thickest portion registers 145–160°F. Slice, and serve immediately.

SERVES 6

Roasted Spring Lamb with Herbs & Madeira Sauce

1 boneless leg of lamb

BREAD CRUMB–HERB–NUT MIXTURE
4½ cups fresh bread crumbs, divided

3 tablespoons minced fresh parsley
or 1 tablespoon dried

3 tablespoons minced fresh chives
or 1 tablespoon dried

1 tablespoon minced fresh thyme
or 1 teaspoon dried

1 tablespoon minced fresh rosemary
or 1 teaspoon dried

1 tablespoon minced fresh garlic

1 tablespoon salt

1 teaspoon freshly ground black pepper

½ cup coarsely chopped pistachio nuts

SAUCE
2 tablespoons butter

2 tablespoons flour

1 tablespoon tomato paste

1½ cups lamb or chicken stock

3 tablespoons Madeira

Salt and pepper to taste

LAMB
Preheat oven to 450°F. Cover roasting pan with foil. Split leg of lamb, and lay out flat to butterfly the lamb leg.

BREAD CRUMB–HERB–NUT MIXTURE
1. Combine all ingredients, and blend well. Reserve 1½ cups for coating.
2. Distribute remaining mixture evenly over butterflied lamb.
3. Roll, and secure by tying with kitchen twine at 2" intervals.
4. Coat exterior surface of lamb with remaining mixture.

CONTINUES →

ROASTING

1. Place lamb on a rack in an open roasting pan. Roast in center of oven 30 minutes. Prepare Madeira sauce while roasting.

2. Reduce heat to 350°F. Roast 20 minutes per pound for medium doneness, until internal temperature registers 140°F on a meat thermometer. If you prefer your lamb more or less rare, adjust cooking times accordingly.

3. Remove lamb from oven, and let stand at room temperature 10 minutes.

4. Remove twine, and slice. Serve with sauce.

SAUCE

In a medium saucepan, cook butter and flour together over medium heat until lightly browned. Whisk in tomato paste, stock and Madeira. Reduce heat to low, and simmer, stirring occasionally until sauce has thickened and reduced slightly. Season with salt and pepper.

SERVES 8–10

"Oven-Fried" Chicken Tenders

CHICKEN
2 pounds chicken tenders

¾ cup mayonnaise

CRACKER COATING
1½ cups finely crushed
Ritz crackers

1 teaspoon garlic powder

1 teaspoon freshly ground
black pepper

1 teaspoon paprika

CHICKEN

Preheat oven to 375°F. Line a jelly-roll pan or rimmed baking sheet with nonstick aluminum foil. Combine the chicken tenders with the mayonnaise. Stir to coat each piece.

CRACKER COATING

Combine all ingredients in a gallon-size zip-top bag. Seal shut, and shake to blend together. Coat chicken tenders with crumb coating, working with 3 or 4 pieces at a time. Place on foil-lined baking pan, allowing a bit of space between each piece. Place in center of oven, and bake 25 minutes.

SERVES 6

Garlic & Rosemary Roasted Pork Loin with Sour Cream & Mushroom Sauce

1 boneless pork loin

RUB

1 tablespoon vegetable oil

1 teaspoon minced garlic

½ teaspoon minced fresh rosemary

½ teaspoon salt

¼ teaspoon freshly ground black pepper

SAUCE

Reserved, defatted pan drippings from roasted pork loin

8 ounces thinly sliced fresh mushrooms

3 tablespoons cornstarch

1 cup cold water

1 cup sour cream

RUB

Blend rub ingredients for each pound of pork loin. (Example: If the pork weighs 3 pounds, triple the ingredients.) Score fatty side of pork in a cross-hatch fashion ½–1" deep. Coat entire loin with rub. Place in zip-top bag; refrigerate, and marinate up to 24 hours.

ROASTING

Preheat oven to 325°F. Place marinated loin on rack in roasting pan. Roast 1–1½ hours, or until a meat thermometer inserted into the center of the roast registers 160°F. Transfer to serving platter, cover with foil, and let stand 5–10 minutes before slicing and serving with sauce.

SAUCE

1. Strain defatted drippings into a saucepan. Bring to a boil.
2. Add mushrooms, and cook 5 minutes.
3. Dissolve cornstarch in the cold water. While stirring, gradually add to sauce. Cook and stir until thickened. Reduce heat to low.
4. Stir in sour cream. Heat through. Do not allow sauce to boil once sour cream has been added.

SERVES 4–6

Vegetarian Pasta Primavera with Smoked Gouda Sauce

1 pound dried pasta

SAUCE
1 medium onion, chopped

1 teaspoon minced garlic

½ cup butter

1 pound asparagus, trimmed, cut into 1" pieces

8 ounces sliced mixed mushrooms

8 cauliflower florets

1 medium zucchini, cut into thin slices

1 medium carrot, cut into thin slices

1 cup heavy whipping cream

½ cup chicken stock

3 tablespoons chopped fresh basil or 1 tablespoon dried

1 cup frozen young green peas, thawed

5 green onions, thinly sliced

Salt and pepper to taste

2 cups (8 ounces) grated smoked Gouda cheese

SAUCE

1. In a large skillet over medium-high heat, sauté onions and garlic in butter until softened.
2. Add asparagus, mushrooms, cauliflower, zucchini and carrot. Sauté 3–5 minutes, stirring often.
3. Add cream, stock and basil. Bring to a gentle boil. Cook 3–5 minutes, stirring often, until liquid is slightly reduced.
4. Stir in peas and green onions. Cook 1 minute.
5. Season to taste with salt and pepper. Stir in grated cheese. Cook until cheese melts.

PASTA

While sauce is being prepared, cook pasta according to package directions.
Drain thoroughly. Add to sauce, and toss gently. Garnish with additional basil, if desired.

SERVES 6

Mixed Mushroom Risotto

2 cups medium-diced Vidalia onion (or other sweet yellow onion)

1 pound fresh mushrooms (use a variety), thinly sliced

3 tablespoons olive oil

4 garlic cloves, minced

1 (16-ounce) package arborio (Italian short-grain) rice

6 cups hot chicken broth

1 cup dry sherry

1 cup heavy whipping cream, room temperature

1 cup freshly grated Parmesan cheese, room temperature

Salt and pepper to taste

1. Sauté onions and mushrooms in hot oil in a Dutch oven over medium heat until tender.

2. Stir in garlic, and sauté 1 minute more.

3. Add rice; stir to coat grains well.

4. Combine broth and sherry in a saucepan until very hot. Add a ladle of hot broth to rice mixture, stirring constantly until almost all liquid is absorbed. Continue to add broth, a ladle at a time, stirring constantly until liquid is absorbed with each addition. This should take approximately 25–30 minutes. Rice should be cooked until it is al dente (still a tiny bit firm in the center of the grain).

5. Remove from heat. Add whipping cream and Parmesan cheese. Stir to combine. Season as desired with salt and pepper. Serve immediately—risotto waits for no one.

SERVES 10

Three-Cheese Macaroni Casserole

1 pound cooked elbow macaroni

2 cups (8 ounces) shredded smoked Gouda, divided

2 cups (8 ounces) shredded sharp cheddar, divided

4 large eggs, beaten

1½ cups milk

1 (8-ounce) package cream cheese, room temperature

1 teaspoon salt

½ teaspoon freshly ground black pepper

Dash cayenne pepper

1. Preheat oven to 350°F.

2. Generously grease a 3-quart casserole or baking dish. Distribute ½ the cooked macaroni in the bottom of the dish.

3. Combine shredded cheeses. Sprinkle 1½ cups cheese mixture over macaroni. Layer with remaining macaroni and an additional 1½ cups cheese mixture.

4. Blend remaining ingredients together. Pour over casserole. Cover tightly, and bake 45 minutes.

5. Remove cover, and top with remaining 1 cup cheese. Return to oven, and bake 10 minutes more.

SERVES 10–12

Southern-Style Green Beans Amandine with Frizzled Bacon & Smoked Almonds

12 ounces thick-sliced pepper-coated bacon, cut into thin strips

3 pounds fresh or frozen whole green beans (if using frozen beans, thaw, rinse, and drain well)

Salt and freshly ground black pepper to taste

1 cup coarsely chopped smoked almonds

Note: Gracious goodness, these are out-of-this-world good! Notice that I didn't say good for you. Save this dish for special occasions, when you're feeling indulgent or when you just want some great comfort food.

In a Dutch oven or very large skillet, cook bacon over medium-high heat until crisp. Remove with a slotted spoon. In reserved drippings, cook green beans until crisp and heated through, seasoning well with salt and pepper. Just before serving, stir in cooked bacon and almonds.

SERVES 10–12

Note: Smoked almonds aren't really smoked. They're roasted almonds coated in a smoky-seasoned salt. You'll find these delicious tidbits in the snack aisle of your grocery store, near the cocktail peanuts and other nuts.

Carolina Red Rice

6 ounces thick-sliced, pepper-coated bacon, cut into thin strips

1 large onion, diced

2 cups converted rice

1 (28-ounce) can diced tomatoes, including juice

2 cups chicken stock or canned chicken broth

Salt and freshly ground black pepper to taste

1. In a large skillet over medium-high heat, cook bacon until crisp.
2. Add onion to skillet, and sauté until transparent.
3. Add rice, and stir to coat the grains. Add tomatoes and chicken stock. Bring to a boil.
4. Reduce heat to simmer. Cover, and cook until liquid is absorbed. Season with salt and pepper. Fluff with a fork before serving.

SERVES 8

Note: Why converted rice? Converted rice has been par-boiled. When you cook with it, all the grains stay separate and never get mushy. Don't make the mistake of buying instant rice.

Sweet Potato Soufflé with Pecan & Oat Streusel Topping

SOUFFLÉ

2 (40-ounce) cans sweet potatoes (yams) packed in syrup, drained well

1 (14-ounce) can sweetened condensed milk

4 eggs, beaten

1 cup heavy whipping cream

1 tablespoon pure vanilla extract

Finely grated zest of 1 orange

½ teaspoon ground cinnamon

½ teaspoon freshly grated nutmeg

½ teaspoon salt

TOPPING

1 ¼ cups chopped pecans

1 packed cup light brown sugar

¾ cup old-fashioned oats

½ cup melted butter

¼ cup all-purpose flour

SOUFFLÉ

1. Preheat oven to 350°F.
2. Grease a 13" × 9" × 2" baking dish or suitable shallow casserole dish.
3. Using a food processor or potato masher, mash potatoes to desired degree of texture.
4. Add remaining soufflé ingredients, and blend well. Pour into prepared pan.

TOPPING

Combine all topping ingredients in a medium mixing bowl, stirring with a fork to blend. Evenly distribute over soufflé. Bake 45 minutes, then let stand 10 minutes before serving.

SERVES 8–10

Note: This recipe is intended to serve a crowd for your holiday meal gathering. If you want to halve the recipe, bake it in an 8" pan for 35 minutes.

Walnut-Crusted Potatoes with Herbs

CRUST

1½ cups French bread cubes

¾ cup walnuts

⅓ cup freshly grated Parmesan cheese

2 tablespoons butter, softened

POTATOES

3 pounds red potatoes

1 tablespoon minced fresh parsley

2 teaspoons minced fresh thyme
or 1 teaspoon dried

1½ teaspoons minced fresh sage
or ½ teaspoon dried

1 teaspoon salt

½ teaspoon freshly ground black pepper

¼ cup olive oil

1 cup chicken broth

CRUST

Combine ingredients in food processor. Blend well, and set aside.

POTATOES

1. Preheat oven to 375°F.
2. Grease a 13" × 9" × 2" baking pan.
3. Thinly slice unpeeled potatoes. Rinse, and drain.
4. Toss with herbs, salt and pepper. Distribute in prepared pan.
5. Drizzle with oil, and add chicken broth.
6. Cover tightly with foil. Bake 25–30 minutes.
7. Remove from oven, and increase oven temperature to 425°F.
8. Remove foil, and distribute crust over top. Bake uncovered 15–20 minutes, until top is golden brown.

SERVES 6–8

SERENITY FARMERS' MARKET

Every good cook knows there's nothing better than using fresh ingredients in a recipe. In summertime here in South Carolina, we're blessed with a bounty of fresh produce from local farmers. Believe you me, I take full advantage of that, whether I'm planning the specials for Sullivan's or just cooking for my family and friends.

Personally, I could be satisfied with one of those amazing beefsteak tomatoes straight from the garden every single day they're in season. Drizzle it with a little balsamic vinegar, add a slice of mozzarella, and you have a tasty salad that rises above the ordinary. But for most folks around here, variety is the spice of life. And why not, with fresh corn, greens, okra, squash, green beans, limas, zucchini and those sweet Vidalia onions available? And then there are the strawberries, blackberries, peaches and apples! Oh, my! Just wandering among the vendors at our local farmers' market is enough to get my mouth watering and my creative juices flowing. I always say that cooking is one part skill and one part inspiration.

Now, it used to be Southern cooks tossed their vegetables into some water, boiled the very life out of them, added enough butter to clog the arteries and then seasoned with more salt than the most lenient dietary recommendations call for. We've wised up in recent years. Now we've found all sorts of new ways to perk up veggies. I promise you, some of these are good enough they'll lure even the most suspicious youngster into gobbling them right up.

You're always free to eat that delicious corn straight off the cob at your backyard barbecue, but how about a hearty bowl of Southern smothered corn chowder as a change of pace? Or maybe a spring pea vischyssoise? Tired of your mama's potato salad? Take a sweet potato tailgate salad next time you head to the ball park.

As for all those delectable fruits that are available in summer, there's nothing quite like berries picked straight from the vine, still warm from sunshine, and popped straight into your mouth with all that sweetness bursting on your tongue. Or a ripe peach just off the tree, its juice dripping as you take that first bite. Heavenly.

But from time to time we all want to impress our guests with something a little fancier. Maybe it's a fruit cobbler or an all-American apple pie. Or just maybe you can earn their praise with an apple salad with a sherry and honey vinaigrette that's both tasty and healthy.

Now, if it were up to me, I'd have my own garden right outside my kitchen, but as a practical matter that's not likely to happen. I just don't have the time to do all that weeding and watering. So, if you can't find a patch of ground to grow your own produce, make sure you plan a visit to your local farmers' market as often as you can.

There are plenty of ideas right here in these pages for using whatever you find that's in season and grown locally. Or just take a walk through the market, draw in a deep breath, and let your imagination soar. With fresh ingredients straight from the garden, I can just about guarantee that whatever you fix for dinner will be extraordinary.

Pickled Green Tomatoes

8 cups thinly sliced green tomatoes

3 large onions, thinly sliced

¼ cup salt

6 pint-size canning jars, lids and screw-on bands

2 broken (3") cinnamon sticks

1 tablespoon black peppercorns

1 tablespoon whole cloves

1 tablespoon whole allspice

1 tablespoon celery seeds

1 tablespoon mustard seeds

3 cups apple cider vinegar

1 pound light brown sugar

2 red bell peppers, thinly sliced

1. In a large glass or plastic bowl, combine tomatoes and onions. Sprinkle with salt. Cover, and refrigerate overnight.

2. The following day, remove from the refrigerator. Add enough cold water to cover tomatoes and onions. Let vegetables stand in water for 1 hour.

3. Sterilize canning jars, lids and screw-on bands in boiling water for at least 5 minutes. Drain well.

4. Make a cheesecloth bundle to enclose the cinnamon, peppercorns, cloves, allspice, celery seeds and mustard seeds. Secure shut with kitchen twine.

5. In a Dutch oven, combine vinegar and brown sugar. Bring to a boil, stirring to dissolve the sugar. Add cheesecloth bundle, reduce heat to simmer, and cook 30 minutes.

6. Add tomatoes and onions. Bring to a low boil, and simmer over low heat 30 minutes. Remove and discard cheesecloth bundle.

7. Evenly distribute tomatoes and onions among canning jars. Evenly divide strips of red bell peppers among jars, standing strips on end around inside perimeter of jar. Divide spiced vinegar syrup among jars, coming to within ½" of tops of jars.

8. Wipe rims clean, and add jar lids, securing with the screw-on bands. Carefully lower the filled canning jars into a large canning pot. Cover jars by at least 1" of boiling water. Boil gently 15 minutes.

MAKES 6 PINTS

Note: One of my guilty pleasures after a long day at the restaurant is a sandwich made using these pickled green tomatoes and thinly sliced smoked cheddar cheese on toasted wheat bread lavished with mayonnaise. Oh, and a heavy grinding of fresh black pepper, too. You gotta trust the chef with this one! It really is a divine (although quirky) combination.

Dana Sue's Pickled Okra

3 (1-pint) wide-mouth canning jars, lids and screw-on bands

9 peeled garlic cloves, divided

3 teaspoons crushed red pepper flakes, divided

3 bay leaves, divided

3 teaspoons dill weed, divided

3 tablespoons sugar, divided

3 teaspoons salt, divided

2 pounds okra

1½ cups water

1½ cups apple cider vinegar

① Sterilize the canning jars, lids and screw-on bands in boiling water for at least 5 minutes. Remove jars, lids and bands from water to drain.

② In the bottom of each jar, layer the ingredients as follows:

1. 3 garlic cloves
2. 1 teaspoon crushed red pepper flakes
3. 1 bay leaf
4. 1 teaspoon dill weed
5. 1 tablespoon sugar
6. 1 teaspoon salt

③ Divide okra among the jars, standing okra upright.

④ Combine water and vinegar. Bring to a full boil. Pour over the okra.

⑤ Wipe rims of jars clean. Place lids on jars, and secure with screw-on bands. Place in a pot of boiling water, making sure water covers the jars by at least 1". Boil for 15 minutes.

⑥ Carefully remove jars from boiling water, and let stand at room temperature 30 minutes. Turn jars upside down, and cool for another 30 minutes. Turn jars upright, and cool completely.

⑦ Check jars for a tight vacuum seal. If any of the jars did not seal, refrigerate for use within 2 weeks. Store sealed jars at room temperature for up to 1 year before using.

MAKES 3 PINTS

Note: Honey, down South we pickle just about anything! This same recipe is great using fresh whole green beans instead of okra, but we Southerners are mighty fond of our okra. Use this pickled okra as a great little nibble—anywhere you would normally use dill pickles. A piece of this pickled okra makes a Bloody Mary extra special.

Pickled Dilly Green Beans

5 pint-size canning jars, lids and metal bands

3 (14-ounce) bags frozen whole green beans, thawed, rinsed and drained well or 3 pounds fresh green beans, stem ends trimmed and discarded

5 whole garlic cloves

5 sprigs fresh dill weed or 5 teaspoons dried

5 small dried hot red peppers or 2½ teaspoons crushed red pepper flakes

2½ cups distilled white vinegar

1 cup sugar

¼ cup salt

Note: These are the ultimate garnish for a Bloody Mary!

1. Wash, rinse, and sterilize 5 jars, lids and metal bands.

2. Pack beans vertically in jars. To each jar, add 1 garlic clove, 1 dill sprig (or 1 teaspoon dried) and 1 hot pepper (or ½ teaspoon pepper flakes).

3. Bring vinegar, sugar and salt to a boil over high heat, stirring to dissolve salt and sugar. Pour hot liquid over the beans.

4. Wipe jar rims clean. Top with lids, and secure tightly with bands. Cool to room temperature. Refrigerate at least 1 week and up to 1 month.

MAKES 5 PINTS

Fresh Apple Cake

1½ cups canola oil

1 pound light brown sugar

3 eggs, beaten

1 teaspoon pure almond extract

1 teaspoon pure vanilla extract

3 cups all-purpose flour

1 teaspoon salt

1 teaspoon baking soda

1 tablespoon apple pie spice

6 cups diced Gala apples, peeled or unpeeled (you decide!)

1 cup chopped walnuts

① Preheat oven to 325°F.

② Grease and flour a 12-cup Bundt pan.

③ In a large mixing bowl, beat oil and sugar 2 minutes. Add eggs and extracts.

④ In a medium mixing bowl, whisk together flour, salt, baking soda and apple pie spice. Add flour mixture to the batter, and blend well. Stir in apples and walnuts by hand using a wooden spoon.

⑤ Spoon batter into prepared pan. Bake 90 minutes, until tester inserted in center comes out clean.

⑥ Cool in pan on rack 10 minutes. Remove from pan, and cool thoroughly. Store airtight at room temperature up to 3 days.

SERVES 16

Note: This cake is quite versatile and so tasty. Serve it as a dessert topped with vanilla bean ice cream and drizzled with warm caramel sauce. It also makes a great after-school snack or breakfast pastry.

Make your own apple pie spice: Combine ½ cup ground cinnamon, 2 tablespoons ground nutmeg, 1 tablespoon ground allspice and 1 tablespoon ground cloves. Whisk together to blend. Store airtight at room temperature to use within 1 year.

Spring Pea Vichyssoise
with Vegetable Confetti

SOUP

2 cups medium-diced sweet onion

2 tablespoons olive oil

1½ pounds peeled russet potatoes, cut into 1" pieces

4 cups chicken broth

1 pound frozen baby peas

1 cup heavy whipping cream, divided

Salt and white pepper to taste

CONFETTI

Tiny-diced multicolored bell peppers

1. In a heavy large saucepan over medium heat, sauté onions in oil.

2. Add potatoes and chicken broth. Bring to a boil. Reduce heat, cover, and simmer until potatoes are very tender, stirring occasionally, about 15 minutes.

3. Add peas, cover, and continue cooking until just tender, about 5 minutes.

4. Working in batches, puree soup in blender. Transfer to a bowl. Cool slightly. Chill uncovered until cold, then cover, and chill. (Can be made 1 day ahead. Keep chilled.)

5. Before serving, whisk in ¾ cup whipping cream. Season with salt and white pepper. Thin soup with more broth, if desired. Ladle soup into bowls. Drizzle remaining ¼ cup whipping cream on top of soup, then garnish with bell peppers.

SERVES 6–8

Note: Although this soup is great served warm, I much prefer to serve it cold in chilled soup bowls. It's so pretty and so good. For the diet conscious, you can substitute fat-free half-and-half for the whipping cream.

Vidalia Onion Canapés

2 cups grated Vidalia onion, squeezed dry

1 cup freshly grated Parmesan cheese

1 cup mayonnaise

½ teaspoon cayenne pepper

1 very thinly sliced 16-ounce loaf cocktail party pumpernickel or rye bread

Paprika

1. Blend first 4 ingredients. Cover, and refrigerate several hours or up to 1 week before using.

2. Preheat oven to 350°F.

3. Spread heaping tablespoon of mixture evenly on each bread slice. Place in single layer on baking sheet. Sprinkle tops lightly with paprika.

4. Bake 15–20 minutes or until topping is puffed and golden. Serve hot or warm.

MAKES ABOUT 40

Lavender Blue Dilly Dilly
Green Bean Salad

SALAD
2 pounds fresh baby green beans, stem ends removed

½ cup thinly sliced radishes

½ cup chopped walnuts

½ cup blue cheese crumbles

1 cup chopped green onions

DRESSING
¼ cup minced fresh dill weed

3 tablespoons sugar

3 tablespoons lemon juice

2 tablespoons Dijon mustard

2 tablespoons minced fresh parsley

2 tablespoons apple cider vinegar

1 teaspoon food-safe dried lavender

¾ cup extra-virgin olive oil

Salt and pepper to taste

SALAD

Steam green beans until crisp tender. Immerse beans in a bowl filled with ice water to stop cooking, and drain well. Combine with remaining salad ingredients in a large serving bowl.

DRESSING

Process first 7 ingredients in blender or food processor. With machine running, pour olive oil in a thin, steady stream through the top, and blend 30 seconds. Season to taste with salt and pepper. Pour dressing over green bean salad, and toss to coat. Refrigerate at least 4 hours or up to 3 days before serving.

SERVES 8–10

Apple Salad with Sherry & Honey Vinaigrette

Kosher salt

Mixed greens (optional)

SALAD

3 Gala apples

1 cup thinly sliced celery

1 cup golden raisins or dried sweetened cranberries

1 cup pecan pieces, toasted

1 (4-ounce) package blue cheese crumbles

VINAIGRETTE

½ cup sherry vinegar or ¼ cup apple cider vinegar + ¼ cup sherry

¼ cup honey

1 tablespoon coarse-grain Dijon mustard

1 garlic clove, minced

1 cup vegetable oil

½ cup extra-virgin olive oil

Freshly ground black pepper to taste

SALAD

1. Fill a bowl halfway with water. Add enough salt to taste like seawater, stirring to dissolve.
2. Core and cut apples into bite-size pieces. Immediately soak in salted water for a couple of minutes to keep apples from turning brown.
3. Drain well, but do not rinse.
4. Toss with remaining salad ingredients, and coat well with sherry & honey vinaigrette. Serve as is or over mixed greens.

VINAIGRETTE

Combine first 4 ingredients in blender or food processor. With machine running, add oils in a thin, steady stream. Season with salt and pepper.

MAKES 2 CUPS

Oven-Roasted Sweet Potato Tailgate Salad

4½ cups peeled, cubed sweet potatoes

6 tablespoons extra-virgin olive oil, divided

Sea salt

¼ cup honey

¼ cup white wine vinegar

1 tablespoon minced fresh rosemary

2 garlic cloves, minced

Salt and pepper to taste

1. Preheat oven to 450°F.

2. Line a 15" × 10" jelly-roll pan with nonstick foil. Toss together potato cubes and 2 tablespoons olive oil in pan. Sprinkle with sea salt. Scatter on pan.

3. Roast 35 minutes or until fork tender. Cool to room temperature.

4. Whisk together remaining ingredients. Add cooled, roasted potatoes, and toss well. Serve slightly chilled or at room temperature. Cover, and refrigerate up to 4 days.

SERVES 6

Note: This recipe is always such a hit. It's especially great for fall picnics and tailgates—and no mayonnaise to worry about!

Lowcountry Seafood Gumbo

¾ cup vegetable oil

¾ cup all-purpose flour

2 cups diced onions, divided

1 cup diced bell pepper, divided

1 cup thinly sliced celery, divided

¼ cup minced parsley, divided

4–6 garlic cloves, minced

1 tablespoon Cajun and Creole seasoning

4 cups fish or chicken stock

1 (20-ounce) package frozen creamed white corn, thawed

1 (14½-ounce) can diced tomatoes

2 bay leaves

1 pound fresh or frozen peeled, deveined shrimp

1 pound fresh or frozen white fish filets

8 ounces fresh crabmeat, picked through

2 tablespoons gumbo filé powder

Salt and freshly ground black pepper to taste

Steamed rice (optional)

ROUX

① In a large Dutch oven over medium-high heat, combine oil and flour. Whisk until smooth. Stir constantly. (Caution: Spattering roux can cause painful burns!)

② When the roux has reached the color of milk chocolate, add half the onions, bell pepper, celery and parsley. Cook and stir 2–3 minutes.

③ Stir in garlic and Cajun and Creole seasoning. Add stock, corn, tomatoes and bay leaves. Bring to a boil. Reduce heat, and simmer 10–15 minutes.

④ Stir in seafood and remaining onions, bell pepper, celery and parsley. Cook just until seafood is cooked through. Season with filé powder, salt and pepper. Serve with or without steamed rice.

SERVES 8–10

Southern Smothered Corn Chowder

2 medium red-skinned potatoes, diced into ½" cubes

3 cups water

6 slices bacon, cut into thin strips

1 cup finely diced onion

2 (20-ounce) packages frozen creamed white corn, thawed

4 cups half-and-half

1 cup chicken stock

⅛ teaspoon ground nutmeg

Salt and pepper to taste

1. Bring potato cubes and 3 cups water to a boil in a large Dutch oven, reduce heat, and cook until potato cubes are cooked through. Remove from heat and set aside. (Do not drain.)

2. Cook bacon in a small Dutch oven or large saucepan until crisp. Using a slotted utensil, remove bacon from pan, and reserve drippings in pan.

3. Sauté onions in drippings until tender. Stir in remaining ingredients. Bring to a boil over medium heat, stirring often.

4. Add potato cubes and their cooking water to the soup. Return to a boil. Reduce heat to low, and simmer 5–10 minutes.

5. Ladle into bowls, garnishing each with the cooked bacon.

SERVES 8

Cornmeal-Crusted Fried Okra

¾ cup cornmeal

¾ cup all-purpose flour

1 tablespoon sugar

2 teaspoons seasoned salt

1 teaspoon freshly ground black pepper

1 pound fresh okra

½ cup buttermilk

1 egg, beaten

¾ cup canola or vegetable oil

1. Combine cornmeal, flour, sugar, salt and pepper in a mixing bowl. Whisk until blended.

2. Trim ends from okra, and discard. Slice okra into ½" pieces. Place sliced okra in cornmeal mixture, and toss to coat. Remove okra from mixture, shaking off excess.

3. Whisk together buttermilk and egg until smooth. Place okra in egg mixture, and toss to coat. Transfer okra back to cornmeal mixture, and toss to coat and cling. Transfer coated okra to a surface lined with paper towels.

4. Heat oil in a heavy skillet over medium-high heat. Test oil to make sure it is hot enough to fry properly. Place a single piece of coated okra in hot oil. It should sizzle and bob around. Working in single-layer batches, carefully place coated okra in hot oil. When golden brown on underside, flip okra over, and cook on other side. When golden brown on both sides, remove from skillet with a slotted utensil, and place on surface lined with paper towels to drain. Sprinkle lightly with seasoned salt or sea salt. Enjoy immediately.

SERVES 6

Note: The coating method in this recipe is known as dry-wet-dry. It is the secret to the cornmeal coating staying on the okra during the frying process. Use this same method for any cornmeal-crusted garden veggie—fried green tomatoes, zucchini, yellow squash, Vidalia onion rings, etc.

Fall Harvest Bisque

2 medium butternut squash, peeled, seeded, diced

6 cups chicken stock

2 cups apple juice or cider

1 (3") cinnamon stick

2 teaspoons minced fresh rosemary

2 cups apple sauce

2 cups whipping cream or half-and-half

¼ cup maple syrup

1 teaspoon vanilla extract

½ teaspoon grated nutmeg

Salt and white pepper to taste

In a Dutch oven, combine first 5 ingredients. Bring to a boil over medium-high heat. Reduce heat and simmer until squash is tender. Remove cinnamon stick. Using blender or food processor, puree in batches. Return mixture to Dutch oven. Add remaining ingredients, and cook until heated through, stirring occasionally. Do not boil.

SERVES 10

Fresh Peach Macaroon Tarts

CRUST

3 large egg whites

1 cup sugar

30 coarsely crushed Ritz crackers

1 cup chopped pecans

1 teaspoon almond extract

FILLING

1 cup cold heavy whipping cream

1 (8-ounce) package cream cheese, softened

1 cup confectioners' sugar

PEACHES

4 large or 6 medium peaches, thinly sliced

½ cup melted peach preserves or jam

1 teaspoon almond extract

TOPPING

1 cup cold heavy whipping cream

¼ cup confectioners' sugar

½ teaspoon almond extract

GARNISH

Grated nutmeg

Cinnamon

CRUST

1. Preheat oven to 350°F.

2. Beat egg whites until frothy. Gradually add sugar, beating all the while. Beat until stiff peaks form.

3. Stir in remaining ingredients.

4. Draw 6 (5") circles on a piece of baking parchment. Turn parchment over, and place on baking sheet. Distribute meringue mixture evenly among the 6 circles, spreading to fill the circles. Bake 20 minutes.

5. Remove from oven, and let cool completely on parchment. Once cooled, store airtight until serving time. Can be prepared earlier in the day.

CONTINUES →

FILLING

Combine ingredients in a medium mixing bowl. Beat until smooth. Cover, and refrigerate at least 1 hour.

PEACHES

Combine ingredients in a medium mixing bowl. Stir gently to coat peaches. Cover, and refrigerate at least 1 hour.

TOPPING

Combine ingredients in a small mixing bowl. Beat until stiff peaks form. Cover, and refrigerate.

ASSEMBLY

Place macaroons on 6 dessert plates. Evenly distribute filling over crusts, and spread to the edges. Spoon peaches over the filling. Top each tart with a dollop of topping.

GARNISH

Dust with freshly grated nutmeg or a sprinkling of cinnamon.

SERVES 6

Sullivan's Smothered Corn with Frizzled Bacon

6 thick slices pepper-coated bacon, cut into thin strips

2 cups medium-diced sweet onion

1 cup medium-diced celery

1 red bell pepper, seeded, chopped

1 tablespoon minced garlic

¼ cup flour

1 tablespoon ham base

½ cup water

2 (20-ounce) packages frozen creamed white corn, thawed

½ teaspoon freshly ground black pepper

1. In a large deep skillet or Dutch oven over medium-high heat, cook bacon until crisp. Using a slotted cooking utensil, carefully transfer cooked bacon to a plate lined with paper towels, and reserve the drippings in the pan. Set aside the bacon.

2. In the drippings, sauté onion, celery, bell pepper and garlic until wilted and slightly cooked.

3. Sprinkle on flour, and stir into sautéed vegetables. Cook and stir constantly 1 minute or so.

4. Dissolve ham base in ½ cup water. Stir into vegetable mixture until smooth.

5. Add corn and black pepper. Reduce heat to medium, and continue to cook 10–15 minutes, stirring occasionally. Add additional water if necessary to prevent sticking to pan. Just before serving, stir cooked bacon into the corn. Serve hot.

SERVES 10–12

Sullivan's Crab Cakes—Page 97

SUNDAY BRUNCH AT SULLIVAN'S

Folks here in Serenity have always had their big meal of the day just after church on Sunday. Some had it at home. Others packed the local restaurants.

For the longest time after I opened the doors at Sullivan's, I went along with tradition, serving the usual sort of Sunday meals with meat and potatoes and piping hot yeast rolls. Or maybe that old staple, fried chicken just like Grandma used to make. Then it occurred to me that Sullivan's has a reputation for shaking things up, doing the unexpected, not serving the exact same Sunday dinners folks could get if they went straight on home, put on their aprons and fixed a meal. The idea of putting a Sunday brunch on the menu, while not exactly revolutionary, was a real eye-opener here in town.

But think about it for a minute. How often do most people really take the time to cook a fancy breakfast these days? In our house, before I had my own restaurant, Ronnie was the one who whipped up a batch of pancakes on Sunday. Weekdays, during those years I was a single mom with Ronnie gone, I barely had time to pour a bowl of cereal or scramble an egg before sending Annie off to school.

But the truth is, most folks I know love a traditional breakfast as long as somebody else is cooking it. In Sullivan's we've taken that reality and kicked it up another notch or two with a mix of breakfast favorites and a few lunch specialties that aren't on our regular menu.

Now you can do the exact same thing when you have company visiting and want to sit right there at the kitchen table and linger over a glass of sweet tea and a few tasty dishes you'd never take the time to fix on an ordinary morning. After all, isn't the best part of having out-of-town guests taking the time to sit and visit over a leisurely meal—something we rarely get to do in our harried lives? I'm even sharing my own favorite sweet tea recipe to add an authentic touch to your Southern brunch.

When folks come into Sullivan's on Sunday, we give them a pastry basket of my almond-filled croissants and cranberry-orange scones with orange glaze and cranberry-orange butter. We offer miniature versions. After all, we certainly wouldn't want them to fill up on those, not with strawberry-topped stuffed French toast on the menu or a country ham and grits quiche. The recipes here are for the full-sized versions, of course. You'll probably want to pick and choose among the recipes. Try them all at once, and you'll be as stuffed as that delicious French toast.

Of course, some folks here at Sullivan's opt for the pineapple chicken salad, especially if they had breakfast at home before going to church. And you can't very well call it brunch if you're not offering a combination of breakfast and lunch choices, so we always include a variety of specials that cater to folks who can't bear to break with their old Sunday traditions.

Whatever you put on your own Sunday brunch menu, just be sure to include a warm helping of Southern hospitality. It'll keep your visitors coming back time and again.

Dana Sue's Almond-Filled Croissants

8 medium croissants

1 cup sliced almonds, divided

½ cup sugar, divided

¼ cup (2 ounces) almond paste

6 tablespoons butter, softened

3 large egg yolks

1 teaspoon pure almond extract

Confectioners' sugar

1. Preheat oven to 350°F.

2. Split croissants in half horizontally. Using a food processor, combine ½ cup almonds and ¼ cup sugar. Process until finely ground. Add almond paste, and process until finely chopped.

3. Using an electric mixer, cream together butter and remaining ¼ cup sugar. Add almond mixture, and beat at medium speed 1 minute. Beat in egg yolks and almond extract.

4. Fill each croissant with 2 tablespoons almond filling, heaping in the center and spreading to the edges. Sandwich croissant together with filling in center. Spread 1 tablespoon filling over top of each croissant. Press tops of each croissant into remaining ½ cup almonds. Place on parchment or foil-lined baking sheet a couple of inches apart.

5. Bake 20 minutes or until tops are deep golden brown and almonds on top are toasted. Serve warm or at room temperature, garnished with a slight dusting of confectioners' sugar.

MAKES 8

Classic Cream Scones

2 cups all-purpose flour

½ cup granulated sugar

1 tablespoon baking powder

1 teaspoon salt

½ cup cold butter, cut into cubes

1 cup heavy whipping cream

1 teaspoon pure vanilla extract

½ teaspoon pure almond extract

Egg wash (1 beaten egg +
2 tablespoons water)

Coarse sugar

1. Preheat oven to 425°F.

2. In a food processor fitted with the chopping blade, combine first 4 ingredients.

3. Add butter and operate food processor in 1-second pulses until butter is the size of small peas. (Alternatively, cut butter into dry ingredients using a handheld pastry blender.)

4. Transfer dry ingredients to a mixing bowl. Make a well in the center of dry ingredients.

5. In a small mixing bowl, combine whipping cream and extracts. Pour into well. Stir just until dough clings together.

6. Transfer dough to a floured work surface. Roll dough to ½" thickness.

7. Using a 2" round cutter, cut out dough. Place on a parchment-lined baking sheet 1" apart. Brush tops with egg wash. Sprinkle tops with coarse sugar.

8. Bake 10–12 minutes until tops are golden.

9. Remove from oven, and transfer to cooling rack. Serve warm.

MAKES 24 PETITE SCONES

Frosted Café Royale

½ gallon (8 cups) double-strength freshly brewed coffee

2 cups sugar

2 cups brandy

1 quart half-and-half

2 cups milk

½ gallon vanilla ice cream

In a gallon-size container, combine coffee and sugar. Stir to dissolve. Add brandy. Bring to room temperature, then cover, and refrigerate until thoroughly chilled. Add half-and-half and milk. Serve over ice cream cut into 1" cubes.

SERVES 20 Recipe halves easily for smaller gatherings.

> *Note: To make a frosted mocha royale, simply substitute 2 cups chocolate milk for the milk, and use chocolate ice cream instead of vanilla.*

Lemon & Poppy Seed Scones

SCONES
2½ cups self-rising flour

½ cup granulated sugar

2 teaspoons baking powder

½ cup cold, cubed unsalted butter

Grated zest of 2 lemons

2 tablespoons poppy seeds

1 cup heavy whipping cream

1 teaspoon vanilla extract

Yellow food coloring (optional)

GLAZE
2 cups sifted confectioners' sugar

Lemon juice

Yellow food coloring (optional)

SCONES

1. Preheat oven to 425°F.

2. In food processor fitted with the chopping blade, combine first 3 ingredients.

3. Add butter and lemon zest. Operate food processor in 1-second pulses until the butter is the size of small peas. (Alternatively, cut butter into dry ingredients using a handheld pastry blender.)

4. Transfer dry ingredients to a mixing bowl. Stir in poppy seeds. Make a well in the center of dry ingredients.

5. In a small bowl, blend together whipping cream, vanilla extract and food coloring. Pour into the well of dry ingredients. Stir until the dough clings together—it will be very stiff!

6. Transfer dough to a floured work surface, and roll to ¾" thickness.

7. Using a 2" round cutter, cut out dough. Place on a parchment-lined baking sheet at least 1" apart.

8. Bake 10–12 minutes or until tops are golden brown. While scones are baking, prepare glaze.

9. Remove from oven, and immediately transfer scones to a cooling rack.

GLAZE

Sift confectioners' sugar into a small bowl. Adding a little bit of lemon juice at a time, stir until a thick glaze is formed. Tint with a few drops of food coloring. While scones are still warm, spread tops with glaze. Let glaze set several minutes. Serve warm.

MAKES 24 PETITE SCONES

Cranberry-Orange Scones with Orange Glaze

SCONES

2½ cups self-rising flour

½ cup granulated sugar

Grated zest of 2 oranges

½ teaspoon ground cinnamon

½ teaspoon ground ginger

¼ teaspoon ground nutmeg

⅛ teaspoon ground cloves

½ cup cubed cold butter

¾ cup pecan pieces

¾ cup dried sweetened cranberries (such as Craisins)

1 cup heavy whipping cream

GLAZE

2 cups sifted confectioners' sugar

Grated zest of 1 orange

2–3 tablespoons orange juice

SCONES

1. Combine first 7 ingredients.
2. Preheat oven to 425°F.
3. Using a handheld pastry blender or a food processor, cut in butter until the butter is the size of small peas.
4. Stir in pecan pieces and cranberries. Make a well in center of dough.
5. Pour whipping cream into the center of the well. Blend until dough comes together, but do not overmix.
6. On a lightly floured surface, divide dough in half, and form each half into a 6" circle. Cut each circle into 6 pie-shaped wedges. Place 2" apart on a greased or parchment-lined baking sheet.
7. Bake 15–18 minutes until tops are golden brown and centers of scones test done. Prepare glaze while scones are baking.
8. Remove from oven, and transfer scones to a cooling rack.

GLAZE

Place confectioners' sugar and orange zest in a small mixing bowl. Add enough orange juice to make a very thick glaze. After scones have cooled for 5 minutes, spread glaze on top of scones. Let glaze harden. Serve warm. Store in an airtight container.

MAKES 12 LARGE SCONES

Gingerbread Scones

2¼ cups all-purpose flour

¼ packed cup light brown sugar

2 tablespoons finely minced crystallized ginger

1 teaspoon baking powder

1 teaspoon ground ginger

1 teaspoon ground cinnamon

½ teaspoon baking soda

¼ teaspoon ground nutmeg

⅛ teaspoon ground cloves

½ cup cubed, cold butter

¾ cup heavy whipping cream

⅓ cup molasses

1. Preheat oven to 425°F.
2. Combine all ingredients except butter, cream and molasses, and whisk to blend.
3. Using a handheld pastry blender, cut butter into dry ingredients until the butter is the size of peas.
4. Whisk together the whipping cream and molasses. Add to the dry ingredients. Stir just until dough clings together.
5. Turn dough out onto a lightly floured work surface, and knead several times.
6. Divide dough into 2 equal pieces. Shape each piece into a flat 6" round. Cut each round into 6 pie-shaped wedges. Place on a baking sheet, spacing a couple of inches apart.
7. Bake in center of oven for about 15 minutes.

MAKES 12

Cranberry-Orange Butter

1 cup butter, room
temperature

½ cup orange marmalade

½ cup finely chopped
sweetened dried cranberries
(such as Craisins)

Combine butter and orange marmalade in a small bowl.
Using an electric mixer, blend well. Add cranberries, and
blend until thoroughly incorporated.

MAKES 2 CUPS

*Note: Serve at room temperature with biscuits, toast
and especially scones! It also makes a deliciously simple
spread for gingersnaps.*

Macaroon Muffins with Dates & Pecans

3 egg whites at room temperature

²/₃ cup sugar

1 cup coarsely crushed vanilla wafers

1 cup chopped pecans

½ cup pitted, chopped dates

1 teaspoon almond extract

½ teaspoon baking powder

1. Preheat oven to 350°F.
2. Beat egg whites until foamy. Continue beating, adding the sugar gradually, until stiff peaks form and most of the sugar has dissolved.
3. Fold in remaining ingredients until well blended.
4. Divide mixture evenly among 12 paper-lined muffin cups.
5. Bake 18–20 minutes or until tops are golden brown and cake tester inserted in center comes out clean.
6. Allow to cool in pan 10 minutes, then remove from pan, and continue cooling on rack. Store airtight.

MAKES 12

Note: To serve these muffins as a wonderful light dessert, omit the dates, and bake as directed. When ready to serve, remove muffins from paper, and split in half. Spoon on fresh fruit (sweetened, if desired) and lots of freshly whipped cream.

Lowcountry Crab Hash

1½ pounds washed red-skinned potatoes, cut into ½" cubes

OLD BAY Seasoning

3 thick slices smoked pepper-coated bacon, cut into thin strips

1 cup medium-diced onion

1 bell pepper, medium-diced

8 ounces fresh crabmeat, picked over

½ cup minced fresh parsley

Freshly ground black pepper to taste

1. Cook potatoes in boiling water seasoned with OLD BAY until just fork tender; do not overcook. Shock in cold water, or pour into a colander and run cold water over potatoes several minutes to stop their cooking. Drain well. (This can be done 1 day ahead and then refrigerated.)

2. In a large skillet, cook bacon until crisp. Remove from skillet, reserving drippings in pan.

3. In drippings, cook onions until translucent. Add bell pepper and potatoes, and heat through, stirring to coat.

4. Just before serving, stir in crabmeat, parsley and cooked bacon. Season to taste with additional OLD BAY Seasoning and freshly ground black pepper.

SERVES 4–6

Note: This hash is a favorite Lowcountry breakfast or brunch dish. It is extra delicious (and indulgent!) to top each serving with a poached egg, then spoon hollandaise sauce on top.

Microwave Lemon Curd

2 cups sugar

12 large egg yolks

1 cup freshly squeezed lemon juice

¼ cup freshly grated lemon zest

1 cup butter, room temperature

Whisk together sugar, egg yolks, lemon juice and lemon zest. Cook in microwave on high (100% power) until mixture boils, stirring well after each minute of cooking. Bring to room temperature. Beat in butter, a couple of tablespoons at a time. Beat until smooth. Cover, and refrigerate up to 1 month.

MAKES 4 CUPS

Stuffed French Toast with Glazed Strawberries

FILLING

1 (8-ounce) package cream cheese, softened

1 cup whole-milk ricotta cheese

¼ cup sugar

FRENCH TOAST

1 large loaf French bread, thinly sliced

1 cup half-and-half

4 eggs, beaten

¼ teaspoon salt

2 teaspoons vanilla

¼ teaspoon ground cinnamon

⅛ teaspoon ground nutmeg

½ cup clarified butter

STRAWBERRIES

1 pound fresh strawberries

¾ cup strawberry jam

¼ cup orange marmalade

FILLING

Blend all ingredients until smooth.

FRENCH TOAST

1. Spread filling on half the number of bread slices. Top with remaining slices, and press together. Arrange a few in a single layer in a shallow pan.

2. Whisk together remaining ingredients except butter. Pour over stuffed bread. Soak briefly on both sides.

3. Fry slices in clarified butter until golden brown, turning once. Transfer to a warm serving platter. Cover.

4. Repeat with remaining stuffed bread slices.

STRAWBERRIES

1. Trim away caps from strawberries and discard. Thinly slice the strawberries.

2. Blend together strawberry jam and orange marmalade. Pour over the sliced strawberries. Stir gently to coat the strawberry slices.

3. Spoon the strawberry and jam topping over each serving of prepared French toast.

SERVES 6–8

Spicy Shrimp & Sausage with Country Ham Cream-Style Gravy over Creamy Yellow Grits

CREAMY GRITS

1 quart half-and-half

1 quart whole milk

2 cups coarsely ground yellow grits

½ cup butter

2 tablespoons sugar

1 tablespoon salt

Pepper to taste

COUNTRY HAM GRAVY

¼ cup butter

½ cup all-purpose flour

1 quart half-and-half

2 tablespoons ham base or bouillon

3 ounces country ham, chopped

SHRIMP & SAUSAGE

1½ pounds andouille or smoked sausage

1½ pounds peeled, deveined shrimp

2 tablespoons butter

2 tablespoons Cajun and Creole seasoning

¼ cup whipping cream

GARNISH (OPTIONAL)

¼ cup chopped fresh parsley

GRITS

1. Combine all ingredients in a large saucepan. Bring to a boil over medium-high heat, stirring frequently and breaking up any lumps with a whisk.

2. Reduce heat, cover, and simmer at least 20 minutes, stirring often. Adjust seasoning if necessary. Prepare the gravy while the grits are cooking.

GRAVY

1. Melt butter in heavy saucepan over medium heat. Add flour, stirring constantly, 2–4 minutes or until lightly browned.

2. Gradually add half-and-half and ham base, whisking constantly. Cook until mixture has thickened. Stir in chopped country ham.

3. Cover, and simmer 10–15 minutes, stirring occasionally. While the grits and the gravy are simmering, prepare the shrimp & sausage.

SHRIMP & SAUSAGE

1. Cut sausage into ½"-thick rounds. In a large skillet, cook thoroughly over medium-high heat. Drain, and set aside.

2. In a large skillet, cook shrimp in butter and Cajun and Creole seasoning over medium-high heat 3–5 minutes, just until shrimp blush and curl.

3. Add sausage and 2½ cups prepared gravy. Cook over medium heat 1–2 minutes.

4. Stir in whipping cream, and cook until heated through. If mixture is too thick, add a bit of milk to thin down.

TO SERVE

Spoon about 1 cup grits into a large shallow bowl or onto a plate, and spoon shrimp and sausage mixture over grits. Sprinkle with parsley. Serve with additional gravy on the side.

SERVES 8

Chicken Salad with Dijon-Dill Dressing & Toasted Almonds

SALAD

¾ cup slivered almonds

3 cups diced, cooked chicken breast

3 stalks celery, thinly sliced

1 bunch green onions (white and light green parts only), thinly sliced

8 leaves Boston or butter lettuce

DRESSING

1 cup mayonnaise

1 tablespoon Dijon mustard

1 tablespoon minced fresh dill weed or 1 teaspoon dried

1 teaspoon salt

½ teaspoon freshly ground black pepper

SALAD

Preheat oven to 350°F. Scatter almonds on a baking sheet. Bake about 10 minutes, just until nuts are lightly browned and begin to smell toasted. Cool to room temperature, and set aside. In a medium mixing bowl, combine chicken, celery and green onions.

DRESSING

In a small mixing bowl, whisk all dressing ingredients together. Transfer dressing to chicken salad. Stir to blend well. Cover, and refrigerate at least 2 hours or up to 3 days before serving.

TO SERVE

Just before serving, stir toasted almonds into chicken salad. Place 2 lettuce leaves on each of 4 salad or luncheon plates. Place a large scoop of chicken salad on top.

SERVES 4

Pineapple Chicken Salad

SALAD
2 medium fresh pineapples
(whole with tops)

2 cups cubed, cooked chicken breast

²/₃ cup thinly sliced celery

²/₃ cup seedless green grapes, cut in half lengthwise

½ cup sweetened flaked coconut

½ cup coarsely chopped, roasted, salted macadamia nuts

DRESSING
1 (8-ounce) package cream cheese, softened

¾ cup mayonnaise

3 tablespoons orange marmalade

SALAD

1. Using a very sharp knife, slice pineapple in half lengthwise. Slice each half into two quarters lengthwise. Repeat with other pineapple.

2. Using a sharp knife, remove most of the flesh of each pineapple quarter, leaving a substantial shell (boat shaped) that will hold the prepared chicken salad. Remove core from each piece of pineapple.

3. Cut remaining pineapple flesh into bite-size cubes. Turn pineapple boats upside down on paper towels to drain.

4. Combine pineapple chunks with all remaining salad ingredients except nuts.

DRESSING

Combine all dressing ingredients, and blend together using a whisk or an electric mixer. Pour over salad ingredients. Stir gently but thoroughly to blend well.

TO SERVE

Scoop an equal amount of prepared chicken salad into each of 8 pineapple boats. Sprinkle macadamia nuts over top. Serve immediately.

MAKES 8

Barbecue Salad with Tangy Coleslaw

COLESLAW

1 (10-ounce) package coleslaw mix

⅓ cup mayonnaise

¼ cup prepared ranch dressing

¼ cup wine vinegar

¼ cup sugar

1½ teaspoons garlic salt

½ teaspoon freshly ground black pepper

BARBECUE SALAD

2 hearts of romaine, thinly sliced

2 cups fully cooked, shredded pork barbecue in sauce, warmed slightly

1. Prepare coleslaw 1 day ahead of serving. Place coleslaw mix in a medium mixing bowl.

2. Combine remaining slaw ingredients in a small bowl. Whisk together.

3. Pour over slaw mix. Stir to coat well. Cover, and refrigerate at least 4 hours.

4. Just prior to serving, arrange lettuce on a serving platter or on 4 individual plates. Spoon warmed barbecue over lettuce. Top with coleslaw.

SERVES 4–6

Note: I usually purchase the pork barbecue at a favorite local barbecue restaurant, but I've also purchased it in grocery stores, in either the frozen food or canned meats section.

Sullivan's Crab Cakes

1 pound fresh lump crabmeat, picked through

1 stack Ritz crackers, coarsely crushed

½ cup mayonnaise

¼ cup chopped fresh parsley

2 eggs, beaten

1 tablespoon OLD BAY Seasoning

Finely grated zest of 1 lemon

Tabasco sauce to taste

¼ cup butter

1. In a mixing bowl, use your hands to carefully combine the crabmeat with the coarsely crushed crackers.
2. In another mixing bowl, whisk together all remaining ingredients except butter.
3. Blend gently with the crab and cracker mixture, being careful not to break up the crabmeat. Cover, and refrigerate at least 30 minutes or up to 1 day ahead.
4. Shape into crab cakes of desired size.
5. Fry in melted butter in a heavy-bottomed skillet over medium-high heat. Turn once when halfway through cooking. Cook until golden brown on both sides.

SERVES 6 as an entrée or 12 as an appetizer.

Note: Chef Erik at Sullivan's serves these yummy crab cakes as a brunch specialty, topping each crab cake with a poached egg and a ladle of sherry hollandaise sauce over the crab cake (see next recipe). On the evening menu, the crab cakes are featured as a starter course and served with our Carolina rémoulade sauce (recipe follows).

Sherry Hollandaise Sauce

6 egg yolks

1 teaspoon salt

¼ teaspoon ground
cayenne pepper

¼ cup sherry

1 cup butter, cubed, room
temperature

Combine all but the butter in the top section of a double
boiler. Stirring constantly, cook over simmering water
until very hot. Whisk in butter one cube at a time
until all butter has been incorporated and sauce
is smooth. Transfer to a bowl or gravy boat.
Cover with plastic wrap, then swaddle in a
kitchen towel to keep warm until serving time
(up to 15 minutes).

MAKES ABOUT 1½ CUPS

*Chef's Tip: To make a traditional hollandaise sauce,
replace the sherry with freshly squeezed lemon juice.
Finely grated lemon zest is a lovely addition as well.*

Carolina Rémoulade Sauce

2 cups mayonnaise

½ cup prepared chili sauce

½ cup finely chopped green onions
(white and light green parts only)

⅓ cup Creole mustard

¼ cup extra-virgin olive oil

¼ cup finely chopped celery

¼ cup finely minced fresh parsley

Finely grated zest and juice of
1 medium lemon

1 tablespoon minced garlic

1 tablespoon minced capers

Salt and Tabasco sauce to taste

Prepare at least 1 hour ahead of serving time. (Best if made a day or so ahead to allow flavors to blend.) Combine all ingredients in a mixing bowl. Whisk to blend well. Cover, and refrigerate up to 2 weeks.

MAKES ABOUT 1 QUART

Note: Okay, here's the scoop on rémoulade sauce. As with most sauces, it is French in origin but reached its height of popularity in New Orleans cuisine. Here in the South, we love this sauce on almost anything, but it is especially wonderful served with crab cakes, spicy boiled shrimp, fried green tomatoes and other fried veggies. It also makes a delicious spread for sandwiches and any fried seafood. Although the recipe makes almost 4 cups, you can prepare just a half batch if desired. Once you taste it, though, you'll wish you had prepared the full recipe.

Country Ham & Grits Quiche with Red-Eye Gravy

QUICHE

6 ounces country ham

½ cup water

½ teaspoon salt

⅓ cup uncooked quick-cooking grits

1 (12-ounce) can evaporated milk

1 cup (4 ounces) shredded sharp cheddar cheese

3 large eggs, beaten

1 teaspoon dry mustard powder

1 teaspoon Tabasco sauce

GRAVY

Pan drippings from country ham

2 cups very strong coffee

2 tablespoons butter

2 tablespoons cornstarch

¼ cup cold water

Salt and freshly ground black pepper to taste

QUICHE

1. Preheat oven to 350°F.

2. Grease a deep-dish 9" pie plate.

3. In a skillet over medium-high heat, place country ham in enough water to cover. Cook 5 minutes, adding additional water as necessary.

4. Remove ham from skillet. Reserve water and pan drippings for gravy. Dice ham, and set aside.

5. In a large saucepan, bring ½ cup water and salt to a boil.

6. Stir in grits. Remove from heat, cover, and let stand 5 minutes (mixture will be very thick).

7. Stir in country ham and remaining ingredients. Pour into prepared pie plate.

8. Bake 30–35 minutes. Let stand 10 minutes before serving. Prepare gravy while quiche bakes.

SERVES 6–8

GRAVY

In the same skillet used to cook the ham, add the coffee and butter to the pan drippings. Cook over medium-high heat until reduced to 1 cup. Dissolve cornstarch in water. Quickly whisk into gravy. Stir constantly until thickened. Season to taste. Serve hot over wedges of quiche.

MAKES 1¼ CUPS

Crustless Broccoli & Three-Cheese Quiche

2 cups milk

4 large eggs, beaten

¾ cup biscuit baking mix (such as Bisquick)

4 tablespoons butter, softened

½ teaspoon freshly ground black pepper

2 cups chopped, steamed crisp-tender broccoli

1 cup canned French-fried onions

1 cup grated Parmesan cheese

1 cup grated Swiss cheese

1 cup grated cheddar cheese

1. Preheat oven to 375°F.
2. Grease a 10" quiche pan.
3. In a large mixing bowl using an electric mixer on low speed, blend together the first 5 ingredients.
4. Stir in broccoli, French-fried onions and the 3 grated cheeses. Transfer mixture to the prepared quiche pan.
5. Place in the center of the oven. Bake 45–50 minutes, until center is set and top is golden brown.
6. Remove from oven, and let stand 5 minutes before serving.

SERVES 6

Caramelized Onion & Bacon Quiche

CRUST
1½ cups finely crushed Ritz crackers

6 tablespoons unsalted butter,
room temperature

FILLING
4 slices thick-sliced bacon, cut into
thin strips

3 cups thinly sliced sweet onions

1 cup half-and-half

3 large eggs

1 teaspoon salt

½ teaspoon freshly ground black pepper

¼ teaspoon freshly grated nutmeg

6 ounces (1½ cups) grated Gruyère
or Swiss cheese

GARNISH (OPTIONAL)
¼ cup minced fresh parsley

CRUST

Preheat oven to 350°F. Combine ingredients until well blended. Press mixture in bottom and 1" up sides of a 9" pie plate. Bake 10 minutes. Prepare filling while crust bakes.

FILLING

1. In a skillet over medium heat, cook bacon until crisp. Reserving drippings, use a slotted spoon to transfer bacon to a plate lined with paper towels.
2. In drippings, cook onions until tender, cooking away all liquid from onions. Arrange onions in cracker crust.
3. Beat half-and-half, eggs, salt, pepper and nutmeg in a medium bowl until blended. Pour egg mixture over onions in crust. Sprinkle cheese and cooked bacon over filling.
4. Bake until knife inserted into center comes out clean, about 40 minutes. Garnish with parsley, and serve.

SERVES 6

Petite Dilly Biscuits

3 cups Bisquick baking mix

1 cup sour cream

½ cup melted butter

2 tablespoons minced fresh dill weed
or 2 teaspoons dried

1. Preheat oven to 425°F.
2. Lightly grease or parchment-line a baking sheet.
3. Combine all ingredients in a medium mixing bowl. Stir to blend using a wooden spoon.
4. Turn dough out onto a lightly floured work surface, and knead several times.
5. Roll dough to ½" thickness. Cut into rounds with a 2" biscuit cutter. Place on prepared pan, allowing 1" space between each.
6. Bake about 8 minutes, until tops are golden brown.

MAKES 24

Note: Serve warm with butter or as a base for Sullivan's crab cakes topped with Carolina rémoulade sauce.

CHEF'S TIP: To make your own baking mix, combine 4½ cups all-purpose flour, 2 tablespoons baking powder, 1 tablespoon salt, 1 tablespoon sugar and 1 cup all-vegetable shortening, then process in a food processor until it becomes the texture of cornmeal. If you don't have a food processor, you can simply blend together using a handheld pastry blender. Store this baking mix airtight at room temperature up to 3 months. If you have the space to store it in the refrigerator, it will last up to 6 months.

Sweet Potato Biscuits

2½ cups all-purpose flour

2 tablespoons sugar

1 tablespoon baking powder

1½ teaspoons salt

½ cup cold butter, cut into small pieces

1 cup cooked, mashed sweet potato, room temperature

1 cup sour cream

1. Preheat oven to 425°F.

2. Lightly grease a cookie sheet.

3. Combine flour, sugar, baking powder and salt. Whisk together. Using a handheld pastry blender or food processor, cut butter into the dry ingredients until the butter is the size of peas.

4. Blend together the sweet potato and sour cream until smooth. Stir into the dry ingredients, just until the dough comes together; do not overmix.

5. On a lightly floured surface, knead the biscuit dough a few times. Roll dough to ¾" thick. Cut into rounds, and place 2" apart on prepared pan.

6. Bake 10–15 minutes until golden brown.

MAKES 12 MEDIUM OR 24 PETITE BISCUITS

Note: To turn these yummy Southern jewels into a more savory dish, add some minced fresh herbs, such as rosemary, sage or thyme, and serve with country ham, baked ham, breakfast sausage patties or pork tenderloin.

Whipping Cream Drop Biscuits

2½ cups all-purpose flour

1 tablespoon baking powder

1 tablespoon granulated sugar

1 teaspoon salt

2 cups heavy whipping cream

1. Preheat oven to 425°F.
2. In a mixing bowl, combine dry ingredients, and stir to blend. Make a well in center of ingredients. Pour whipping cream into well. Stir just until the dough is well blended.
3. Onto a baking sheet, drop dough into 12 mounds of equal size, allowing about 2" in between.
4. Bake in center of oven for about 20 minutes, until tops of biscuits are light golden brown and bottoms are golden brown.

MAKES 12

Strawberry Preserves
with Rose Geranium & Vanilla Essence

This recipe is a favorite creation of mine. My mother is a purist and believes perfection (like traditional strawberry preserves) shouldn't be messed with. Well, the chef in me (or is it the rebel?!) screams out to try new things. I grow my own scented geraniums and use them to flavor these preserves. Also, I love to make scented sugars by placing the scented geranium leaves in sugar. Leave alone a month and then discard the leaves. Use the sugar in baked goods like sugar cookies and pound cakes. The taste is subtle but memorable.

8 half-pint canning jars, lids and screw-on bands

7 cups sugar

5 cups very thinly sliced, hulled ripe strawberries

8 rose-scented geranium leaves

1 teaspoon butter

1 (3-ounce) pouch liquid fruit pectin

2 teaspoons pure vanilla extract

1. Sterilize jars, lids and screw-on bands in boiling water for at least 5 minutes. Drain well just before filling jars with prepared preserves.

2. In a saucepan, combine sugar, strawberries, geranium leaves and butter (the little bit of butter helps reduce foaming). Bring to a boil, stirring often. Remove geranium leaves, and discard.

3. When you reach a rolling boil (one that you can't stir down), add pectin all at once. Stir well. Return to a boil, and boil exactly 1 minute. Remove from heat.

4. Stir in vanilla extract. Pour into hot, sterilized jars. Wipe rims of jars clean. Secure lids with screw-on bands.

5. Process jars of preserves in a boiling water bath for 10 minutes.

6. Carefully remove from water bath, and let stand at room temperature to cool.

7. In a few hours, check to be certain all jars are vacuum sealed. Store at room temperature up to 1 year. If you have a jar that didn't vacuum seal, refrigerate, and use within 1–2 weeks.

MAKES 8 JARS

Note: Rose geranium is a nonflowering plant found at a nursery, usually with the herbs. The leaves make this plant special because they are scented like roses. (There is also a lemon geranium variety.) You can also substitute 1 tablespoon food-safe rosewater.

Peach Cobbler Jam

9 half-pint canning jars, lids and screw-on bands

7½ cups granulated white sugar

4 cups coarsely chopped peaches and their juice

¼ cup freshly squeezed lemon juice

2 tablespoons freshly grated gingerroot

1 tablespoon butter

1 teaspoon ground cinnamon

½ teaspoon freshly grated nutmeg

1 (3-ounce) pouch liquid fruit pectin

1. Sterilize jars, lids and screw-on bands in boiling water for at least 5 minutes. Drain well just before filling jars with prepared preserves.

2. In a large saucepan, combine everything but the pectin. Bring to a boil over medium heat, stirring often to keep from scorching.

3. When you reach a rolling boil (one that you can't stir down), add pectin all at once. Stir well. Return to a boil, and boil exactly 1 minute while stirring constantly. Remove from heat.

4. Pour into hot, sterilized jars. Wipe rims of jars clean. Secure lids with screw-on bands.

5. Place jars of preserves in a boiling water bath for 10 minutes.

6. Carefully remove from water bath, and let stand at room temperature to cool.

7. A couple of hours later, check to be certain all jars vacuum sealed. Leave undisturbed. It may take up to 2 weeks for the gel to completely set. Store at room temperature up to 1 year. If you have a jar that didn't vacuum seal, refrigerate, and use within 1–2 weeks.

MAKES 9 JARS

Jingle Bell Candied Cranberries

1 pound washed fresh cranberries, picked through

2 cups granulated sugar

¼ cup high-quality bourbon

---

1. Preheat oven to 350°F.

2. Fully line the interior of a jelly-roll pan with foil. Spray with nonstick spray. Scatter cranberries in pan.

3. Sprinkle evenly with sugar. Cover tightly with foil.

4. Bake 1 hour. Remove from oven, and drizzle bourbon over cranberries. Let stand 10 minutes. Transfer to a bowl. Store tightly covered in the refrigerator.

MAKES 3 CUPS

Note: Don't you just love it when a recipe has so many uses?! These candied cranberries are truly special and enhance so many dishes. Serve this dish simply as your holiday dinner cranberry dish. Then think of the other ways to enjoy these spiked, candied bits of bliss: as a topping for mixed green salads with blue cheese dressing, with a variety of fine cheeses and crackers, as a topping for baked brie, scattered over roasted poultry, ...

Southern Christmas Ambrosia

SALAD

6 oranges, peeled, cut into sections, or
2 large cans mandarin orange sections,
drained well

1 fresh pineapple, peeled, cored,
cut into 1" chunks

1 cup red seedless grapes, cut in half

2 apples, cored, cut into 1" chunks

1 cup coarsely chopped pecans

1 (6-ounce) package frozen coconut, thawed

½ cup golden raisins or dried cranberries

½ cup thinly sliced celery

DRESSING

2 cups sour cream

½ cup golden or cream sherry

1 packed cup light brown sugar

SALAD

Combine all salad ingredients, and toss well.

DRESSING

Combine all dressing ingredients, and stir until sugar dissolves. Pour dressing over salad. Stir gently. Cover, and refrigerate at least 4 hours or up to 2 days before serving.

SERVES 12

Uptown Down-South Cheese Grits

½ gallon milk

¼ cup butter

2 teaspoons salt

2 cups grits

1 cup whipping cream

6 ounces (1½ cups) grated smoked Gouda cheese

Tabasco sauce to taste

1. In a large saucepan, combine milk, butter and salt. Bring to a boil over medium-high heat.

2. Whisk in grits. Continue to whisk 1 minute more. Reduce heat, cover, and simmer until grits are tender and liquid has been absorbed. Whisk or stir often to discourage lumps and prevent sticking.

3. Add whipping cream, and stir to blend.

4. Stir in cheese, and blend well. Season to taste with Tabasco sauce and additional salt, if needed.

SERVES 8–10

Smoky Pork-Filled Tamales—Page 120
Roasted Corn & Mixed Bean Salsa—Page 126

MAMA CRUZ'S RECIPE FILE

When Helen, Maddie and I decided to open The Corner Spa, not a one of us knew a thing about proper exercise or working out. Oh, we'd take a jab at jogging from time to time or lifting an occasional weight over at Dexter's gym, but we were far from being experts. Truth be told, we weren't all that enthusiastic about exercise. That's when we decided we'd better hire personal trainer Elliott Cruz as an independent contractor to run the fitness side of our business.

I'd like to tell you we made that decision based solely on his résumé, which was rock-solid, but it was his equally rock-solid abs that really won us over. That man could be the poster boy for fitness! I swear, half the women who joined the spa did so just so they could watch him giving lessons. Even our seniors take a weekly jazzercise class just to ogle him and make the sort of smart remarks that make him blush. I'm not kidding! They'll tell you that themselves. Helen's mother, Flo Decatur, is the leader of this outrageous pack.

Still, it was mostly a business relationship (honest!) until Elliott started romancing Karen Ames, a struggling single mom who worked for me at Sullivan's. Then we all discovered the man could cook, and everything he'd learned in the kitchen, he'd learned from his mamacita, Maria Cruz.

As I understand it, Mama Cruz has always kept a tightfisted grip on her recipe secrets, using them as leverage to guarantee that all her children and their families show up every week for Sunday dinner. Karen says her mother-in-law has always sworn she'd take her blend of peppers and spices for her incredible mole sauce to the grave with her just to be sure they come visit the cemetery in the hope she'll communicate it from the great beyond. Somehow, though, Karen managed to wrestle it away from her to include here. Just wait till you taste Mama Cruz's enchilada casserole with classic mole sauce.

Elliott's the one who forked over the seafood paella recipe, a meal that makes good use of all the fresh Lowcountry seafood we have available around here. Add a salad and a nice white wine, and you have the makings for a fabulous party!

Since she's been married to a man who definitely likes a little spice in his life and in his food, Karen's taken to doing her own experimenting here in the Sullivan's kitchen, stealing a page right out of Mama Cruz's book. Her jalapeño mac and cheese has become a local favorite…and it's been quite a boon for our beverage sales, too! First Elliott and now his wife can't seem to go anywhere without generating plenty of heat.

Though I'm all about Southern cooking with a twist at Sullivan's, personally there's nothing I'd like better than having more ethnic specialties available right here in Serenity. When I was growing up, pizza and spaghetti were about as exotic as we got. A Chinese take-out place opened a few years ago. Now that I've sampled a few of Mama Cruz's specialties, I'm thinking there ought to be an authentic Mexican restaurant here in town. Maybe Karen and I need to talk. I wouldn't mind an exciting new business opportunity. Try these recipes, and see what you think.

Dulce De Leche Cheesecake Bars

CRUST

1¼ cups finely crushed Mexican "Maria" cookies, vanilla wafers or graham crackers

½ cup butter, melted

FILLING

1 (8-ounce) package cream cheese, softened

1 cup sugar

3 eggs, room temperature

1 tablespoon vanilla extract

½ teaspoon salt

1 (14-ounce) can dulce de leche

CRUST

① Preheat oven to 350°F.

② Grease a 13" x 9" x 2" baking pan.

③ Combine ingredients and press into bottom of prepared pan. Bake 15 minutes. While crust is baking, prepare filling.

FILLING

① Cream together cream cheese and sugar. Beat in eggs.

② Stir in vanilla and salt, then spread the mixture on the hot baked crust.

③ Heat dulce de leche until very hot and melted, then drizzle it over cheesecake layer. Using a skewer or the tip of a knife, swirl dulce de leche into cheesecake layer.

④ Cover pan tightly with foil and place in a large roasting pan. Add boiling water to roasting pan until water comes halfway up the sides of the baking pan. Bake 1 hour.

⑤ Remove from oven. Carefully lift pan out of water bath and place on a cooling rack, then remove the foil. Let cool to room temperature.

⑥ Cover and store in the refrigerator until ready to serve. Cut into 24 squares.

MAKES 24

Chicken Enchilada Casserole with Speedy Mole Sauce

CASSEROLE

6 boneless, skinless chicken breast halves (about 2¼ pounds total)

1 envelope dry taco seasoning

2 tablespoons vegetable or canola oil

12 ounces shredded Mexican cheese blend

1 (15-ounce) can black beans, rinsed, drained well

1 (15-ounce) can whole-kernel corn, drained well

10 (6-inch) corn tortillas

1½ cups sour cream

SAUCE

1 large medium-diced sweet onion

2 tablespoons vegetable or canola oil

3 tablespoons cocoa powder

1 envelope dry taco seasoning

2 (10¾-ounce) cans tomato soup concentrate

2 (10-ounce) cans mild RO·TEL tomatoes

1 milk chocolate Hershey's bar (no nuts)

GARNISHES (OPTIONAL)

Finely diced fresh jalapeño peppers

Minced fresh cilantro

Sour cream

Guacamole

CASSEROLE

1. Place chicken breast halves on a plate. Sprinkle both sides of each breast with taco seasoning.

2. In a skillet over medium heat, heat oil until hot but not smoking. Add chicken breast halves to skillet. Brown chicken on both sides, turning halfway through cooking, for a total cooking time of about 10 minutes.

3. Remove chicken from pan, and let stand 5 minutes before cutting into thin slices.

SAUCE

1. Sauté onion in oil until crisp tender. Add cocoa powder and taco seasoning.

2. Stir together tomato soup and tomatoes. Add to the sauce, and blend well.

3. Cook over medium heat 5 minutes, stirring often.

4. Remove from heat, and crumble chocolate bar over top. Let stand for several minutes, then stir melted chocolate into the sauce.

ASSEMBLY

1. Preheat oven to 350°F.

2. Grease a 13" × 9" × 2" baking pan.

3. Combine half of the sauce with the thinly sliced chicken breasts. Add half of the cheese blend along with the black beans and corn. Stir to combine.

4. Spoon half of the remaining sauce in the bottom of the prepared pan. Set aside remaining sauce.

5. Divide chicken mixture among the 10 tortillas. Roll tightly.

6. Crowd the filled enchiladas in the pan on top of the sauce. Spoon all remaining sauce over top. Drop sour cream in dollops over the sauce.

7. Cover tightly with foil, and place in center of oven. Bake 40 minutes.

8. Remove casserole from oven, and remove foil. Raise oven temperature to 400°F. Scatter remaining cheese over top of casserole. Return casserole to oven, and cook an additional 10 minutes, until cheese melts and begins to brown.

TO SERVE

Remove casserole from oven, and let stand at least 5 minutes before serving with desired garnishes.

SERVES 6–8

Jacked-Up Tex-Mex Macaroni & Cheese

1 pound breakfast sausage

1 cup chopped onion

1 envelope taco seasoning

1 (14-ounce) can spicy RO·TEL tomatoes

1 cup sour cream

1 pound elbow macaroni, cooked in salted water until al dente, drained well

8 ounces grated cheddar cheese

8 ounces grated Monterey Jack cheese

4 cups milk

6 large eggs, beaten

Salsa of your choice

1. Preheat oven to 350°F.
2. Generously grease a 13" × 9" × 2" baking dish or other suitable casserole dish.
3. In a large skillet over medium-high heat, cook sausage, stirring to crumble.
4. Add onion and taco seasoning. Cook until onion is softened. Remove from heat, and stir in tomatoes and sour cream. Set aside.
5. In bottom of prepared dish, distribute half of the macaroni. Evenly spoon on half of the meat and then half of each cheese. Repeat layering once more.
6. Whisk together milk and eggs. Slowly pour over entire casserole contents.
7. Cover tightly with foil, and bake 45 minutes. Remove foil, and bake an additional 15–20 minutes, until cheese is melted and top is golden brown.
8. Remove from oven, and let stand 7–10 minutes before serving. Serve with salsa.

SERVES 6–8

Pico de Gallo

7 finely chopped jalapeño peppers, ribs and seeds removed

3 Roma tomatoes, seeded, diced

1 small white onion, finely chopped

¼ cup minced fresh cilantro

Juice of 1 lime

Salt to taste

Combine all ingredients, and stir to blend. Cover, and refrigerate up to 1 week.

MAKES 2 CUPS

Note: Brace yourself because this is one brazen pico! Fresh jalapeño peppers have so much flavor. By removing the seeds and ribs from these peppers, about 70% of their heat is removed. If you like this pico hotter still, leave in some of the seeds and ribs.

Smoky Pork-Filled Tamales

1 (8-ounce) package dried corn husks

FILLING
1 (1¼ pounds) pork tenderloin

2 cups large-diced onion

3 garlic cloves, roughly chopped

1 (12-ounce) can beer

SAUCE
1 dried ancho chili pepper

1 tablespoon vegetable oil

1 tablespoon flour

½ cup cooking liquid from pork

1 tablespoon smoked paprika

1 garlic clove, minced

1 teaspoon red wine vinegar

1 teaspoon ground cumin

1 teaspoon fresh oregano or
½ teaspoon dried

½ teaspoon crushed red pepper flakes

Seasoned salt to taste

TAMALE DOUGH
1 cup lard

1 teaspoon salt

3 cups masa harina

1½ cups cooking liquid from pork

HUSKS

Place corn husks in a large bowl. Cover with hot water, and let soak about 3 hours (while the pork filling cooks). Use a dinner plate to help keep the corn husks submerged in the water.

FILLING

1. Place pork tenderloin, onion and garlic in a large pot. Add beer and enough water to cover tenderloin. Bring to a boil.

2. As soon as water boils, reduce heat to simmer, and cover pot with a lid. Simmer at least 3 hours, until pork is tender.

3. When pork is done, remove from pot, reserving 1½ cups of the cooking liquid. Once the pork is cool enough to handle, shred the pork using two forks, then coarsely chop.

SAUCE

1. Toast the ancho in a skillet over medium-high heat. Keep a close eye on the pepper so it doesn't burn. Remove from heat, and let cool until you can handle it.

2. Remove the stem and seeds from the ancho. Crumble and grind in a clean coffee grinder or with a mortar and pestle.

3. Heat oil in a medium saucepan over medium heat. Add flour, and cook until the mixture has browned somewhat and begins to smell nutty.

4. Add ½ cup cooking liquid from pork, stirring until smooth. Add ground ancho and remaining sauce ingredients.

5. Reduce heat to simmer, and add shredded pork. Cover with lid, and let simmer 30 minutes.

TAMALES

1. Using an electric mixer on high speed, blend together lard and salt until light and fluffy.

2. Add masa harina in several additions, and blend at low speed until fully incorporated.

3. Add remaining pork cooking liquid, a little at a time, enough to form a spreadable dough, similar to a soft cookie dough.

4. Remove the corn husks from their soaking water. Working with 1 tamale at a time, flatten out a corn husk. Have the narrow end facing you. Place a dollop (about 2 tablespoons) of dough in center of corn husk. Leaving an outer margin of about ⅓ the husk, spread dough to cover the remaining husk.

5. Spread a heaping tablespoon of pork filling down the center of the tamale. Roll up the corn husk, starting at one of the long sides. Fold the narrow end of the husk onto the rolled tamale, and secure with kitchen twine.

6. Layer tamales in a steamer basket. Steam over boiling water 1 hour. Add water to the steamer as needed during the cooking time.

SERVES 6–8

Note: It's true love and indeed a labor of love when Mama Cruz makes tamales. She normally triples the recipe to feed the crowd. Any leftovers (yeah, right!) can be stored covered in the refrigerator up to 3 days, then steamed again to reheat.

Southern Seafood Paella

4½ cups chicken broth

1 (10-ounce) bottle clam juice

¾ cup white port or dry sherry

2 star anise (do not omit this seasoning)

2 teaspoons sea salt

1 teaspoon smoked paprika

¾ teaspoon crushed red pepper flakes

½ teaspoon saffron threads

1 pound arborio rice

4 tablespoons extra-virgin olive oil

2 large onions, cut into medium dice

4 ounces Spanish chorizo sausage, casing removed, thinly sliced

3 ounces country ham, trimmed, cut into small dice

3 ounces smoked bacon, cut into thin strips

4 garlic cloves, minced

4 ounces fresh green beans, trimmed, cut into 1" pieces

¾ cup frozen peas

10 large sea scallops, cut in half

12 ounces grouper, cut into 1" chunks

18 raw jumbo shrimp, shelled, deveined

1 pound live mussels, scrubbed, beards removed

1 (10-ounce) jar roasted red peppers, drained, cut into strips

1 lemon, thinly sliced

½ cup minced fresh parsley

For sanity's sake, have all ingredients prepped and ready before starting this dish.

1. In a medium saucepan, combine first 8 ingredients to make stock. Bring to a boil, then lower heat to a simmer, and cook at least 15 minutes. Remove star anise from broth. Meanwhile, proceed with recipe.

2. Rinse rice under running water until water runs clear. In a standard (12") paella pan or heavy-bottomed skillet of similar size, heat olive oil until hot but not smoking over medium-high heat. Sauté onions until crisp tender.

3. Add chorizo, country ham and bacon. Cook 2–3 minutes.

4. Stir in garlic, and sauté briefly.

5. Add drained rice, green beans and peas; stir to coat with oil.

6. Add seasoned stock to the rice mixture. Bring to a boil, stirring constantly. Reduce heat to low, and simmer for 15 minutes, cooking uncovered and without stirring.

7. Cover pan with lid or foil, and cook 5 minutes more. Most of the liquid should now be absorbed. If not, cover, and cook an additional 5 minutes.

8. Arrange all of the seafood on top, ending with the shrimp and mussels. Re-cover, and let simmer for an additional 5 minutes, or until the shrimp turns pink, the mussels open, and all liquid has been absorbed. Discard any mussels that do not open.

9. Arrange the red pepper strips and lemon slices over the top. Sprinkle with parsley, and serve immediately.

SERVES 6–8

Note: Don't let the long list of ingredients scare you away from this recipe—it is heavenly! This classic Spanish dish gets all gussied up Southern style. The intense flavors, vibrant colors and festive presentation are a feast for the eyes as well as the palate. This is truly special-occasion fare at its finest!

Black Bean Chili

1 pound ground pork breakfast sausage

1½ cups diced onion

1 tablespoon minced garlic

1 envelope taco seasoning

1 tablespoon dried oregano

1 teaspoon ground cumin

3 cups water

3 (15-ounce) cans black beans, rinsed well, drained

1 (15-ounce) can diced tomatoes

1 (15-ounce) can crushed tomatoes

1 tablespoon red wine vinegar

① In a large soup pot, brown the sausage over medium-high heat, stirring to crumble.

② Add onion, and cook until crisp tender.

③ Add garlic, and cook 1 minute before adding the taco seasoning, oregano and cumin.

④ Add the remaining ingredients. Bring to a boil, then lower heat, cover pot, and let simmer at least 15 minutes.

SERVES 6

Note: Can you keep a secret? Mama Cruz sure can! This is her quick-and-easy—but oh, so tasty—recipe for a super yummy and hearty black bean chili. The flavors are so well balanced and complex that you would swear she had been slaving over a hot stove all day. In truth, it can be made and served in about half an hour—start to finish! Another great thing about this chili is that the ingredients can be easily doubled (or tripled!) to suit your size gathering. Any leftovers freeze well.

Roasted Corn & Mixed Bean Salsa

3 ears corn, shucked, silks removed

1 (15-ounce) can black beans, rinsed, drained

1 (15-ounce) can small red beans, rinsed, drained

3 green onions, minced

1 bell pepper, seeded, diced

2 jalapeño peppers, minced (remove seeds and ribs for milder salsa)

1 cup diced tomato

½ cup balsamic vinaigrette

¼ cup minced cilantro

2 garlic cloves, minced

Salt and pepper to taste

Grill corn on all sides until done. Remove from grill to cool. Cut kernels from cob. Combine with remaining ingredients. Chill thoroughly. Serve with tortilla chips.

SERVES 8–10

Caution: Wear plastic gloves when working with hot peppers, and avoid contact with face.

Tex-Mex Appetizer Cheesecake

CRUST

1½ cups crushed Ritz crackers

¼ cup melted butter

FILLING

2 (8-ounce) packages cream cheese, softened

3 large eggs, beaten

1 envelope taco seasoning

1 (4-ounce) can diced green chili or chipotle peppers, drained well

1 (4-ounce) jar diced pimentos, drained well

8 ounces (2 cups) shredded Mexican cheese blend

1 cup sour cream

GARNISHES (OPTIONAL)

Salsa

Guacamole

Corn chips

CRUST

Preheat oven to 325°F. Spray a 9" springform pan with cooking spray. Stir together cracker crumbs and butter. Press firmly into the bottom of the pan. Bake 15 minutes.

FILLING

1. In a medium mixing bowl, blend together the cream cheese and eggs until smooth.
2. Stir in taco seasoning, peppers and pimentos. Add the shredded cheese, and stir just until incorporated. Pour mixture over baked crust.
3. Bake 30 minutes.
4. Remove from oven. Immediately spread sour cream over cheesecake. Cool to room temperature. Cover, and refrigerate at least 4 hours or up to several days before serving.
5. Release cheesecake from pan. Slice into wedges, and top with your favorite salsa and/or guacamole. Serve with sturdy corn chips.

SERVES 16

Tres Leches Cake

CAKE
6 large eggs, separated

2 cups granulated sugar

2 cups all-purpose flour

2 teaspoons baking powder

¾ teaspoon salt

½ cup whole milk

1 teaspoon vanilla extract

SOAKING LIQUID
1 (14-ounce) can sweetened condensed milk

1 (14-ounce) can evaporated milk

1 cup heavy whipping cream

TOPPING
2 cups heavy whipping cream

¼ cup sugar

1 teaspoon pure vanilla extract

GARNISH
1 pound fresh strawberries, sliced or cut in half

CAKE

1. Preheat oven to 350°F.
2. Lightly grease and flour a 13" × 9" × 2" baking pan.
3. Using an electric mixer, beat egg whites until frothy. Add sugar gradually, beating all the while, until stiff peaks form. Add egg yolks, 1 at a time, beating well after each addition.
4. Whisk together flour, baking powder and salt.
5. Add the flour mixture to the batter alternately with the milk, beginning and ending with the flour mixture. Stir in vanilla extract.
6. Transfer the batter to the prepared pan, and spread the batter level. Bake about 25 minutes, until golden and tester inserted in center comes out clean.
7. Remove from oven, and place on a cooling rack. Pierce cake all over with a wooden skewer.

SOAKING LIQUID

Whisk together the soaking liquid ingredients, but do not incorporate any air into the liquid. Pour mixture over the hot cake in several additions, letting each soak in before adding more. When all the liquid has been absorbed, cover with plastic food wrap, and refrigerate at least 6 hours or up to 3 days before serving.

TOPPING

Combine all topping ingredients in a large mixing bowl. Using an electric mixer, beat on high speed until stiff peaks form. Spread over top surface of cake.

GARNISH

Arrange strawberries on cake or on each individual serving.

SERVES 12

Southern Supreme Red Velvet Cake—Page 134

CHEF ERIK'S DECADENT DESSERTS

When I hired Erik Whitney straight out of the Atlanta Culinary Institute as my pastry chef here at Sullivan's, I suspected he wouldn't stay in Serenity for long. He was a big city guy through and through, an ex-paramedic who'd gone to culinary school after his wife died. He'd done it mostly to shake himself out of his grief. I think he was as shocked as anyone when it became his career destiny.

Despite his claim that he'd found his niche in the world, I figured he'd tire of cooking, grow weary of small-town life or, because he's absolutely fantastic, be hired away by some fancy gourmet restaurant over in Charleston. Believe me, any one of those things could have happened, but I hadn't taken into account the impact my friend Helen would have on him.

It seems the uptight, control-freak lawyer had finally met her match, the one man on Earth who wouldn't take any of her nonsense and trampled right on over her defenses. I claimed an emergency and begged her to help out in the kitchen at Sullivan's more than once just to watch the fireworks between those two! They kept Maddie and me entertained for months as they fought the attraction. They're now happily married and the parents of the most adorable little girl you've ever seen. Feisty little Sarah Beth, the perfect blending of their strong-willed personalities, is going to give them headaches when she hits her teens, I guarantee it.

Though Erik's my sous-chef now, he still specializes in pastry. Believe me, there's no one in these parts who does it better. I'm just waiting for the day when a customer comes in, skips right over the main courses that are my personal pride and joy and goes straight to the dessert menu and orders everything!

Who could resist that traditional Southern favorite, a moist red velvet cake with a frosting that melts in sugary, buttery heaven on the tongue? Then there's the personal favorite of some of my friends, Erik's baked apple bread pudding with homemade cinnamon ice cream and caramel sauce. One of our standbys that's always a hit is the warm walnut brownie, served à la mode with hot fudge sauce. It takes an easy treat and turns it into something divine.

Since I've had my issues with a family history of diabetes, every now and again I push for desserts that even I can eat without guilt. Erik created his no-sugar-added chocolate amaretto cake just for me. Trust me, it makes up for needing to steer clear of some of those other options. Well, maybe not the bread pudding. I've always had a fondness for that. It's something my grandma used to make, though hers couldn't hold a candle to Erik's.

And because I need to watch my sugar intake, here's a little tip I've learned about dessert. Sometimes just a taste or two is enough.

I'm looking into experimenting with those tiny dessert samplers served in some restaurants, no more than a couple of bites in a two-ounce shot glass. I like to call them desserts without guilt or temptation. I figure there aren't enough calories or sugar to throw most diets into a tailspin. And since there's no great big dessert sitting on a plate to tempt you to eat more than you should, well, it just makes life easier.

I'll bet your guests would appreciate that, too. Think about those portion sizes next time you have folks over, and remember that sometimes a little can go a long way when it comes to sweet, heavenly decadence!

Pluff Mud Fudgy Bottom Peanut Butter Icebox Pie

FUDGE
½ cup heavy whipping cream

6 ounces semisweet chocolate chips

CRUST
1 (6-ounce) prepared chocolate cookie crumb crust

FILLING
8 ounces cream cheese

1 cup granulated sugar

1 tablespoon vanilla extract

1 cup creamy peanut butter

1 cup heavy whipping cream, whipped firm

6 coarsely chopped regular-size Reese's peanut butter cups

GARNISHES (OPTIONAL)
Whipped cream

Chopped peanuts

Chopped Reese's peanut butter cups

Chocolate or caramel sauce

FUDGE

1. Heat whipping cream until almost boiling. Remove from heat.
2. Stir in chocolate chips. Cover, and let stand 5 minutes.
3. Whisk until smooth. Spoon ¾ cup into bottom of pie crust, and set aside.
4. Cover, and refrigerate the remaining chocolate sauce. It will be used at serving time as a topping.

FILLING

1. In a mixing bowl, combine cream cheese, sugar and vanilla. Beat until smooth.
2. Beat in peanut butter.
3. Stir in whipping cream until no white streaks appear.
4. Stir in Reese's cups.
5. Spoon into crust over chocolate layer. Cover, and refrigerate (or freeze!).

TO SERVE

Place a wedge of pie in center of dessert plate. Heat remaining fudge until hot and liquid. Spoon or drizzle over pie. Then, top with any desired toppings.

SERVES 6–8

Note: What's not to like here?! Because this dessert is so rich (like cheesecake!), small servings are a must. If you choose to freeze the pie, just remove from freezer 30 minutes before slicing and serving. Yummy!

Southern Supreme Red Velvet Cake

CAKE

1½ cups granulated sugar

½ cup shortening

1 teaspoon vanilla

2 eggs

2 tablespoons cocoa powder

2 ounces red food coloring

2½ cups all-purpose flour

1 teaspoon salt

1 cup buttermilk

1 tablespoon white vinegar

1 teaspoon baking soda

ICING

1¼ cups milk

6 tablespoons flour

1½ cups granulated sugar

1 cup butter, room temperature

1 teaspoon pure vanilla extract

CAKE

1. Preheat oven to 350°F.
2. Grease and flour two 9" round cake pans.
3. In a large mixing bowl, using an electric mixer, cream together sugar, shortening and vanilla. Add eggs, 1 at a time.
4. Make a paste by stirring together cocoa and food coloring. Add to the creamed mixture.
5. Sift together flour and salt. Add alternately with buttermilk to batter, beginning and ending with flour.
6. Combine vinegar and baking soda. Stir into batter.
7. Divide batter evenly between prepared pans. Firmly rap cake pans on countertop to level batter.
8. Bake 30–35 minutes or until a cake tester inserted in center comes out clean. Prepare frosting.
9. Cool in pans 10 minutes on rack. Remove from pans. Cool thoroughly.
10. Split cake layers in half horizontally, making 4 layers total.

CONTINUES →

ICING

① Whisk together milk and flour. Pour through a wire mesh strainer (to remove any lumps) into a medium saucepan. Add sugar to the saucepan.

② Cook mixture over medium heat, stirring constantly, until the mixture thickens and begins to boil. Continue to stir and cook for 2 minutes.

③ Remove from heat and transfer mixture to a mixing bowl. Place in refrigerator about one hour, stirring mixture several times during the cooling period. (Cool mixture to approximately 70°F.)

④ Using an electric mixer, blend the cooled flour/milk/sugar mixture with the room temperature butter. Add vanilla. Beat until light and fluffy, scraping down the bowl several times while beating.

ASSEMBLE

Spread ¼ of the icing between each layer and on the top of the cake. Do not frost sides of cake. Store covered in the refrigerator (or at room temperature during colder months).

SERVES 16–20

Note: This is one of Chef Erik's signature desserts. The icing is just so ethereal, so light and fluffy. If, however, you prefer a cream cheese frosting with your red velvet cake, by all means...

Buttermilk-Glazed Carrot Cake with Orange Cream Cheese Frosting

CAKE

2 cups all-purpose flour

2 teaspoons baking soda

2 teaspoons ground cinnamon

½ teaspoon salt

2 cups sugar

¾ cup vegetable oil

¾ cup buttermilk

3 eggs, beaten

2 teaspoons pure vanilla extract

2 cups grated carrots

1 (8-ounce) can crushed pineapple, drained well

1 cup chopped walnuts

1 (3½-ounce) can flaked coconut

GLAZE

1 cup sugar

½ cup buttermilk

½ cup butter

1 tablespoon light corn syrup

½ teaspoon baking soda

1 teaspoon pure vanilla extract

FROSTING

12 ounces cream cheese, softened

¾ cup butter, softened

3 cups sifted confectioners' sugar

1 tablespoon orange juice concentrate, thawed

1½ teaspoons vanilla extract

1½ teaspoons freshly grated orange zest

CAKE

① Preheat oven to 350°F.

② Grease and flour two 9" round cake pans.

③ Sift together flour, baking soda, cinnamon and salt.

④ In a large mixing bowl, combine sugar, oil, buttermilk, eggs and vanilla. Beat 2 minutes at medium speed using an electric mixer.

⑤ Add flour mixture, and blend. Stir in remaining ingredients.

⑥ Pour batter into prepared pans. Bake 35–40 minutes or until wooden pick inserted in center comes out clean.

⑦ Remove from oven, and place pans on cooling rack.

CONTINUES →

GLAZE

① Combine all ingredients except vanilla in a small saucepan. Bring to a boil, and cook 5 minutes, stirring often.

② Remove from heat, and stir in vanilla.

③ Spread over cakes while cakes are still hot. Cool in pans 15 minutes.

④ Carefully remove from pans, and let layers cool completely.

FROSTING

① Using an electric mixer, blend together cream cheese and butter.

② Add remaining ingredients, and beat until smooth. You may need to refrigerate icing to firm and reach desired spreadable consistency.

③ Spread between cake layers and on the sides and top.

④ Cover, and refrigerate up to 4 days before serving.

SERVES 16–20

Coconut Cream Tart in Pecan Shortbread Crust

CRUST

3 cups pecan sandie cookie crumbs (the size of bread crumbs or slightly more coarse)

½ cup confectioners' sugar

½ cup melted butter

FILLING

1 (15-ounce) container whole-milk ricotta cheese

1 (8-ounce) package cream cheese, softened

1 (4-serving) package coconut instant pudding

1 cup cream of coconut (such as Coco Lopez)

1 cup sifted confectioners' sugar

1 (3½-ounce) can coconut, divided

CRUST

Combine crust ingredients, and mix well. Spoon mixture into a 9–10" tart pan with removable bottom. Press mixture firmly and evenly up sides and in bottom of pan. Refrigerate to firm up and fill later, or proceed.

FILLING

In a medium mixing bowl, combine all ingredients except canned coconut. Beat with an electric mixer until mixture is smooth and creamy. Stir in ⅔ can of coconut. Spoon filling into tart shell, and sprinkle on remaining coconut. Refrigerate until serving time.

SERVES 8

Southern Cream Cheese Pound Cake

3 cups granulated sugar

1 (8-ounce) package cream cheese

1 cup (2 sticks) butter (not margarine)

6 large eggs

3 cups lightly measured cake flour

1 tablespoon pure vanilla extract

1 tablespoon pure almond extract

Finely grated zest of 1 lemon

Note: 1 hour before making pound cake, remove butter, cream cheese and eggs from refrigerator, and let stand at room temperature for only 1 hour.

1. Preheat oven to 325°F.
2. Using a bit of butter and flour, grease and flour either a 12-cup 1-piece tube pan or a 12-cup Bundt pan.
3. In a large bowl, using an electric mixer on medium speed or a standing mixer on medium-low speed, cream together sugar, cream cheese and butter. Blend about 5 minutes.
4. Add eggs, 1 at a time, blending well after each addition.
5. Sift flour 3 times. Add flour in 3 additions to batter, scraping sides and bottom of bowl after each addition. Do not beat batter. Blend just briefly until all flour is incorporated.
6. Stir in extracts and lemon zest.
7. Pour batter into pan. Drop pan onto countertop to level batter and to help remove any air bubbles.
8. Place in center of oven, and bake about 90 minutes, until wooden pick or cake tester inserted into center comes out clean.
9. Remove from oven, and place pan on cooling rack. Let cool 10 minutes.
10. Remove cake from pan, and place on cooling rack. Let cake cool thoroughly. Slice and serve. Store airtight at room temperature.

SERVES 16–20

Cinnamon Roll Bread Pudding with Whipped Vanilla Bean Crème

BREAD PUDDING

2 (11½-ounce) packages store-bought cinnamon rolls with icing

1 quart half-and-half, heated until very warm

1¾ cups sugar, divided

½ cup melted butter

4 eggs, beaten

1 tablespoon pure vanilla extract

½ teaspoon salt

TOPPING

1 (8-ounce) package cream cheese, softened to room temperature

½ cup sugar

1 vanilla bean

1½ cups cold heavy whipping cream

BREAD PUDDING

① Preheat oven to 350°F.

② Grease a 13" × 9" × 2" baking dish.

③ Tear cinnamon rolls into 1" chunks, and set aside.

④ In a large mixing bowl, combine half-and-half, 1½ cups sugar and remaining ingredients. Blend well.

⑤ Add torn cinnamon rolls, and stir to blend.

⑥ Pour mixture into prepared pan. Cover tightly with foil, and bake 45 minutes.

⑦ Remove foil. Sprinkle top with remaining ¼ cup sugar. Return to oven, and bake an additional 15 minutes.

Note: Reheats easily in the microwave.

TOPPING

In a small mixing bowl, beat cream cheese and sugar until sugar is dissolved. Split vanilla bean in half lengthwise. Remove seeds from the inside by scraping with the tip of a knife. Place vanilla bean seeds in with cream cheese and sugar. Add whipping cream slowly, and using an electric mixer, blend on high speed until medium-firm peaks form. Serve on each individual serving of bread pudding.

SERVES 8–10

Note: You'll flip over the simplicity of this dessert, and do back-flips over the taste!!

Baked Apple Bread Pudding with Cinnamon Ice Cream & Caramel Sauce

BREAD PUDDING

1 (10-ounce) loaf stale French bread, thinly sliced

3 cups sugar

3 cups half-and-half

4 eggs, beaten

½ cup melted butter

1 tablespoon pure vanilla extract

1 teaspoon ground cinnamon

½ teaspoon freshly grated nutmeg

1 (20-ounce) can apple pie filling

ICE CREAM

½ gallon vanilla bean ice cream

2 teaspoons ground cinnamon

SAUCE

1 firmly packed cup light brown sugar

½ cup dark corn syrup

6 tablespoons unsalted butter

1½ cups heavy whipping cream

1 teaspoon pure vanilla extract

BREAD PUDDING

1. Preheat oven to 350°F.
2. Generously grease a 13" × 9" × 2" baking pan.
3. Tear bread into pieces, and set aside.
4. Combine sugar, half-and-half, eggs and butter. Beat well.
5. Stir in vanilla, cinnamon and nutmeg. Add apple pie filling and bread pieces. Blend well.
6. Pour into prepared pan. Cover tightly with foil, and bake 1 hour.
7. Remove foil. Return to oven, and bake an additional 15–20 minutes, or until knife inserted in center comes out clean.
8. Cool briefly before serving. Serve alone or topped with cinnamon ice cream and warm caramel sauce.

SERVES 12

ICE CREAM

Remove ice cream from freezer, and let stand at room temperature 5–10 minutes. Stir in cinnamon. Return to freezer to firm up.

SAUCE

1. In a large, heavy saucepan, stir together brown sugar, corn syrup and butter. Cook over medium heat, stirring often, until butter and sugar are melted and the mixture is smooth.

2. Add whipping cream and vanilla. Increase heat to high, and bring to a boil. Continue to boil until caramel is somewhat reduced and reaches 225°F.

MAKES 2½ PINTS

Pumpkin Cake Roll

CAKE

3 eggs

1 cup sugar

¾ cup firmly packed canned pumpkin

¾ cup all-purpose flour

2 tablespoons finely minced crystallized ginger

2 teaspoons ground cinnamon

1 teaspoon baking powder

1 teaspoon ground nutmeg

½ cup chopped pecans

Confectioners' sugar

FILLING

1 (8-ounce) package cream cheese, softened

1 cup confectioners' sugar

4 tablespoons butter, softened

1 teaspoon vanilla

CAKE

① Preheat oven to 375°F.

② Grease 15" × 10" × 1" jelly-roll pan. Line bottom with wax paper or parchment.

③ Using an electric mixer, beat eggs on high speed 5 minutes. Add sugar very gradually, beating until thick. Fold in pumpkin.

④ Combine all dry ingredients except pecans and sugar. Fold into batter.

⑤ Pour into pan, and spread evenly. Sprinkle with chopped pecans. Bake 12–15 minutes.

⑥ Sift confectioners' sugar liberally over a kitchen towel. Turn cake out onto towel. Carefully peel off parchment. Using a pizza wheel, trim away edges. Cool on rack 10 minutes.

⑦ Starting at one of the short sides, roll cake up, towel and all, while cake is still warm. Place seam-side down on cooling rack. Cool thoroughly.

FILLING

Combine all ingredients, and beat until light and fluffy. Carefully unroll cake. Spread with filling. Roll up, peeling away towel from cake as it rolls. Wrap roll securely in plastic wrap. Place seam-side down on tray. Refrigerate several hours or up to 3 days. Freezes well up to 1 month.

TO SERVE

Remove plastic wrap, and place seam-side down on serving platter. Sprinkle with confectioners' sugar. Serve with slightly sweetened whipped cream and a dusting of nutmeg, if desired.

SERVES 8–10

Chocolate Sugarplum Truffles

1½ cups heavy whipping cream

¼ cup high-quality cognac

2 (12-ounce) bags semisweet chocolate chips

½ cup coarsely chopped dried, sweetened cranberries

¼ cup finely chopped dried apricots

¼ cup dried currants

European-processed cocoa powder

1. In a microwave-safe dish, combine whipping cream and cognac. Heat just to a boil.

2. Remove from microwave, and stir in chocolate. Let stand 5 minutes.

3. Whisk until melted and smooth. Stir in dried fruits. Cool to room temperature.

4. Cover, and refrigerate until firm.

5. Shape into 1" balls, and roll in cocoa. Cover, and refrigerate up to 1 month.

MAKES ABOUT 4 DOZEN

Note: This recipe calls for you to roll the prepared truffle in cocoa powder. If you prefer your truffles to have a hard chocolate shell, you can freeze the truffles first, then dip the frozen truffles, one at a time, into melted chocolate. Let harden completely before storing airtight.

Deep-Dish Apple Pie with Crunchy Crumb Topping

CRUST

1½ cups all-purpose flour

5 tablespoons shortening or lard

4 tablespoons butter, cut into cubes

½ teaspoon salt

3 tablespoons ice water

FILLING

5 cups very thinly sliced, peeled, cored Granny Smith apples

¼ cup flour

½ packed cup light brown sugar

½ cup granulated sugar

1½ teaspoons apple pie spice

TOPPING

¾ cup flour

⅓ cup sugar

½ cup butter, softened

Note: This recipe includes a no-fail pie crust!

CRUST

1. At least 30 minutes before making the pie crust, combine the first 4 ingredients in the bowl of a food processor fitted with the metal blade, and chill for at least 30 minutes. (This cold method ensures a flaky crust.)

2. When the ingredients are cold, place the bowl on the food processor, and pulse a few times to incorporate the ingredients.

3. With the machine running, add the water through the top of the machine. Do not overwork the dough. Process it just until the dough becomes quite crumbly and does not gather up into a ball in the food processor.

4. Gather the dough into a ball with your hands. You may squeeze the dough to help it stay together. If it still won't form a ball, you can add a tiny bit more ice water. Shape the ball into a flat disc. Wrap in plastic food wrap, and refrigerate at least 30 minutes.

5. On a cool, lightly floured surface, roll dough out to fit your deep-dish pie plate. Transfer dough, and fit into the pie plate, turning edges under and crimping the rim of the crust.

FILLING

Preheat oven to 350°F. Toss the apple slices with the flour. Add sugars and apple pie spice to the apples. Transfer mixture to the pie crust.

TOPPING

Using your hands, combine the flour and sugar. Work in the butter until you have large clumps. Distribute evenly over the apple filling.

PIE

Place pie in center of oven. Bake about 1 hour, covering top of pie with foil if the crust edge and/or crumb topping seems to be browning too quickly. Remove from oven, and let cool for at least 30 minutes before slicing.

SERVES 6–8

Valentine's Special Decadence Cake
(flourless chocolate cake)

CAKE

¾ cup butter, cut into small pieces

1 (12-ounce) bag semisweet chocolate chips

6 large eggs, separated

12 tablespoons sugar, divided

2 teaspoons pure vanilla extract

GLAZE

½ cup heavy whipping cream

½ cup dark corn syrup

1 (12-ounce) bag semisweet chocolate chips

CAKE

1. Preheat oven to 350°F.

2. Grease a 9" springform pan. Line bottom with parchment or wax paper. Wrap entire outside of pan with heavy-duty foil.

3. Melt butter, and bring to a boil.

4. Place chocolate chips in a medium mixing bowl. Pour hot butter over chocolate, and let stand 5 minutes. Stir until smooth.

5. Using an electric mixer, beat egg yolks and 6 tablespoons sugar in a large bowl until mixture is thick and pale, about 3 minutes.

6. Add chocolate mixture and vanilla to yolk mixture. Stir until smooth.

7. Using clean, dry beaters, beat egg whites in a large bowl until soft peaks form. Gradually add remaining 6 tablespoons sugar, beating until stiff. Fold into chocolate mixture in 3 additions.

8. Pour batter into prepared pan. Bake 1 hour. Cake top will be puffed and cracked when done.

9. Cool cake in pan on cooling rack 15 minutes. Cake will fall.

10. Using a spatula or the back of a large spoon, press edges of cake to be level with the center. Leave cake in pan until thoroughly cooled.

11. Run thin knife around inside edge to loosen cake. Remove wall of springform pan. Invert cake onto a 9" cardboard round. Peel off parchment.

CONTINUES →

GLAZE

1. In a medium saucepan, bring cream and corn syrup to a boil.

2. Remove from heat, and add chocolate. Let rest 5 minutes.

3. Gently stir until smooth; you do not want to create any air bubbles in the glaze.

4. Cover a work surface with parchment or foil. In the center of your prepared work surface, elevate the cake (on the cardboard round) by placing it on top of a bowl smaller than the cardboard round.

5. Spread 1 cup glaze over cake top. Pour glaze over cake sides. Using an icing spatula, scrape up glaze that has dripped onto parchment to reuse. Repeat glazing the cake top and sides until almost all glaze is used. Wipe clean the bottom rim of cardboard round. Place cake on a platter, and chill at least 1 hour or until glaze is firm. Can be made up to 3 days ahead.

TO SERVE

Serve with lightly sweetened, freshly whipped cream or fresh berries. Add garnish if desired.

SERVES 12

GARNISH (OPTIONAL)

Pour a few ounces of melted chocolate into a freezer-strength zip-top bag. Snip a tiny hole in corner of bag. On parchment or waxed paper, drizzle chocolate into desired shapes. (I think a heart shape is romantic.) Let chocolate harden. Carefully peel away from parchment. Or make chocolate curls and sprinkle with confectioners' sugar.

Note: Beware, chocoholics—you may have met your match here!!

Warm Walnut Brownie à la Mode with Hot Fudge Sauce

BROWNIE

2 cups sugar

1½ cups all-purpose flour

¾ cup cocoa powder

1 teaspoon salt

1 cup melted butter, cooled a bit

5 eggs, beaten

1 teaspoon vanilla

1½ cups chopped walnuts

6 ounces semisweet chocolate chips

HOT FUDGE SAUCE

⅓ cup heavy whipping cream

⅓ cup light corn syrup

6 ounces semisweet chocolate chips

BROWNIE

1. Preheat oven to 350°F.
2. Grease a 13" × 9" × 2" baking pan.
3. In a large mixing bowl, combine first 4 ingredients.
4. Whisk together butter, eggs and vanilla. Add wet ingredients to dry ingredients, and stir. Do not overmix. Add walnuts and chocolate chips.
5. Pour batter into prepared pan. Spread batter level. Bake 30 minutes.
6. Cool 30 minutes before slicing and serving with ice cream and hot fudge sauce. Store airtight up to 2 days.

HOT FUDGE SAUCE

In a microwave-safe bowl, combine whipping cream and corn syrup. Cook on high power until mixture comes to a boil. Add chocolate chips, and let stand at room temperature 5 minutes. Whisk until smooth. Serve warm over anything that could stand a deep, rich chocolate sauce. This keeps for up to 6 months covered in the refrigerator and can be reheated.

SERVES 12

Candied Orange Peel

6 large oranges

Cold water

3 cups granulated sugar, divided

1. Wash oranges. Using an orange peeler or knife, score orange into quarters. Remove orange peel, keeping peel intact. (Save oranges for another use.) Slice peel diagonally into thin strips.

2. Place in a large saucepan or Dutch oven. Fill pot ¾ full with cold water. Bring to a boil, and boil for 1 minute. Drain oranges.

3. Return orange peel to pot, and repeat procedure 4 more times. (This removes the bitterness from the peel.) Have ready baking sheets lined with paper towels.

4. Bring 2 cups granulated sugar and 1 cup water to a boil, stirring until sugar is dissolved.

5. Add drained orange peel to syrup. Cook orange peel in syrup about 10 minutes, stirring constantly. The peel will absorb most of the syrup.

6. Drain off any remaining syrup. Using tongs, transfer candied orange peel to prepared baking sheets, arranging in single layers and allowing a bit of space between each piece. Dry at room temperature at least 4 hours.

7. Coat candied peel in remaining 1 cup granulated sugar, shaking off excess. Store airtight at room temperature up to 1 week or in the freezer up to 2 months. Use in recipes calling for candied orange peel.

MAKES ABOUT 6 CUPS

Note: Although time consuming, this recipe isn't hard to make and is well worth the effort. For a special Christmas treat, take the candied peel (but not sugar coated), and dip the pieces in melted dark chocolate. After letting the chocolate harden on the candied peel, store airtight at room temperature for up to 1 month.

Southern Pecan Toffee

1 stack saltine crackers

1 cup unsalted butter

1 packed cup brown sugar

1 cup chopped pecans

1 (8-ounce) bag brickle bits
(Heath bar toffee chips)

1 (12-ounce) bag milk chocolate chips

1. Preheat oven to 375°F.

2. Completely line the interior of a 15" × 10" × 1" jelly-roll pan with aluminum foil. Smooth out all wrinkles, and spray with nonstick cooking spray. Place saltines in pan side by side.

3. In a medium saucepan, melt butter. Stir in brown sugar and pecans. Bring to a boil. Stirring occasionally, let mixture boil 5 minutes only.

4. Remove from heat. Pour mixture over saltines. Bake 10 minutes.

5. Remove from oven, and place on cooling rack. Immediately sprinkle half the bag of brickle bits over hot toffee. Evenly distribute chocolate chips over hot toffee. Let stand several minutes.

6. Using an off-set spatula, spread chocolate over toffee. Immediately sprinkle remaining brickle bits over melted chocolate. Cover tightly with foil, and let cool until firm. (Note: You can speed this up by placing in the refrigerator; just make sure that it is tightly covered with foil so it doesn't pick up any humidity.)

7. Remove from refrigerator, and break into pieces like peanut brittle. Store airtight at room temperature.

SERVES 20

Warning: This stuff has to be as addictive as any substance ever imagined. There surely is a support group out there somewhere whose members, although anonymous, all have melted chocolate in the corners of their mouths and bits of toffee stuck in their back teeth!

Chocolate Amaretto Cake
(no sugar added)

CAKE

1 cup milk

½ cup canola or vegetable oil

2 large eggs

1 teaspoon pure almond extract

1 teaspoon pure vanilla extract

2¼ cups baking Splenda

1¾ cups all-purpose flour

¾ cup cocoa powder

1 teaspoon salt

½ teaspoon baking powder

½ teaspoon baking soda

½ cup boiling water

½ cup amaretto

TOPPING

¾ cup thinly sliced almonds

1 cup heavy whipping cream

2 tablespoons baking Splenda

½ teaspoon pure almond extract

CAKE

1. Preheat oven to 350°F.

2. Grease and flour two 8" round cake pans.

3. In a mixing bowl, combine milk, oil, eggs and extracts. Blend together.

4. In a separate bowl, whisk together Splenda, flour, cocoa, salt, baking powder and baking soda. Add to the wet ingredients.

5. Using an electric mixer, beat on medium speed for 2 minutes.

6. Combine boiling water and amaretto. Add slowly to batter, and blend thoroughly. Batter will be very thin.

7. Divide batter evenly between the two cake pans. Bake 10 minutes.

8. Turn cake layers out of pans onto cooling racks. Let cool thoroughly.

TOPPING

After the cake layers come out of the oven, scatter the almonds on a baking sheet, and bake at 350°F about 8 minutes, until lightly browned and almonds begin to smell toasted. Set aside to cool. In a medium mixing bowl, combine whipping cream, Splenda and almond extract. Beat on high speed until firm peaks hold.

TO SERVE

Cut cake layers into wedges or chunks. Place cake on dessert plates. Top with the whipped cream and toasted almonds.

SERVES 12

Vidalia Onion Vinaigrette—Page 161

THE CORNER SPA'S LOW-CAL HEALTHY SELECTIONS

When Maddie was going through her divorce, tensions were running pretty high among the Sweet Magnolias. I'd been divorced from Ronnie for a while, but I knew better than anyone that what Maddie really needed was a challenge. Not that being a single mom to three children isn't difficult enough, but Helen and I knew Maddie needed to get her legs back under her. What she needed most of all was a boost to her self-esteem.

And what we all needed was a pleasant place to exercise. I mean, it's not as if a one of us could work up any enthusiasm for the treadmill in the first place, but at least it needed to be located someplace that wasn't a dump. Dexter's gym was all Serenity had, and sweet as he is, Dexter had let the place get so run-down, only the desperate would go there for a workout.

What Serenity needed—or at least what the women in town needed—was a place not only to get fit but to be pampered too. The minute the idea came to me and Helen, we were all over it, but Maddie took a whole lot of convincing, especially since she had only sweat equity to contribute. I think once she realized how difficult it was going to be to create a business plan, deal with renovations and get the doors open, she started feeling a whole lot better about her contribution. She was, after all, putting in the hard work. All Helen and I did was give her a budget to work with. She made The Corner Spa the success it is today, and she did it practically single-handedly, which not only assured us a healthy bottom line but also gave her self-esteem just the boost it needed.

Despite all the credit that belongs to Maddie, I'd like to think at least part of The Corner Spa's success is due to the little café we created so women could take a break after working out or getting a massage or mani-pedi. Of course, the menu had to be healthy. And since we weren't going to have a kitchen on the premises, it had to be simple, special things that could be prepared fresh at Sullivan's each day or easily blended right on the premises.

Our smoothies are one of the most popular items we serve. Who wouldn't enjoy sitting under a big ol' shade tree on our brick patio with a tropical fruit smoothie after a hard workout? Or how about a bowl of spicy, chilled gazpacho? Talk about refreshing!

Because every woman tends to feel incredibly virtuous after an hour or so of exercise, there's no reason to spoil that mood with something heavy. Our low-fat chunky apple muffins with a glass of tea seem faintly decadent, but they won't break the calorie bank.

My personal favorite for the woman who needs to grab something quick on the go after using her lunch hour to work out is our chicken Caesar salad wrap. It's low-calorie and filling but light enough that it won't ruin that high that comes from putting in some time on the treadmill.

In fact, that's what all the recipes in this section are about: healthy eating, whether it's after a workout or just an alternative on a hot summer evening. And these just go to prove that tasty doesn't have to be loaded down with fat!

Corner Spa Tortilla Soup (low-fat)

8 ounces boneless, skinless chicken breasts, cubed

2 cups frozen whole-kernel corn, thawed

2 (14½-ounce) cans fat-free chicken broth (low-sodium preferred)

1 (10¾-ounce) can tomato puree

1 (10-ounce) can diced tomatoes and green chilies

1 large onion, chopped

2–3 garlic cloves, pressed or minced

1 tablespoon sugar

2 teaspoons ham base or bouillon

2 teaspoons ground cumin

1 teaspoon chili powder

⅛–¼ teaspoon cayenne pepper

2 bay leaves

4 (5½") corn tortillas

GARNISHES (OPTIONAL)
Chopped fresh cilantro

Fat-free or low-fat sour cream

Note: This recipe can be prepared in a slow cooker or on the stovetop.

SLOW COOKER

Combine all ingredients except the tortillas in a 4-quart slow cooker. Cover, and cook on high 6–8 hours.

STOVETOP

Combine all ingredients except the tortillas in a Dutch oven, and bring to a boil over medium-high heat, stirring occasionally. Reduce heat to low, and simmer 1 hour minimum.

1. Preheat oven to 375°F.
2. Remove and discard bay leaves.
3. Cut tortillas into ¼"-wide strips, and place on baking sheet. Bake 5 minutes.
4. Stir and rearrange tortillas on baking sheet. Bake additional 5 minutes or just until crisp.
5. Ladle soup into soup bowls. Sprinkle tops with crispy tortilla strips, and garnishes.

SERVES 8–10

Summer Gazpacho

2 large vine-ripe tomatoes or 6 Roma tomatoes, peeled

1 cucumber, peeled, seeded

½ bell pepper, seeded

½ cup fresh parsley

1 (46-ounce) can tomato juice

¼ cup extra-virgin olive oil

¼ cup red wine vinegar

1 tablespoon Worcestershire sauce

½ teaspoon Tabasco sauce

Salt and pepper to taste

1 lemon, thinly sliced

1 cup sour cream

GARNISH (OPTIONAL)
Minced cilantro or parsley sprigs

1. Place tomatoes, cucumber, bell pepper and parsley in a food processor or blender, and process until finely minced.
2. Add tomato juice, olive oil, vinegar, Worcestershire sauce, Tabasco, salt and pepper, and stir to combine well.
3. Add lemon slices, and stir into soup.
4. Refrigerate, and allow flavors to develop several hours until mixture is thoroughly chilled.

TO SERVE
Ladle into chilled soup bowls, and place a dollop of sour cream on top. Garnish with minced cilantro or additional parsley.

SERVES 8

Vidalia Onion Vinaigrette
(fat-free)

1 large Vidalia onion or
other sweet onion

½ cup white wine
Worcestershire sauce

½ cup water

¼ cup honey

2 tablespoons coarse-grain
Dijon mustard

Celery salt and freshly
ground black pepper to taste

Combine all ingredients in container of food processor
or blender. Blend until smooth. Cover, and refrigerate
up to 1 week.

MAKES 2½ CUPS

Corner Spa Cream of Carrot Soup
(low-fat)

2 cups chicken or vegetable stock

1 pound carrots, peeled, thinly sliced

1 medium onion, diced

1 cup sliced celery

2 tablespoons minced fresh mint or 2 teaspoons dried, crushed

2 cups soy milk

1 teaspoon MAGGI liquid seasoning*

Salt and pepper to taste

GARNISHES (OPTIONAL)

Sour cream

Minced fresh mint

In a Dutch oven, combine the first 5 ingredients. Bring to a boil over high heat. Cook until vegetables are tender. Using a blender, puree mixture (in batches if necessary). Combine pureed mixture with soy milk. Heat through. Season with MAGGI seasoning, salt and pepper. Garnish with a drizzle of sour cream and minced fresh mint.

SERVES 6

*NOTE: MAGGI liquid seasoning can be easily found in the soup aisle of most grocery stores.

Cucumber Cooler

1 cucumber, peeled, seeded, coarsely grated

1 quart cold water

1 (1-liter) bottle chilled lemon-lime soda

1 (1-liter) bottle seltzer or sparkling water

GARNISHES (OPTIONAL)

Thin cucumber slices

Lemon slices

Lime slices

In a pitcher, combine grated cucumber and water. Cover, and refrigerate at least 2 hours or up to 24 hours before serving. Strain, and discard cucumber. When ready to serve, combine cucumber essence water with remaining ingredients. Serve in tall glasses over crushed ice. Garnish with cucumber, lemon and lime slices.

MAKES ABOUT 3 QUARTS

Note: Talk about refreshing—this cooler is a girl's best friend after a good workout at The Corner Spa.

Southern Legacy Apple & Mint Spritzer
(no sugar added)

4 cups water

1 packed cup mint leaves

Grated zest from 1 lime

4 cups apple juice

Freshly squeezed juice of 1 lime

1 (2-liter) bottle diet lemon-lime soda, chilled

GARNISHES (OPTIONAL)
Lime slices

Apple wedges

Mint sprigs

Bring water to a boil. Remove from heat. Add mint and lime zest. Cover and let steep at least 30 minutes. Strain, and discard lime zest and mint. Cool the flavored water. When ready to serve, combine the flavored water with the remaining ingredients. Serve in tall glasses over ice. Garnish with lime slices, apple wedges and mint sprigs.

MAKES ABOUT 1 GALLON

Fuzzy Navel Smoothie

1 (6-ounce) container fat-free, no-sugar-added peach yogurt

1 cup frozen peach slices

1 cup freshly squeezed orange juice

Place all ingredients in a blender. Process until smooth. Serve immediately.

SERVES 2

Chunky Apple Bran Muffins
(low-fat)

1½ cups wheat bran

1 cup low-fat buttermilk

1 cup all-purpose flour

½ packed cup brown sugar

1 teaspoon cinnamon

1 teaspoon baking soda

½ teaspoon salt

2 egg whites

1 teaspoon pure vanilla extract

2 medium apples, cored, medium diced

1. Preheat oven to 350°F. Line a 12-cup muffin tin with paper liners, or use a nonstick cooking spray.

2. Whisk together wheat bran and buttermilk. Set aside to soak for 10 minutes.

3. In a mixing bowl, mix together flour, brown sugar, cinnamon, baking soda and salt. Whisk egg whites and vanilla into the bran mixture.

4. Combine the wet and dry mixtures, and blend briefly. Stir in the apples by hand.

5. Divide batter among the muffin cups. Bake 18–20 minutes, until a pick inserted in center comes out clean.

MAKES 12

Almond Biscotti

¾ cup sugar

½ cup butter, softened

2 eggs, beaten

2 teaspoons almond extract

2½ cups all-purpose flour

1 tablespoon baking powder

¾ teaspoon salt

²/₃ cup coarsely chopped toasted almonds

Milk

1. Preheat oven to 350°F.
2. Line cookie sheet with nonstick aluminum foil or parchment.
3. In a large mixing bowl, using an electric mixer, cream sugar and butter until light and fluffy.
4. Add eggs and almond extract. Mix well.
5. Combine dry ingredients except nuts, and add to dough. Dough will be very stiff. Stir in nuts by hand.
6. With floured hands, divide dough in half. Shape each half into a log measuring 14" × 3". Place logs, several inches apart, on prepared cookie sheet. Smooth the top of each. Brush with milk, then sprinkle with additional sugar.
7. Bake 25–30 minutes, until golden brown.

CONTINUES →

8. Remove from oven. Reduce oven temperature to 300°F.

9. Carefully transfer loaves to cooling rack. Cool 10 minutes.

10. Carefully transfer to cutting board. Using assertive force, slice on the diagonal into ¾" slices.

11. Place upright on baking sheet, allowing a bit of space between pieces. Bake at reduced temperature 20 minutes (to dry out biscotti).

12. Remove from oven, and transfer to cooling racks. Cool thoroughly. Store airtight up to 1 month. Freezes beautifully.

MAKES 3 DOZEN

Note: These Italian twice-baked cookies are simple to make. They're a bit time consuming but well worth the effort. They are best enjoyed with a cup of coffee, cappuccino, hot tea, port or dessert wine. Go ahead and dunk them. Although the little old genteel ladies of Charleston might not agree, it's well accepted to do so.

Chicken Caesar Salad Wraps

1 pound boneless, skinless chicken breast halves

1 tablespoon garlic salt

1 tablespoon minced fresh rosemary

1 teaspoon freshly ground black pepper

1 large head romaine lettuce, torn into bite-size pieces

1 cup low-fat garlic croutons

1 cup homemade or store-bought Caesar salad dressing

6 (8") flour tortillas

½ cup freshly grated Parmesan cheese

GARNISHES (OPTIONAL)

Fresh fruit

Celery slices

Thinly sliced carrots

1. Rinse and pat dry chicken. Lay side by side on a surface lined with paper towels.

2. Blend together garlic salt, rosemary and pepper. Evenly divide among the chicken breasts, and rub into the chicken.

3. In a large skillet over medium-high heat, cook chicken breasts about 10 minutes, turning halfway through cooking. Chicken is thoroughly cooked at 165°F. (Every cook should have at least 1 instant-read thermometer.)

4. Remove chicken from skillet, and let cool to room temperature.

5. Once cooled, cut chicken into very thin strips. Combine with lettuce, croutons and salad dressing.

6. On a clean kitchen work surface, lay tortillas side by side. Divide the salad mixture among the tortillas. Sprinkle Parmesan over the salad. Wrap each sandwich like a burrito. Wrap in parchment paper, and refrigerate up to 8 hours before serving.

TO SERVE

Leaving the parchment paper wrapping on the sandwich, cut sandwich in half diagonally. Serve with a fresh fruit garnish and a few pieces of celery and thinly sliced carrots.

Mixed Salad with Strawberry & Basil Vinaigrette

VINAIGRETTE

1 cup sliced strawberries

4 packets Splenda

$1/3$ cup white balsamic vinegar

2 tablespoons minced fresh basil
or 2 teaspoons dried

1 cup vegetable oil

Salt and freshly ground black pepper
to taste

SALAD

Mixture of baby lettuces and crisp lettuce
(such as red leaf, romaine or Bibb)

1 red onion, very thinly sliced and separated
into rings

GARNISH (OPTIONAL)

Caramelized almonds

VINAIGRETTE

In food processor or blender, combine strawberries and their juice, along with Splenda, with vinegar and basil. With machine running, add oil in a thin, steady stream. Process 1 minute more. Season with salt and pepper to taste.

SALAD

Combine ingredients, and serve with strawberry vinaigrette and caramelized almonds.

SERVES 6–8

Balsamic Vinaigrette
(fat-free)

2 teaspoons cornstarch

1 cup water

¾ cup balsamic vinegar

¼ cup orange marmalade

¼ cup dried minced onion

1 tablespoon minced fresh garlic

1 tablespoon minced fresh basil

2 teaspoons seasoned salt

1½ teaspoons minced fresh thyme or ½ teaspoon dried

1½ teaspoons minced fresh oregano or ½ teaspoon dried

½ teaspoon freshly ground black pepper

1 bay leaf

Dissolve cornstarch in water. In a blender, combine dissolved cornstarch with remaining ingredients except bay leaf. Process until smooth. Transfer to a small saucepan, and add bay leaf. Bring to a boil over medium heat, stirring occasionally. Remove from heat, and cool thoroughly. Remove bay leaf. Cover, and refrigerate up to 1 month.

MAKES 2 CUPS

Gold Nugget Chicken & Pasta Salad

SALAD

3 pounds boneless, skinless grilled chicken breasts, cut into chunks

8 ounces whole-grain rotini pasta, cooked according to package directions, drained well

1½ cups thinly sliced celery

½ cup finely diced fresh pineapple

½ cup chopped dried papaya

½ cup chopped dried mango

½ cup golden raisins

DRESSING

1 cup low-fat mayonnaise

2 teaspoons curry powder

Salt and freshly ground black pepper to taste

GARNISH

1 cup roasted, salted cashew halves

In a large mixing bowl, combine all salad ingredients. Whisk together the dressing ingredients. Spoon dressing over salad, and stir well to blend. Cover, and refrigerate at least 4 hours or up to 4 days before serving. Garnish each serving with a sprinkling of cashew halves.

SERVES 8

Old-Fashioned Molasses Cookies—Page 213

HOLIDAYS & GET-TOGETHERS

In Serenity, there's nothing we love more than our holiday celebrations and community events. Whether it's the annual Fourth of July parade with its accompanying hoopla, backyard barbecues and fireworks, our fall festival or Christmas with Santa on the town green, we'll use any excuse to gather and celebrate.

The Sweet Magnolias are no different. Not every gathering is a margarita night. We bring our whole families together for everything, from birthday parties to cookouts at the drop of a hat, just the way I'm sure you do with your friends and neighbors. If you don't, then start making time for these relaxing get-togethers.

With so many of us these days, along with our growing number of children and grandchildren, it's quite a crowd. We dole out assignments, and everyone brings along a specialty, made in quantities large enough to feed a lot of people. Some things are traditional, and we simply couldn't have a party without them.

It's gotten to be a huge joke around town that no Serenity Christmas tree-lighting ceremony would be complete without eggnog. Believe you me, that raised a few eyebrows at first, especially with newcomers to Serenity, but we serve an alcohol-free version that suits the town's holiday spirit just fine. It makes our police chief and town manager happier, too.

Right after the annual Fourth of July parade, no barbecue at my place would be complete without front porch sippin' lemonade. There's nothing better on a hot summer day, and around these parts you can just about guarantee there will be heat and humidity on the Fourth. After watching all the former members of the armed forces, elaborate floats and bands march through town, that lemonade is the perfect antidote to being parched. It also gives us just enough refreshing oomph to pay a visit to all the vendors who come to town for the occasion before we settle down with our burgers, hot dogs and potato salad.

Usually we like to stick to the traditional barbecue on the Fourth, but at least once during the summer we get together for a backyard Lowcountry seafood boil. Oh, my! All that fresh, succulent seafood just reminds us how blessed we are to live in this area. Now you'll be able to try it wherever you are.

Whenever we're getting together, just us Sweet Magnolias, for a baby or wedding shower, for instance, we like to pull out all the stops and do something a little special. The amaretto and pecan baked brie makes eyes light up. The last time we were together, I made Erik's grilled cheese panini with a pecan-pesto mayonnaise and spicy tomato jam. Once you've tried it, you'll never look at a plain old grilled cheese sandwich the same way again. I guarantee it.

And, of course, no New Year's celebration down South would be complete without hoppin' John New Year's salad. They say it brings luck throughout the whole year. I can't swear there's any truth to that, but I do know that the Sweet Magnolias have had more than their share of luck over the years. Oh, we've had our trials and disappointments, but I'd have to say we've faced them all with courage and grace. And, most important of all, of course, we've not once faced them alone.

Down here in Serenity, we like to set a table loaded down with incredible food whenever we get together. It's a key ingredient to the Southern hospitality on which we all pride ourselves. But, if you ask me, the most important ingredient of all is friendship. With a glass of sweet tea or a margarita and a friend by your side, there's not a thing in the world that can keep you down for long! Try it, and see if that's not so.

Christmas Festival Eggnog
(alcohol-free)

4 cups whole milk

8 whole cloves

2 (3") cinnamon sticks

1 whole nutmeg, broken into bits using a rolling pin or meat mallet

12 egg yolks

1²/₃ cups sugar, divided

4 cups half-and-half

1 tablespoon rum extract

2 cups heavy whipping cream

1 teaspoon pure vanilla extract

½ teaspoon freshly grated nutmeg

1. Combine milk, cloves, cinnamon sticks and nutmeg in a large saucepan. Cook over medium-low heat, stirring often. Bring to a low boil.

2. In a large bowl, combine egg yolks and 1⅓ cups sugar. Beat together until fluffy.

3. Whisk the hot milk mixture into the egg yolk mixture very slowly.

4. Return mixture to the saucepan. Cook over medium heat 3–5 minutes, stirring constantly until mixture thickens. Do not allow mixture to boil.

5. Strain mixture through a fine-wire mesh strainer. Let cool at least 1 hour.

6. Stir in half-and-half and rum extract. Cover, and refrigerate until thoroughly chilled or up to 4 days before serving.

7. Just before serving, beat together heavy cream, remaining ⅓ cup sugar and vanilla until soft peaks form.

8. Pour eggnog into a small punch bowl. Drop whipped cream into the mixture in dollops, then fold into the eggnog. Add freshly grated nutmeg to float on top.

MAKES 1 GALLON

Poinsettia Punch

2 (12-ounce) bags frozen raspberries, thawed

1 (12-ounce) can frozen pink lemonade concentrate, thawed

½ cup sugar

1 (750-milliliter) bottle white zinfandel wine, chilled

1 (2-liter) bottle raspberry-flavored or regular ginger ale, chilled

In a food processor, blend together raspberries, lemonade concentrate and sugar. Process 1 minute. Pour mixture through a wire mesh strainer, pressing mixture against the sides of the strainer. Discard seeds. Refrigerate raspberry mixture until thoroughly chilled. When ready to serve, blend with wine and ginger ale.

MAKES 1 GALLON

Note: This gorgeous punch has a low alcohol content and is the perfect choice when you want to serve up just a little holiday "spirit." You may also leave out the wine totally, replacing it with an equal amount of cran-raspberry juice cocktail.

Golden Wassail
(alcohol-free)

½ gallon apple cider

1 (46-ounce) can pineapple juice

2 (12-ounce) cans apricot nectar

4 cups water

1 cup sugar

1 (6-ounce) can frozen orange juice concentrate, thawed

1 (6-ounce) can frozen lemonade concentrate, thawed

24 whole cloves

6 (3") cinnamon sticks

In a Dutch oven, combine all ingredients. Bring to a boil. Reduce heat, cover, and simmer 45 minutes to 1 hour. Strain, and discard spices. Serve hot. Refrigerate up to 2 weeks.

MAKES ABOUT 5 QUARTS

White Sangria

1 (2-liter) bottle lemon-lime soda, chilled

1 (750-milliliter) bottle white wine, chilled

2 (12-ounce) cans guanabana nectar (found in Mexican food section in grocery stores and in Mexican markets)

1 (12-ounce) can frozen lemonade concentrate, thawed

1 (12-ounce) can frozen limeade concentrate, thawed

1 (10-ounce) can frozen piña colada drink mix, thawed

1–2 cups vodka (you decide!)

GARNISHES (OPTIONAL)
Lemon slices

Lime slices

Fresh pineapple chunks

Combine all ingredients, and serve cold with lemon, lime and pineapple.

MAKES 5 QUARTS

Note: Don't you just love sangria?! This is not *your ordinary sangria. Because it is light in color, it makes a beautiful presentation in a pitcher or punch bowl with all the lemon and lime slices and chunks of fresh pineapple. It's great for sipping the summer away. Make a nonalcoholic version for the kids simply by replacing the wine and vodka with more lemon-lime soda.*

Front Porch Sippin' Lemonade

2 pounds lemons, washed

2 cups boiling water

1½ cups sugar

Cold water

(1) Using a vegetable peeler, remove zest from lemons. Add lemon zest to boiling water. Cover, and let steep 30 minutes.

(2) Remove and discard lemon zest. Add sugar to warm lemon water. Stir to dissolve. Let lemon syrup cool to room temperature.

(3) Transfer lemon syrup to a 2-quart pitcher.

(4) Cut lemons in half, and squeeze out their juice. This should yield about 1½ cups freshly squeezed lemon juice. Stir lemon juice into the lemon syrup.

(5) Add enough cold water to equal 8 cups lemonade. Stir well. Refrigerate until serving time. Serve in tall glasses with lots of ice.

MAKES 2 QUARTS

Note: This recipe makes one smooth but strong lemonade—perfect for leisurely afternoons and front porch sippin'. The melting ice will not dilute it too much. For an adult libation, add a jigger of your favorite gin to each glass.

Iced Almond-Lemonade Tea

8 cups boiling water

4 family-size iced tea bags

1 cup sugar

1 (12-ounce) can frozen lemonade concentrate, thawed

1 tablespoon pure almond extract

Cold water

Pour boiling water over tea bags, and let steep 5–10 minutes. Remove and discard tea bags. Add sugar, and stir until dissolved. Stir in lemonade concentrate and almond extract. Add enough cold water to measure 1 gallon.

MAKES 1 GALLON

Hot Cocoa

½ cup sugar

⅓ cup unsweetened dark cocoa powder (European style/Dutch processed)

½ teaspoon salt

4 cups whole milk

1½ cups heavy whipping cream

GARNISHES (OPTIONAL)
Freshly whipped cream

Marshmallows

In a blender or food processor, thoroughly combine sugar, cocoa powder and salt. Transfer to a medium saucepan. Slowly whisk in milk and whipping cream until smooth. Heat over medium heat, stirring often, until very hot but not boiling. Ladle into mugs, and serve topped with freshly whipped cream or marshmallows (preferably homemade—see next recipe).

SERVES 4–6

Note: This is fabulous cocoa—sure to chase away the winter blahs. Feel free to add a bit of your favorite liqueur, such as amaretto, Grand Marnier, framboise, Frangelico or peppermint schnapps. Yummy!!

Homemade Marshmallows

4 envelopes unflavored gelatin

1½ cups water, divided

3 cups sugar

1¼ cups light corn syrup

¼ teaspoon salt

1 teaspoon pure almond extract

1 teaspoon pure vanilla extract

1 pound confectioners' sugar

1. Lightly oil a 13" × 9" × 2" baking dish. Line with foil, and smooth out all wrinkles. Generously oil the foil. Coat the oiled foil with a generous sprinkling of confectioners' sugar.

2. In the bowl of an electric mixer, soften the gelatin in ¾ cup water.

3. In a heavy saucepan, combine the remaining ¾ cup water, sugar, corn syrup and salt. Bring to a boil, and cook over high heat until the syrup reaches 234–240°F on a candy thermometer.

4. Remove from heat. Stir in the extracts.

5. With the whisk attachment of the mixer at full speed, add the hot syrup in a thin, steady stream to the softened gelatin. Beat at highest speed at least 5 minutes, until very thick and full volume.

6. Pour mixture into prepared pan. Let rest uncovered 10–12 hours at room temperature.

7. Sift a layer of confectioners' sugar on a large cutting board. Turn stiffened marshmallow mixture onto sugar. (Note: If marshmallow sticks to foil, lift marshmallow on foil from pan. Trim edges, and peel foil from marshmallow.)

8. Using oiled cookie cutters or a knife, cut into desired shapes. Coat all cut surfaces of marshmallows in confectioners' sugar to prevent sticking. Store airtight at room temperature up to 2 weeks.

MAKES 60 MEDIUM MARSHMALLOWS

Crabgrass

2 (10-ounce) packages frozen chopped spinach

¼ cup butter

1½ cups chopped mild onions

1 pound lump crabmeat, picked over

1 (8-ounce) package cream cheese, softened

1 cup sour cream

1½ cups freshly grated Parmesan cheese

⅛ teaspoon cayenne pepper

1. Thaw spinach, drain, and squeeze dry.

2. In a skillet, melt butter, and sauté onions about 4–5 minutes.

3. Add spinach, and sauté another 2–3 minutes.

4. Add the remaining ingredients. Heat through, and serve in a chafing dish with crackers or melba toast rounds.

SERVES 12-16 as a hearty appetizer.

Note: This is also a great spread to fill a hollowed-out bread round. Wrap tightly with foil, and bake at 350°F for 30–40 minutes. Serve with torn pieces of bread for dipping.

Mulled Wine Punch

½ gallon apple cider

2 (750-milliliter) bottles
dry red wine

2 cups water

½ cup honey

4 (3") cinnamon sticks

1 teaspoon whole cloves

1 teaspoon whole allspice

In a Dutch oven, combine all ingredients.
Bring to a boil over high heat. Reduce heat,
and simmer 15–20 minutes. Strain,
and discard spices. Serve hot.

MAKES 1 GALLON

Spicy Pickled Shrimp

½ cup cane or malt vinegar

¼ cup Creole mustard

3 tablespoons sugar

1 tablespoon OLD BAY Seasoning

1 teaspoon cayenne pepper

1 cup extra-virgin olive oil

1 cup diced onion

1 cup green onions, thinly sliced on the diagonal

1 chopped bunch fresh parsley

1 tablespoon minced garlic

2 pounds cooked, peeled, deveined large or extra-large shrimp

In a blender or food processor, combine first 5 ingredients. With machine running, add oil in a thin, steady stream. Combine remaining ingredients in a large glass bowl. Pour dressing over all. Stir well. Refrigerate at least 12 hours or up to 3 days before serving.

SERVES 12

Orange & Toasted Pecan Appetizer Torte

FIRST LAYER

2 (8-ounce) packages cream cheese, softened

2 tablespoons mustard-mayonnaise sauce

8 ounces (2 cups) shredded sharp cheddar cheese

1 (7-ounce can) crushed pineapple, drained

½ cup chopped green onions

2 teaspoons dried mint

1½ cups chopped pecans, toasted

SECOND LAYER

2 (8-ounce) packages cream cheese, softened

¾ cup orange marmalade

1 tablespoon mayonnaise

Grated zest from 1 orange

2–3 teaspoons orange extract

TOPPING

½ cup orange marmalade

½ cup chopped, toasted pecans

1. Line a 9" round cake pan with plastic wrap.
2. In a medium mixing bowl, combine first 6 ingredients for first layer. Beat well.
3. Spread in bottom of prepared pan. Lightly press pecans into first layer.
4. In medium mixing bowl, combine ingredients for second layer. Beat well.
5. Spread over pecans. Cover surface with plastic wrap. Refrigerate 8 hours or up to 3 days.

TO SERVE

Remove plastic wrap from surface. Invert onto serving platter. Remove pan. Top with orange marmalade and pecans. Serve with gingersnaps and crackers.

SERVES 30 as an appetizer spread.

Amaretto & Pecan Baked Brie

1 (14–16-ounce) wheel of brie

¾–1 cup chopped pecans

3 tablespoons brown sugar

3 tablespoons amaretto

GARNISHES (OPTIONAL)
Gingersnaps

Apple slices

1. Preheat oven to 350°F.
2. Line jelly-roll pan with foil or parchment. Slice brie in half horizontally, and place on prepared pan.
3. Combine remaining ingredients, and divide over cheese halves.
4. Bake 5–8 minutes until cheese is soft.

TO SERVE
Serve warm with gingersnaps and apple slices for dipping.

SERVES 10–12

Port Wine & Apple Cheddar Spread

¹/₃ cup port

1 cup finely chopped dried apple

10 ounces shredded sharp or extra sharp cheddar cheese

1 (8-ounce) package cream cheese, softened

1 teaspoon garlic powder

½ teaspoon salt

¼ teaspoon ground cayenne pepper

In a small bowl, pour port over dried apple. Cover, and let stand at room temperature for several hours or overnight. Combine cheddar, cream cheese and seasonings. Blend well. Add port and apples to mixture. Blend well. Cover with plastic wrap, and refrigerate several hours or up to 1 week before serving.

SERVES 10–12

Note: Serve at room temperature with a selection of hearty crackers, toasts and sliced breads. This is a festive and tasty appetizer spread. It's great for autumn picnics and tailgate parties.

Rolled Stuffed Turkey Breast

STUFFING

2 cups soft bread crumbs

2 garlic cloves, minced

1 tablespoon fresh thyme or
1 teaspoon dried

1 tablespoon minced fresh rosemary or
1 teaspoon crushed dried

1 teaspoon salt

½ teaspoon freshly ground black pepper

1 pound uncooked pork sausage, removed
from casing

⅓ cup minced onion

1 egg, beaten

TURKEY

1 (3-pound) whole boneless, skin-on
turkey breast

4 tablespoons butter

¼ cup brandy

STUFFING

Combine first 6 ingredients in a food processor. Process 1 minute. Transfer bread crumb mixture to a mixing bowl. Add sausage, onion and egg. Using a sturdy spoon, blend ingredients together.

TURKEY

To butterfly whole turkey breast, lay breast flat, skin-side down. Remove tendons, and trim fat. From center, cut horizontally (parallel with countertop) through thickest part of each breast side, almost to outer edge. Fold top pieces outward to enlarge breast. Using the smooth side of a meat mallet, flatten to more even thickness.

ASSEMBLY

1. Preheat oven to 425°F.
2. Evenly distribute stuffing over turkey, leaving a 1" margin. Fold the extended breast pieces back toward the center. Roll stuffed breast jelly-roll fashion. Tie securely with kitchen twine at 1" intervals. Place seam-side down, skin-side up, on rack in roasting pan.
3. Combine melted butter and brandy. Baste turkey.
4. Roast 30 minutes, basting often.

5. Reduce oven to 350°F. Roast 30–40 minutes more, basting often, until meat thermometer registers 170°F.

6. Remove from oven, and let stand 10 minutes. Remove twine, and slice.

SERVES 10

FOOD SAFETY GUIDELINES:
- *Never place hot or warm stuffing inside poultry.*
- *Do not leave the stuffing inside the turkey for more than 30 minutes before cooking.*

Honey-Kissed Hot Apple Cider with Ginger

½ gallon apple cider   ⅓ cup thinly sliced gingerroot
½ cup honey

Combine all ingredients. Heat gently, stirring to dissolve honey, until desired temperature is reached. Strain, and discard ginger. Serve warm.

MAKES ½ GALLON

Hoppin' John New Year's Salad

2¼ cups cooked Uncle Ben's converted white rice

1½ cups cooked, drained black-eyed peas

¼ cup chopped red onion

¼ cup chopped celery

½ large red bell pepper, seeded, chopped

½ hot pepper (such as jalapeño), seeded, minced

2 tablespoons minced fresh basil

1 garlic clove, minced

Freshly squeezed juice of 1 large lemon

3 tablespoons extra-virgin olive oil

Salt and freshly ground black pepper to taste

Mix together first 8 ingredients. Whisk together remaining ingredients. Stir into salad. Cover, and refrigerate several hours or up to 3 days.

SERVES 6

Pepperoni Chips

6 ounces thinly sliced pepperoni

1 cup freshly grated Parmesan cheese

Preheat oven to 350°F. Line a jelly-roll pan with foil or parchment. Arrange pepperoni in a single layer. Sprinkle with Parmesan cheese. Bake 8–10 minutes, until crisp. Drain briefly on paper towels. Serve warm.

SERVES 6–8

Note: This is a great snack for game day in front of the television. Everyone loves it, so make plenty!

Chili Bacon Sticks

20 slices good-quality
thinly sliced bacon

20 (8") hard, dry
breadsticks

⅓ cup brown sugar

1 tablespoon chili powder

1. Preheat oven to 350°F.
2. Line the bottom part of a broiler pan with foil. Place the food rack part of the broiler pan on top of the foil-lined pan.
3. Wrap a piece of bacon around a breadstick spiral fashion. Repeat.
4. Mix together brown sugar and chili powder. Roll bacon-wrapped breadsticks in brown sugar mixture.
5. Place on broiler rack. Bake 20 minutes.
6. Cool several minutes on pan before removing. Serve at room temperature.

SERVES 10

Backyard Lowcountry Seafood Boil

3 tablespoons shrimp and crab boil (such as OLD BAY Seasoning)

3 tablespoons salt

1½ gallons water

2 pounds medium red potatoes, cut into quarters

2 pounds smoked sausage, cut into 2" pieces

12 ears freshly shucked corn, broken into 3–4" pieces

4 pounds fresh shrimp

GARNISH
Chopped parsley

Note: Do not wait for the liquid to come to a boil when timing the sausage, corn and shrimp.

1. In a large stockpot, add shrimp boil and salt to water. Bring to a boil.
2. Add potatoes. Return to a boil, and cook 10 minutes.
3. Add sausage, and cook 5 minutes.
4. Add corn, and cook 5 minutes.
5. Stir in shrimp, and cook 3 minutes. Drain immediately. Garnish with chopped parsley if desired.

SERVES 8

Note: Traditionally, this one-dish meal is dumped onto a newspaper-lined table set with paper plates and lots of paper towels. Serve with butter and loaves of warm, crunchy French bread.

Pecan-Crusted Chicken Breasts with Pralines & Cream Sauce

CHICKEN

6 boneless, skinless chicken breast halves

3 cups water

3 tablespoons seasoned salt

3 tablespoons sugar

2 cups all-purpose flour

1 cup finely chopped pecans

1 teaspoon salt

1 teaspoon freshly ground black pepper

1 teaspoon dried thyme

1 teaspoon dried basil

1 cup milk

1 egg, beaten

¼ cup vegetable oil

¼ cup butter

SAUCE

½ cup chopped pecans

2 cups heavy whipping cream

¼ cup praline liqueur

Salt and freshly ground black pepper to taste

CHICKEN

1. Place chicken breast halves in a gallon-size zip-top food storage bag.

2. In a medium mixing bowl, combine water, seasoned salt and sugar; stir to dissolve. Pour over chicken breast halves, and seal bag, removing as much air as possible. Let chicken marinate in brine 8–12 hours.

3. Remove chicken from brine, and pat dry.

4. In a shallow container suitable for breading, combine next 6 ingredients.

5. In another shallow container, combine milk and egg.

6. In a large skillet over medium-high heat, heat oil and butter until hot but not smoking. Dredge each piece of chicken first in dry mixture, then egg wash, and then again in dry mixture (dry-wet-dry method). Panfry chicken in skillet until golden brown on both sides, about 7–10 minutes total.

7. Remove chicken from skillet to a platter. Cover with foil to keep warm. Reserve 2 tablespoons of drippings in skillet. Proceed with sauce.

SAUCE

In drippings in skillet, sauté pecans over medium-high heat 2 minutes. Add whipping cream and liqueur. Increase heat to high, and bring sauce to a boil. Reduce sauce by half. Season with salt and pepper to taste. Serve warm sauce over chicken.

SERVES 6

Note: The praline liqueur used in this recipe is an ingredient that is sometimes hard to find in liquor stores. What's a girl to do? Dana Sue shares her own recipe for making your own praline liqueur (see next recipe).

Praline Liqueur

1 pound pecan pieces	4 cups vodka
1 pound dark brown sugar	2 cups brandy
3 cups water	1 cup amaretto
4 vanilla beans	

1. Preheat oven to 350°F.

2. Scatter pecan pieces on a baking sheet. Place in center of oven, and bake 8–10 minutes, until pecans release a toasty aroma and are toasted a bit. Do not overcook. Cool to room temperature.

3. Combine brown sugar and 3 cups water in a saucepan. Bring to a boil, stirring to dissolve sugar. Remove from heat.

4. Split vanilla beans lengthwise, and place in a large crock or bowl with the toasted pecans. Pour hot syrup over vanilla beans and pecans. Let cool to room temperature.

5. Add vodka, brandy and amaretto. Stir to blend.

6. Cover airtight with plastic wrap, and let develop at room temperature at least 2 weeks.

7. After 2 weeks, strain liquid through a fine-wire strainer. (For further clarification of liquid, if desired, you can strain the liquid through coffee filters to remove all debris. Because this is a time-consuming process, I normally skip this step.)

8. Pour into bottles, and seal tightly. Attractively label the bottles for gift giving, and store at room temperature.

MAKES 10 CUPS. Keep some—share some.

Note: This stuff is absolutely divine. Not only is it the key ingredient for the praline cream sauce for the pecan-crusted chicken breasts recipe, but also it is so delicious when added to coffee or drizzled over pound cake and ice cream. To make a super yummy adult treat, blend with equal parts milk (or half-and-half—how indulgent), and serve over ice. This recipe has won the hearts of all the Sweet Magnolias. Keep some of the liqueur, and share the rest.

Pastel Butter Mints

1 pound 10X confectioners' sugar	6–12 drops peppermint oil
5 tablespoons butter, softened	1 drop food coloring (optional)
2 tablespoons cold water	

Combine all ingredients in a heavy-duty mixer or food processor. Blend until dough comes together and forms a smooth ball. Shape into small balls, and place on waxed paper 1" apart. Flatten with the tines of a fork, dipping in additional confectioners' sugar, if necessary, to prevent sticking. Dry for several hours at room temperature. Store airtight in the refrigerator, or freezer up to 3 months, with wax paper separating the layers.

MAKES 50

Note: These mints are so delicious, cool and creamy. Serve them at bridal showers, baby showers and weddings. Use food coloring to suit the occasion: pink for baby girls and blue for boys; leave white for weddings. Remember to use just a drop or two of the food coloring, keeping the shade subtle.

Erik's Grilled Cheese Panini with Pecan-Pesto Mayo & Spicy Tomato Jam

PESTO

²/₃ cup pecan halves

1 packed cup fresh basil leaves

½ cup freshly grated Parmesan cheese

2 garlic cloves, minced

¹/₈ teaspoon ground cayenne pepper

¹/₃ cup extra-virgin olive oil

Salt to taste

JAM

1 cup sugar

1 cup peeled, finely chopped tomatoes

1 teaspoon freshly grated lemon zest

1 tablespoon lemon juice

¼ teaspoon ground cinnamon

¼ teaspoon allspice

¼ teaspoon cloves

¼ teaspoon cayenne pepper

PANINI

2 slices Italian bread

2 ounces grated smoked mozzarella cheese

2 tablespoons extra-virgin olive oil

1 peeled garlic clove

PESTO

1. Preheat oven to 350°F.

2. Scatter pecans on baking sheet. Bake 8–10 minutes, until nutty smelling. Let cool to room temperature.

3. In the bowl of a food processor, combine pecans, basil, Parmesan, garlic and cayenne. With the machine running, add the olive oil through the top in a steady stream. Season with salt. Refrigerate for use within 2 weeks.

CONTINUES →

JAM

1. Combine all ingredients in a small saucepan. Bring to a boil, then reduce heat to simmer. Continue to cook, stirring often, until reduced somewhat. Jam will thicken as it cools.

2. Cover, and refrigerate for use within 2 weeks.

PANINI

1. Preheat panini press.

2. Place bread slices side by side. On 1 side of 1 slice, smear a liberal amount of pesto. On the other slice, spread jam, and sprinkle on the cheese. Sandwich the 2 slices together. Using a pastry brush, brush the exposed sides of bread slices with olive oil.

3. Place the sandwich on panini press, and close lid, pressing down a bit to slightly weigh down the sandwich. Cook until golden brown and toasted.

4. Remove, and let cool until easily handled. Rub garlic clove over toasted sides. Slice in half on the diagonal.

MAKES 1

Chocolate Cloud Cookies

6 ounces semisweet chocolate chips

3 large egg whites

1 teaspoon pure vanilla extract

½ teaspoon salt

¾ cup sugar

1 cup chopped pecans

1 cup broken vanilla wafers

1. Preheat oven to 350°F.
2. Grease and flour cookie sheets or line them with parchment.
3. Place chocolate chips in microwave-safe dish. Cook at high power until chocolate melts, stirring every 30 seconds. Stir until smooth. Cool slightly.
4. Using an electric mixer, beat egg whites, vanilla and salt until frothy. Gradually beat in sugar until firm peaks hold. Fold in melted chocolate until smooth. Stir in pecans and broken wafers.
5. Drop ¼ cup mounds, 2" apart on prepared pans. Bake 12–15 minutes.
6. Remove from oven. Let cool on pan 5 minutes. Transfer to cooling rack. Cool completely. Store airtight.

MAKES 18

Sunburst Lemon Bars

CRUST

1 cup butter, softened

½ cup confectioners' sugar

2 cups all-purpose flour

FILLING

2 cups sugar

4 large eggs

⅓ cup flour

Freshly grated zest of 2 lemons

⅓ cup fresh lemon juice

½ teaspoon baking powder

GARNISH

Confectioners' sugar

CRUST

① Preheat oven to 350°F.

② Cream butter and sugar together in a mixing bowl. Add flour all at once, and mix until thoroughly combined.

③ Place in a parchment-lined 9" × 13" × 2" metal baking pan, and press evenly to cover entire bottom. (Note: I often place a piece of plastic wrap on top of the dough when pressing it out to keep the dough from sticking to my hands.)

④ Bake 20 minutes. Prepare the filling during the last 5 minutes of the crust baking.

FILLING

① Combine all filling ingredients, and mix well.

② Remove crust from oven. Pour filling over baked crust, return to the oven, and bake an additional 33–35 minutes.

③ Remove pan from the oven, and let cool completely on a cooling rack.

④ When cooled, lift out of the pan by the overhanging parchment paper, and place on a cutting board. Trim off edges with a large, long sharp knife, and discard (chef's treat!). Cut into squares of desirable size. Dust tops with confectioners' sugar.

MAKES 48 MINIATURE LEMON BARS, 24 MEDIUM OR 12 JUMBO

Fall Festival Munch Mix

1 pound miniature pretzels

1 pound roasted, salted peanuts

1 (12-ounce) box original flavor cheese cracker squares (such as Cheese Nips)

1 (9½-ounce) box miniature buttery crackers filled with peanut butter (such as Ritz Bits)

¾ cup butter

1 packed cup light brown sugar

½ cup light corn syrup

2 teaspoons vanilla extract

1 (1-pound) bag candy-coated peanut butter candies (such as Reese's Pieces)

2 (12-ounce) bags candy corn

1. Preheat oven to 250°F.

2. Using a nonstick cooking spray, coat a very large roasting pan or disposable foil pan. Combine first 4 ingredients in prepared pan.

3. In a medium saucepan, melt butter. Add brown sugar and corn syrup. Bring to a boil, stirring occasionally. Boil 5 minutes.

4. Remove from heat. Whisk in vanilla. Pour over pretzel blend. Stir gently to coat.

5. Bake 1 hour, stirring once every 15 minutes.

6. Place on a cooling rack. Stir several times during cooling to avoid clumps. Once cooled, stir in candies. Store airtight.

MAKES 20 CUPS

Note: This recipe makes 20 cups!! You may be asking yourself, What am I going to do with 20 cups of this party mix? Be warned: This stuff magically disappears. It's a favorite of the Sweet Magnolias and our families.

Old-Fashioned Molasses Cookies

1½ cups sugar

1 cup butter, softened

1 cup molasses

2 eggs, beaten

4 cups all-purpose flour

4 teaspoons baking soda

2 teaspoons cinnamon

1 teaspoon salt

1 teaspoon ground ginger

Additional sugar

1. Preheat oven to 350°F.
2. In a large mixing bowl, cream sugar and butter until light and fluffy. Add molasses and eggs; blend well.
3. In a medium mixing bowl, whisk together flour, baking soda, cinnamon, salt and ginger.
4. Add dry ingredients to the creamed mixture. Blend until well incorporated.
5. Shape tablespoons of dough into balls, and coat in sugar. Place 2" apart on parchment-lined or greased baking sheets. Flatten tops slightly.
6. Bake 10–12 minutes.

MAKES 100

CONVERSION CHARTS

Weight

1 ounce	28 grams
4 ounces or ¼ pound	113 grams
⅓ pound	150 grams
8 ounces or ½ pound	230 grams
⅔ pound	300 grams
12 ounces or ¾ pound	340 grams
1 pound or 16 ounces	450 grams
2 pounds	900 grams
2.2 pounds	1 kilogram

Temperature

Fahrenheit	Celsius	Fahrenheit	Celsius
212°	100°	375°	190°
250°	120°	400°	200°
275°	140°	425°	220°
300°	150°	450°	230°
325°	160°	475°	240°
350°	180°	500°	260°

Volume

1 teaspoon	5 milliliters	¾ cup or 6 fluid ounces	180 milliliters
1 tablespoon or ½ fluid ounce	15 milliliters	1 cup or 8 fluid ounces or ½ pint	240 milliliters
1 fluid ounce or $^1/_8$ cup	30 milliliters	1½ cups or 12 fluid ounces	350 milliliters
¼ cup or 2 fluid ounces	60 milliliters	2 cups or 1 pint or 16 fluid ounces	475 milliliters
$^1/_3$ cup	80 milliliters	3 cups or 1½ pints	700 milliliters
½ cup or 4 fluid ounces	120 milliliters	4 cups or 2 pints or 1 quart	950 milliliters
$^2/_3$ cup	160 milliliters	4 quarts or 1 gallon	3.8 liters

ABOUT THE AUTHORS

With her roots firmly planted in the South, **Sherryl Woods** has written many of her more than 100 books in that distinctive setting, whether in her home state of Virginia, her adopted state, Florida, or her much-adored South Carolina. She is the *New York Times* and *USA TODAY* bestselling author of the Sweet Magnolias series and is best known for her ability to create endearing small-town communities and families. She divides her time between her childhood summer home overlooking the Potomac River in Colonial Beach, Virginia, and her oceanfront home with its lighthouse view in Key Biscayne, Florida. Visit her at SherrylWoods.com.

Teddi Wohlford is the chef and owner of Culinary Creations in Macon, Georgia. Her catering company offers a unique assortment of Southern cuisine. She specializes in fare that she calls "uptown down South," updated and upscale versions of timeless Southern classics. Teddi is the Fine Foods Writer for the *Telegraph* (Macon, Georgia) and a frequent guest chef on 13WMAZ television. With family in the upstate of South Carolina and in-laws in the Lowcountry, Teddi spends as much time as possible in her "heart's home" of South Carolina and travels the South teaching gourmet cooking classes.

INDEX

A

B

C

H

I

J

K

L

M

T